On The Spot

Derek Shackleton

A Biography

Best Wishes

Derek Shackleton

On The Spot

Derek Shackleton

A Biography

By

David Matthews

Foreword by Colin Ingleby-Mackenzie

Former Hampshire Captain and President of the MCC

Blackberry Downs Books Lincombe Lee Devon EX34 8LL

First Published in the UK in 1998 by
Blackberry Downs Books
Lincombe
Lee
Devon
EX34 8LL

A catalogue record for this book is available from the British Library

ISBN 0 9532827 0 8

Printed and bound in Great Britain by

Bishops Printers Limited
Goldsmith Avenue
Portsmouth
Hampshire
PO4 0BT

Acknowledgements

I am greatly indebted to the following for their help in the compilation of this book.

The following former Hampshire players gave up their valuable time in seeing me to let me have their reminiscences:

Mike Barnard, Vic Cannings, Bob Cottam, Jimmy Gray, Leo Harrison, Malcolm Heath, Gerry Hill, Henry Horton, Charles Knott, Vic Ransom, Alan Rayment, Neville Rogers, Peter Sainsbury, Bryan Timms, Alan Wassell, David White.

I also corresponded with Neil McCorkell in South Africa.

The views of the following former England players were obtained by correspondence, telephone conversations or at a meeting:

Dennis Amiss MBE, Trevor Bailey CBE, Geoffrey Boycott OBE, Tom Cartwright, The Rt Hon the Lord Cowdrey of Tonbridge CBE, Ted Dexter, Tom Graveney OBE, The Rt. Rev the Lord Sheppard of Liverpool, and MJK Smith OBE.

Colin Ingleby-Mackenzie for kindly meeting me and writing the foreword

Vic Isaacs for supplying the statistical information relating to Derek Shackleton's Hampshire career.

Other statistics were confirmed by the Association of Cricket Statisticians and Historians together with research in Wisden Almanack.

Others have been invaluable in different ways; Stephen Chalke, Peter Jeffs, Andrew Renshaw, Raychel Woodham.

The Hampshire Cricket Society and the Hampshire County Cricket Club have given me their full support and encouragement.

Photographs have been supplied by Patrick Eagar, Susanne Marlow, Derek Shackleton, Central Press Photos, Southern Daily Echo, Sport and General.

My very grateful thanks to the Shackleton family for being so very co-operative and for their patience.

Select Bibliography

H S Altham, John Arlott, EDR Eagar, Roy Webber: *Hampshire County Cricket, The Official History* (Phoenix House) 1957
Denis Compton Annual 1953 (Stanley Paul Ltd) 1953
Phil Edmonds: *100 Greatest Bowlers* (MacDonald Queen Anne Press) 1989
Colin Ingleby-Mackenzie: *Many A Slip* (Oldbourne Books) 1962
Roy Marshall: *Test Outcast* (Pelham Books) 1970
Christopher Martin-Jenkins: *The Complete Who's Who of Test Cricketers* (MacDonald Queen Anne Press) 1987
Peter Wynne-Thomas: *The History of Hampshire County Cricket Club* (Christopher Helm) 1988

Hampshire County Cricket Club, The Handbooks
Playfair Cricket Annuals 1954-1962
Todmorden Cricket Club 1837-1987, 150th Anniversary Souvenir
Wisden Almanack (John Wisden and Co Ltd., Guildford)
Wisden Anthology

Invaluable research has been obtained from the following sources and publications

Hampshire County Cricket Club
Dorset County Cricket Club
MCC
Todmorden Cricket Club

Todmorden Town Council
Todmorden, The Official Guide

Daily Telegraph
The Times
The Guardian
The Cricketer
Hampshire, The County Magazine
Southern Daily Echo
The News, Portsmouth
Todmorden News

Contents

Foreword

By Colin Ingleby-Mackenzie
President of the MCC and former Hampshire captain

"Shack - A Captain's Dream"

If I had won a lottery in the spring of 1958, and had been given the option of buying any first class cricketer to play for Hampshire in my first year as captain, I would not have hesitated; Derek Shackleton is the name.

My first match was at Bradford against Yorkshire. That was bound to be a tough initiation. It rained for the first two days, and on the third morning I won the toss. There was no chance of a result but in those days, first innings lead was worth a good few points. In a naive way I decided we should bat to give us a little practice in the middle - and, out of good manners in a foreign county, we decided to declare at 105. This gave them no chance with but 55 minutes left.

Oh dear! Fred Trueman had other ideas and Derek's analysis was 7 overs 0-64. I should never have allowed such a senior bowler to be submitted to such horrific treatment. Derek was not wound up, and Fred was dynamic. I was amazed Shack ever spoke to me again!

He was unmoved, finishing the season as top wicket taker in the country with 165 wickets at 15.44 each. A truly remarkable man and we should have won the county championship.

He came to Hampshire as a batsman, and was always a useful contributor down the order. An excellent fielder away from the wicket, and a safe catcher, he, above all, was the man who won us the championship in 1961. Roy Marshall with the bat, Derek with the ball - no captain could have asked for more.

He was the real team man, through and through. Always dressed immaculately without a hair out of place, he performed day after day with unerring accuracy. Like all great men he was modest, with a subtle sense of humour.

He deserved a bumper benefit, but Hampshire was not renowned for such things in those days. I remember in his benefit match at Bournemouth he asked me what to do with his collection. I said "put it on the Thomson Jones good thing at Yarmouth". He sensibly refused, but it won at 100-8!

David Matthews has written an excellent biography of the great man. Anyone who has cricket at heart must read it. Derek is the glowing example for young and old alike - always dressed up to give his best - and he did.

INTRODUCTION

The date ... Friday 1st September 1961. The time ... just after four o-clock. The place ... Dean Park, Bournemouth. Bob Taylor, the Derbyshire and future England wicket-keeper, struck a mighty blow off Peter Sainsbury. The ball seemed to be reaching for the heavens and, after an agonising wait, fell from the sky to be safely held on the mid wicket boundary by Danny Livingstone. Hampshire, the county which produced the Hambledon club, became champions for the first time in their history.

Leading the Hampshire players into the pavilion through a packed mass of excited supporters, was a tall handsome man, of immaculate appearance notwithstanding having spent several hours in the warm late summer sunshine. Shirt sleeves neatly rolled to the elbows, and short sleeve sweater and flannels so clean that it gave the appearance of a man just about to enter the field of play. Not even a hair out of place.

Derek Shackleton had, in fact, contributed more than any other Hampshire player on that final afternoon towards such a crucial victory.

The match against Derbyshire was the penultimate one of a long hard season, and the clinching of the county championship, temporarily at least, broke the Surrey/Yorkshire domination of the preceding nine seasons - although Yorkshire were to win five further championship trophies during the remainder of the 1960s.

It had been a closely fought championship race, and during the last month of the season any one of four counties had a chance of winning the trophy. The issue was complicated because nine counties had been allocated twenty eight matches and the remaining eight, including Hampshire, were to play thirty two games. League positions were, therefore, decided on an average of points per matches played.

Apart, obviously, from Hampshire supporters, to most neutral cricket lovers it was a popular victory. The first unfashionable county to do so since Glamorgan in 1948.

Hampshire's achievement had resulted from many years of hard work and commitment from a very dedicated body of people, and the final reward was, in every sense of the word, a team effort led by an inspirational and charismatic captain, Colin Ingleby-Mackenzie.

Basically, the team that season was selected from just fourteen players (two others played two games each) and this contributed greatly to the undoubted team spirit and consistency which were to prove such important ingredients in the ultimate achievement. Crucially, there was also a great self belief which had been absent in the past.

All the players made important and positive contributions throughout the season and the side was a very good mix - a thoroughly well balanced team. In view of this it would, perhaps, be unfair to pick out an individual, or individuals, as being indispensable, but in a season when there were many extremely close victories, the general consensus then was, and indeed looking back thirty five years later is, that any extended absence of their premier bowler would have severely jeopardised the county's chance.

Ingleby-Mackenzie has been rightly praised for his bold declarations, but he would be the first to acknowledge that many of his decisions were made less of a risk due to the fast scoring abilities of the West Indian batsman, Roy Marshall, and to Shackleton, the most accurate and effective seam bowler of his generation.

"Shack", as he was commonly and affectionately called, was aged 37 during that season but bowled more overs than any other player in the country, took the second highest number of wickets (158), conceded only 2 runs per over, and more than one third of his overs were maidens.

In that championship deciding match against Derbyshire, the visitors were in a very strong position at one time with a score of 212 for two following Hampshire's first innings total of 306. Shackleton and the young left arm spinner, Alan Wassell, then proceeded to take the remaining 8 wickets between them to restrict Derbyshire's lead to just 12 runs.

Fast scoring in Hampshire's second innings, especially from Marshall, Sainsbury, and Mike Barnard, enabled Ingleby-Mackenzie to declare leaving Derbyshire a target of 252 in 192 minutes.

As always, the ball was immediately given to Shackleton and in his first 8 overs he took 4 wickets for 8 runs. The Derbyshire innings was in tatters and in a situation from which they never recovered. He took 6-39 and it has been said that he had not, at any time, bowled better. It is perhaps more pertinent to say that such was his incredible consistency that he never bowled badly, and his performance at

Bournemouth, especially on that final day, was exactly what those who knew him would have expected.

"Shack" was calmness personified, but even he would have experienced a few "butterflies" when he began his very important spell of bowling on that Friday afternoon. The county wanted to wrap up the championship that day as their next and final match was against Yorkshire of all people, and who were to finish close runners up. So much depended on him bowling not only a long accurate spell, but with a win essential he would also have to make a quick breakthrough.

Bournemouth, at that time, did not generally favour seam bowling and indeed in four previous matches on that ground in 1961 Shackleton had only taken 7 wickets at a cost of 35 runs apiece. He more than rose to the occasion therefore to ensure such an important victory; with typical modesty he merely said afterwards "I just bowled straight". There was really nothing more to add but he was of course greatly understating a quite extraordinary skill in the oft criticised art of seam bowling.

Derek Shackleton, a quiet, unassuming young man from the then West Riding town of Todmorden, was for more than twenty years Hampshire's premier bowler, and statistically, the most successful in the county's history. When he joined the army towards the end of the Second World War and served in the South of England, it was to prove one of the most significant and luckiest of postings for Hampshire County Cricket Club.

Chapter One

Towards a New Dawn

Derek Shackleton signed professionally for Hampshire in July 1947 but it is relevant to delve back to the preceding summer, the first season of post war cricket.

Following the cessation of hostilities in 1945 the first full cricket season commenced a year later with a visit by the Indian tourists. The weather in 1946 resulted in one of the coldest and wettest summers on record but, notwithstanding this, crowds flocked to watch cricket in large numbers. Many ground attendance records were broken and the counties reported a big rise in membership. Normal pursuits, enjoyed so much in peacetime, had been cruelly disrupted during the war years and sport played a major part in easing the very painful memories of those recent times.

It was to be the start of a relatively brief period when cricket and soccer attendances reached unprecedented levels and, apart from (in cricket's case) test matches and one day Internationals, are not likely to be repeated.

The vast majority of the population expected a period of austerity at that time and material expectations were not high. The car was still a dream for all but the wealthy and mass television and foreign holidays were many years away.

It quickly became apparent that, together with the cinema, the major spectator sports of soccer and cricket would provide a very welcome outlet for leisure. The start of the 1945/1946 football season (although still classed as a 'wartime' competition) followed by the first post war cricket season were awaited with enormous anticipation.

A tremendous onus was placed on the Indians, being the first touring side to visit England since 1939. It is to their outstanding credit that, not only did they achieve excellent results on the tour, winning eleven and losing just four of their twenty nine first class matches, but during a turbulent political period in their own history, were perfect ambassadors for their country. Their sportsmanship and modesty were as much admired as their cricketing successes.

The Indians must have found the English climate completely alien that year and it is generally considered that their results would have been even better if there had been at least a modicum of decent weather. The only advantage they did have was that, during the war years, cricket in the subcontinent had been largely unaffected whereas the first class game in England had lain virtually dormant for six years.

It was to be expected that the overall standard of the game in 1946 would not be as high as in 1939. Mercifully cricket suffered relatively few casualties during the war, the most notable being Hedley Verity, the Yorkshire and England left arm spinner, Ken Farnes, the Essex and England fast bowler, and Maurice Turnbull, who captained both Cambridge University and Glamorgan and played on nine occasions for England.

During that fateful weekend at the end of August and beginning of September 1939, the consequences of which were to claim Verity's life, it is a poignant reminder that the great spinner's last bowling analysis was 6-1-9-7 against Sussex at Hove.

Sadly, Hampshire lost two players during the war - D.F. Walker, a patient reliable batsman who had joined the county in 1937 having previously played in Surrey's second X1, and J.P. Blake who played just a few games between 1937 and 1939.

In that last pre-war season Hampshire finished a very disappointing fifteenth in the county championship with only the desperately weak Northamptonshire and Leicestershire sides below them. No Hampshire player featured in the leading averages and prospects for the future looked bleak, albeit no one realised then that play would not re-commence for seven years.

The immensely powerful Yorkshire side so dominated the 1930s that they won seven championships in that decade. Hampshire were so outplayed by them in 1939 that they lost by an innings and 129 runs with the ignominy of Yorkshire losing only one wicket in the match. Len Hutton and Herbert Sutcliffe shared an opening stand of 315 and, when the declaration came, Hutton was still undefeated on 280.

When the championship re-commenced in 1946 most counties had to rely, to a very large extent, on their pre-war staff and with Yorkshire and Middlesex finishing first and second again it seemed very little had changed. However, with players being almost seven years older, it was immediately apparent that the search must start to unearth fresh talent. This would not have been easy as little cricket at a first class level had been played. A certain number of British Empire matches had been staged, mainly at Lord's and other games were organised when members of the armed forces were home on leave. Largely, though, little serious competitive cricket had been played for six years.

Hampshire were no exception in the quest for new faces. Of the eleven most regular players in 1946 eight were in their thirties with three of those being only two years short of their fortieth birthdays. The three regulars under thirty were Neville Rogers who, for several seasons would be the county's most consistent batsman, Desmond Eagar, who was to prove such an inspired choice as captain and secretary and Tom Dean who promised much as a leg break bowler but who only made a few appearances for the county in subsequent years. Even Rogers and Eagar were 28 in 1946 and a youth policy was a matter of the utmost urgency. It is to the team's great credit that, as an unfashionable side, they should finish as high as tenth with no fewer than eight victories. Ironically they inflicted on Yorkshire their only defeat of the season gaining some consolation for the humiliation of 1939.

The basic X1 in 1946, together with ages, was as follows :

John Arnold	38
Neil McCorkell	34
Arthur Holt	35
Jim Bailey	38
Desmond Eagar	28
Gerry Hill	33
Neville Rogers	28
"Lofty" Herman	38
Tom Dean	25
Charles Knott	31
George Heath	33

With the exception of Rogers and Eagar all had played for Hampshire in that final pre-war season although Eagar had been playing for Gloucestershire and Oxford University. Leo Harrison was not a regular player in 1946 but had played a handful of matches before the war at the age of 17. His best years were to come.

Hampshire were reasonably pleased with tenth and with a little more consistency in the batting could have achieved an even better position. In championship games only Arnold and the all rounder Bailey scored 1000 runs and the bowling honours were shared by Knott and Herman, each of whom took 100 wickets. However, with Herman then aged 38 and no other bowler taking more than 50 wickets danger signs about the lack of a quality seam attack were very apparent.

Certain years evoke particular memories and when a season is mentioned it can be immediately remembered as a time when something very special happened. The regaining of the Ashes in 1953, Laker's torture of the Australians in 1956 and Botham's colossal performances in 1981 are three such years. Sometimes, as time passes, events are exaggerated and nostalgia becomes a powerful force in the memory but there was something special about 1947.

It will forever be remembered because of the dominance of the Middlesex "Twins" Denis Compton and Bill Edrich and for the long hot summer. Memories have played slight tricks with the weather as the hot dry spell did not start until July and the summer as a whole did not measure up to the exceptional summer of 1921 nor to the subsequent years of 1975, 1976 and 1995. It was, though, a year which produced glorious cricket conditions, both for playing and watching, during the main holiday periods. Compton and Edrich brought a gaiety to the game probably not seen previously nor in subsequent years. The joy they evoked was so important to the Nation at that time.

The year did not start on an optimistic note. Austerity was still very much to the fore and the winter of 1946/1947 was a truly bleak one. It was, at the time, the coldest, longest winter of the century and only 1963 in later years bears dubious comparison. It was so cold that snow ploughs were used in London, the sea froze off Kent and, for weeks, many parts of the country were impassable. Power supplies almost broke down completely with over two million people thrown out of work. One of the main reasons for the extreme misery was coal, or indeed the lack of it, because it could not be moved. Early in 1947 the Government estimated that there would later be a manpower shortage of 600,000, although there were still over one and a half million in the Forces, including young Derek.

Against this background there was concern in South Africa, whose side were due to commence their tour in April, that, in view of the manpower crisis, the British Government would ban mid week sport. However, because of all the other miseries the Government probably felt it prudent to avoid such drastic action considering instead that sport could prove to be an important morale booster.

The South Africans duly arrived in bitterly cold weather and not having played test cricket for eight years. England, as well as the series against India in 1946, had undertaken an arduous tour of Australia and New Zealand in 1946/1947. Whilst the players picked for that tour probably relished the chance to miss an English winter, one which ultimately proved to be truly awful, it had been a tour which had been reluctantly agreed to being so soon after the cessation of hostilities. It was under strong pressure from the Australian Board of Control that the MCC gave way. The players spent eight months away from home, a period which included at least six weeks on board ship - there were no 24 hour flights in those days. The series was easily won by Australia but the tour was very much a success as it not only revived cricket interest in Australia but whetted the appetite for cricket lovers in England who were awaiting the 1947 season with great anticipation.

It was to become a vintage summer, one of misty eyed nostalgia for a generation who had endured a truly horrendous period. The aftermath of the First World War, the Depression, the unemployment of the 1930s and then the devastation of the Second World War had understandably taken its toll. Even after the ending of the war there were still many uncertainties and the future was unpredictable, but cricket was back !

After two early reversals against Worcestershire (in a snow affected match) and the MCC, when Compton gave a hint of what was to come with an innings of 97, the tourists were only to suffer defeats at the hands of England, losing the test series by a 3-0 margin. They came close to winning the first test at Trent Bridge and there is a valid argument for the theory that if either Compton or Edrich had swapped sides the tourists may well have won the series. Only once were they beaten when neither of these players made a significant contribution. On a difficult wicket at Headingley the South Africans were twice dismissed cheaply and Len Hutton gave a masterful display of batting to turn the match in England's favour. Compton and Edrich "failed" with scores of 30 and 43. Their final batting averages for the series were 94.12 and 110.40 respectively and, in addition, Edrich took 16 wickets at 23.12. Six of Compton's record breaking eighteen 100s in 1947 were against the tourists, four in the tests.

The 1947 county championship was won by Middlesex but only after stiff competition from the unfancied Gloucestershire side whose premier batsman for so long, Wally Hammond, had announced his retirement following the tour to Australia the previous winter.

It was no surprise that, on what would become hard, true wickets and fast outfields, batsmen would dominate and ten players had averages in excess of 60 with sixteen scoring over 2000 runs. Compton scored a record breaking 3816 and Edrich 3539. It is perhaps now overlooked that they were genuine all-rounders at that time with 73 and 67 wickets respectively and this added to their overall dominance of English cricket that season. And in such sparkling fashion.

It could have been expected that with such a glut of runs there would be many drawn games with bowlers achieving little success. There was also, however, a very positive attitude towards reaching a clear cut result whenever possible and of the fifty two championship matches played by Middlesex and Gloucestershire only seven were drawn. Many bowlers could also look back on 1947 with great affection especially the 46 year old Gloucestershire off-spinner, Tom Goddard, who took a staggering 238 wickets at only 17.30. It was generally the spinners who had most success that year and all six bowlers who took more than 150 wickets were of the slower variety.

In spite of the high scoring later in the season the first matches in May contained only modest totals with Middlesex themselves being dismissed in the second innings of their first match for just 78 with Somerset winning by one wicket. They, crucially as it would turn out, beat Gloucestershire in their next game by an innings and 178 runs with the elegant Jack Robertson scoring a fine century. The south west county were totally outplayed and there was no hint of how successful they would be during the remainder of the season.

In the return match at Cheltenham in August Middlesex won a close, low scoring contest to virtually clinch the championship. The Metropolitan county had been deprived of the services of Compton and Robertson who had been selected for the fifth test but Edrich was available. He was considered not to be fully fit for the test team, largely because his bowling would have been restricted, but Middlesex were very happy indeed that he could take his place in the county side.

Twenty one wickets fell on a blisteringly hot first day with the gates shut on a record crowd of 14,500. Spinners dominated the match but, although Goddard took 15 wickets in 42 overs, it was to be the Middlesex spinners who had the final say with the occasional off-break bowler Harry Sharp, who played in only three matches that season, taking 3 wickets in seven deliveries.

Officially Middlesex had to wait ten further days to clinch the championship with victory over Northamptonshire at Lord's but Cheltenham was really where Gloucestershire realised that their brave attempt had come to an end. It must be very rare for a bowler to take 15 wickets at an average of 10 and yet end up on the losing side ! If just one of their two defeats by Middlesex had been reversed the championship would have been Gloucestershire's. The margin between success and near miss or failure can be so close, and so cruel.

For Hampshire it was a largely disappointing season, the main bonus being the improved and consistent form of Neville Rogers, who would prove to be their leading batsman until 1955. Rogers, born in Oxford in 1918, signed for Hampshire in 1939 on the recommendation of a former Hampshire player, Alec Bowell. The outbreak of war halted his career before it had even started and, like so many others, six important years were lost.

After defeating Yorkshire in the last match of 1946 Hampshire started the 1947 campaign with an encouraging win against Sussex at Portsmouth giving optimism (soon to prove unfounded) that there may be further improvement. However, whereas in 1946 the batsmen had been disappointing, there was little penetration by the bowlers this next season.

Neil McCorkell, John Arnold and Rogers all scored over 1500 runs with Desmond Eagar, Jim Bailey and Gerry Hill only just falling short of 1000 runs in championship matches. The main wicket takers of 1946, Charles Knott and Lofty Herman, could only take 66 wickets between them due to absences through injury and, in the case of Knott, to business commitments. The wickets, during what was to become a very hot summer, did not suit Knott and age was catching up on Herman's performances.

Some action was taken to improve the bowling when Vic Ransom, a strong medium pacer, was signed under special registration. An amateur, he had been playing club cricket in London with Malden Wanderers and had served in the Royal Navy during the war. He had played two friendly matches for Sussex but was persuaded to sign for Hampshire by Giles Baring, who had played for the county in the 1930s. Ransom played a major part in that initial victory over Sussex with match figures of 8-112 in 47 overs. He finished top of the bowling averages with 54 wickets at 27.22 but 1947 was a hard toil for what had become an elderly attack.

Probably the most influential figure in the development of Hampshire cricket in the immediate post war years was Desmond Eagar. A decent enough player his great strengths lay in strong leadership and his enormous enthusiasm in trying to help build a Hampshire side to be truly reckoned with but one which would play within the true spirit of the game. As an Oxford Blue he scored 58 runs for once out in the Varsity match of 1939 and was good enough to play for Gloucestershire on a few occasions just before the war. He must have gained tremendous experience playing alongside people like Wally Hammond, Charles Barnett, Charlie Parker and Tom Goddard. Playing for Oxford against Gloucestershire in 1939 he top scored in the first innings with 74 against an attack which included Goddard. In the next match he produced an even more impressive performance hitting 67 in the second innings against Yorkshire, an innings in which Verity took 6-73. In that final pre-war season Eagar scored over 700 runs for the University at an average of 40 against relatively strong county opposition.

Eagar had intended to take up a full time career in the army but later changed his mind. He applied for the position of secretary and captain of Hampshire and was appointed in preference to Freddie Brown. Immediately recognising the dangers of an ageing side he made a very determined and, what was to prove, a highly successful attempt to improve the fielding which had become slow and cumbersome. Endeavours to put the batting and bowling on a higher plane would take longer to achieve.

A new era was under way and, although changes were not dramatic and progress only modest, it was very real.

After the Sussex victory Hampshire were outplayed by Gloucestershire at Bristol and were well beaten by Kent in the annual Whitsun Bank Holiday fixture at Southampton. The disastrous run continued with innings defeats by Leicestershire and Middlesex. In the match against the county ultimately to become champions Jack Robertson, driving both powerfully and elegantly, hit a six and 20 fours in a score of 229, the first double century of his career. For Hampshire McCorkell, recovering from his disappointments of 1946, top scored in both innings with 43 and 66.

A respite came with a seven wicket victory over Derbyshire, again at Portsmouth where Hampshire were to secure all three of their home victories. The win was not a comfortable one and it took a magnificent stand of 163 in under two hours by McCorkell (top scoring in both innings for the second consecutive match) with 103 not out, and Eagar, also undefeated on 88 to see them home. There was also a sterling performance by the veteran seamer George Heath who, bowling unchanged in the first innings, took 7-49 and, in 37 overs in the second innings, 6-103.

A very creditable draw with Yorkshire at Bradford followed this victory with McCorkell's fine run continuing. Although dismissed for 0 in the first innings he top scored in the second with 82 not out. Significantly in this match Cliff Walker, making his debut for Yorkshire, scored 91 and 21 not out ; significant because he would later sign for Hampshire under the Special Registration Rule of 1949. He had made a great impression on Eagar during that match and would become part of the jig saw which was beginning to be put together.

Hampshire then completed the double over Sussex with a comprehensive innings victory at Chichester. Rogers scored a fine 90 on an awkward pitch, his fourth score of 90 or more and yet to score his first hundred. Sussex were dismissed for only 90 in less than 19 overs in seventy five minutes. Their application must be questioned.

In a high scoring game against Cambridge University Rogers finally reached his first century, a match in which a young Doug Insole scored 161 not out.

After the second win of the season over their nearest neighbours Hampshire's final sixteen championship matches produced just one win and the first tied game in their history. Of the seven defeats in this period many were by considerable margins. Sides were rarely bowled out cheaply and the bowling was reaching crisis proportions. Herman, Heath and Bailey were fast coming to the end of their careers and two others, Knott and Ransom, were in their thirties and appearances limited due to business commitments.

Although neither he nor the county realised it a young man, still in the army and stationed not too far away, would soon be signed to greatly alleviate this problem.

The final victory of 1947 was once again achieved at Portsmouth, a lucky ground for them that year. Surrey, who finished sixth, had been more successful with their team building. A fore-runner of the powerful, dominant side of the next decade the Surrey team of 1947 already contained many fine batsmen and two bowlers, Jim Laker and Alec Bedser who were undoubted test class. Hampshire scored a relatively modest 186 with Rogers hitting a fine 70 playing Laker's off breaks with confidence. Laker took 8-69, on three occasions taking 2 wickets with successive deliveries. Surrey's reply was an even more modest 136 with Hampshire's three seamers doing the damage. Batsmen then dominated - Hampshire declaring on 394 for four with Rogers scoring 178, his highest to date. Set 445 to win Surrey greatly improved on their first innings performance and, although always well behind the clock, made a very respectable effort to save the game. Hampshire won with seven minutes to spare.

A dull draw followed against Warwickshire at Southampton but there was some significance attached to the match.

Vic Cannings was a Hampshire born seam bowler who had signed for Warwickshire in 1947. He had a very useful and promising first season taking 61 wickets at 28.13 but his opportunities for his adopted county were soon to be limited. In this particular game Eagar scored his first century for the county and he must have made a mental note about Cannings' bowling for he would sign for Hampshire in 1950. Cannings had taken 4 wickets in 35 overs.

Although the sun continued to shine relentlessly during August Hampshire's fortunes did not improve and the only real excitement came at the end of the month in a match against Lancashire at Bournemouth resulting in their first ever tie.

A week earlier Hampshire had been beaten by an innings by Lancashire at Old Trafford in two days. In the return game Hampshire fared much better and were in a strong enough position to declare in their second innings setting Lancashire a target of 221 in just over two hours. A superb opening stand of 142 in just ninety minutes by Cyril Washbrook and Winston Place put the North Countrymen on course for victory but strange things frequently happen in cricket. Jim Bailey then took 6 wickets in as many overs and, when Hill began the last over, one run was needed with 9 wickets down. The Lancashire number ten batsman, Barlow, was run out off the fourth delivery.

The final match of the 1947 season resulted in a draw at

Bournemouth against Yorkshire. The last three matches were all played at Dean Park before large crowds. With the glorious weather continuing batsmen were in their element and nearly 3,500 runs were scored. For Yorkshire, Hutton hit a masterful 270 not out, the highest individual innings of the season. Throughout his career Hutton reached three figures twice against Hampshire - 280 in 1939 and, with his 270 in 1947, he obviously relished the Hampshire attack once he was set.

It had been a quite extraordinary summer and one which many were reluctant to see come to an end. The glorious weather made watching and playing cricket so enjoyable and helped to expunge the grim memories of the previous winter. The English cricket spectator is a remarkably stoical individual and, on occasions especially in April and May when a north easterly may be blowing, positively masochistic. Once the summer of 1947 really got under way, however, all was fine with the world.

Notwithstanding the heavy defeat inflicted by the Australians during the winter the Nation's premier summer sport appeared to be in fine fettle and already the 1948 visit by Australia was being eagerly anticipated, especially as it would almost certainly be the final trip, as a player, by the "Don".

Unfortunately, for Hampshire, it had generally been a very disappointing year and, finishing sixteenth in the championship, meant that only Northamptonshire were below them.

The bowling was now a problem of major proportions. Admittedly it had been a batsman's summer but Hampshire's attack rarely caused problems for the opposition and it is being kind to describe the bowling that year as quite ordinary. This is not meant to be a criticism of the individuals themselves but, simply, age was not on their side. The average age also hampered the improvement to the fielding which Eagar had made his first priority, although he himself had set a fine example at short leg. The general feeling during those first two post war years was that, if new blood could not be immediately found to raise the standard of the batting and bowling, at least something could be done in the field.

Although there appeared to be no tangible evidence of optimism for the future a few signings were made in 1947 which would have a distinct bearing on the fortunes of the county. The early pieces of the jig saw towards the ultimate dream of a first championship title were starting to fit together.

In April a young man was signed who was to become one of the unluckiest, yet one of the most humorous, good natured men ever to have played for Hampshire. Mervyn Burden was only 16 and would not make his debut for several years. He was the first of a new crop of young prospects born locally and had been a pupil at the King Edward V1 school in Southampton, although he spent much of his school days in evacuation quarters in Poole. At the time his main prowess was on the football field but he was spotted bowling medium pace seamers at an indoor school at Swaythling by Eagar and the coach, Sam Staples. Much to his amazement and delight Burden, who apparently had not played in an organised cricket match since he was 13, was asked to join the Hampshire ground staff. Needless to say he accepted without hesitation. His own account of his first appearance at the County Ground in Southampton is well known and is akin to the chaotic situations in a Tom Sharpe novel:

> "I've never been so nervous in my life. I went up and bowled my first ball and it flew clean over the top of the nets and smashed one of the windows in the old dining room. Someone gave me another one and as I walked back to bowl my next ball I was wondering what the dickens I should do this time. But I didn't have to worry. Johnny Arnold was batting in the next net and, as I turned to run in, he hit an off drive. I had my back to him and never saw it coming ; it caught me a terrific crack on the ankle and I couldn't bowl for a fortnight. Still, I thought I had better show willing, so I turned up the next morning to see if there was anything I could do and they sent me to help Ernie on the pitch. You know, I hadn't been there a couple of minutes before I kicked a bucket of whiting across the square. So they sent me home until my ankle was better"

Attending the same school as Burden, but four years older, was another budding sportsman who was to become a vital member of the county side for almost two decades. Jimmy Gray, like Burden, was a fine footballer, indeed good enough to be signed as a full back for Arsenal, although he never made it to the first team in view of the experience and stature of Walley Barnes and Laurie Scott. Later, Gray had three years with Bedford Town in the old Southern League and finally three years with Salisbury in the Western League. He had been playing cricket for Deanery Colts, a local Southampton side, and was recommended to Hampshire by A.E."Sam" Pothecary, whose own career with Hampshire had ended in 1946.

Although it certainly was not realised at the time a signing of huge significance took place just a few weeks before the end of the season. Whilst the elderly Hampshire attack was being frequently exposed and the county were in the middle of that desperately disappointing run in the second half of the season little did the committee realise that a saviour was close at hand.

A tall modest man of slender build Derek Shackleton, from the Yorkshire town of Todmorden, was signed as a batsman and, in the words of Desmond Eagar, "bowled temperamental leg spinners".

He was to embark on a phenomenally successful career with his adopted county but not as a batsman, nor as a leg break bowler.

With the signings of Burden, Gray and Shackleton, and the return from the Services of Harrison things were looking up.

Chapter Two

Young Man from Tod

Derek was born on 12th August 1924 in the West Riding town of Todmorden to Walter and Ethel Mary Shackleton.

It was a year in which Ramsay MacDonald became Britain's first Labour Prime Minister and a year when the Government rejected the idea of a Channel tunnel ! It was a difficult and extremely uncertain period for the country still carrying the scars of the carnage of the Great War and with the Depression on the horizon.

In the sporting world of 1924 England defeated South Africa 3-0 in the test series with the tourists being ignominiously dismissed for only 30 in their first innings at Birmingham, still the lowest ever total in a test match in this country. Arthur Gilligan, in his first experience as England's captain, took 6 wickets for 7 runs and Maurice Tate had figures of 4-12. The innings lasted just forty five minutes. Apparently the attendances were low due to the half crown charge for admission, a large and prohibitive amount in those days. Domestically, Yorkshire were county champions and dominated the game to such an extent that they won twelve championships between the wars.

In football Newcastle United beat Aston Villa 2-0 in the F.A. Cup Final at Wembley and Huddersfield Town won the first of three consecutive league championships.

The eighth Olympic Games were held, for the second time, in Paris in conditions of extreme heat which obviously suited the swimmer and future Hollywood "Tarzan", Johnny Weissmuller who took three gold medals.

Derek was to be an only child and was born at home at 76, Well Street, a typical Victorian terraced house so prevalent in towns at that time, particularly in the north. Parts of the original Well Street remain but number 76 was demolished some years ago.

Both his parents were weavers at a time when the textile industry was declining and when hard financial times were to come, and this is something which would have a great bearing on Derek's character and natural caution which would become so evident in later years.

Todmorden grew in size and importance with the coming of the Industrial Revolution and, in particular, the textile industry. Until that time most inhabitants in the area had settled in the hillsides surrounding what was, until the 18th Century, a small hamlet. The town straddles the rivers Calder and Roch and stands at the meeting of three valleys. Ideally situated with roads, railways and the canal to transport cotton goods to the ports, and hence to world markets, it became a very important town in the last century.

It was obvious that, with the mills being the dominant places of employment in Todmorden, most families would have some connection with cotton and Derek's parents were no exception, both working at the Waterside Mill which was owned by an eminent local family - the Fieldens.

The Fieldens were extremely important in that part of Lancashire which borders on West Yorkshire. Their roots spanned many generations and they were responsible for the building of the first cotton mill in the area in 1786 and they quickly became heavily involved in the development and prosperity of Victorian Todmorden. The Shackleton home was very close to the Unitarian church which was erected in memory of John Fielden who, somewhat unusually for that period, was an important social reformer. As Member of Parliament for Oldham he was instrumental in the Passing of the "Ten Hour Act" of 1847 which made it illegal for anyone under 18 or any woman to work for more than ten hours a day in the factories.

When Derek's origins have been the subject of discussion, certainly in his early days with Hampshire, doubts have been expressed as to whether Todmorden is in Lancashire or Yorkshire. At one time the boundary of the two counties passed right under the town hall but, from 1888, the town has, for administration purposes, been wholly in, first the West Riding of Yorkshire, and then from 1974 within West Yorkshire.

For many years Derek was classified as a Lancastrian in all cricket reference books and he, himself, had no reason to question this fact. He now accepts, quite happily, that he was born a Yorkshireman. It is not something which has ever bothered him unduly but it has been an interesting topic of discussion from time to time and, in any case, he has lived contentedly in the south since 1948. The question of his birthplace appears to have been resolved during the Edgbaston test of 1963 when Yorkshire claimed him as "one of their own". What is certain is that both Lancashire and Yorkshire missed out on signing one of England's finest ever seam bowlers and one who would have been an ideal opening partner for either Brian Statham or Fred

Trueman.

Derek had a happy childhood in humble surroundings in the largely Victorian town. Todmorden was not, and still isn't, a large place, and there was a general friendliness and community spirit which made it a comfortable environment in which to live, although materially people did not have too much. Being an only child could have made him isolated, especially as he was naturally quiet, but Derek mixed well with other youngsters and it was a distinct advantage in being good at sport. Boys tend to look up to those who have a natural aptitude for games, in particular football and cricket at which he was already making quite an impression. It might have been more difficult for an only child if he did not have these interests. Also, Derek was not the type to make enemies, nor indeed did he do so later in life.

When the school day was over the streets became the venues for full scale football and cricket matches and great skills were learned at a young age at both sports with the aid of tennis balls. Most of the finest of footballers and cricketers of that generation, and before, benefited from this early training. Too many boys have been put off playing cricket due to being hit painfully by a hard ball before the rudiments of the game have been mastered.

Derek's early skills at both games became quickly apparent and were encouraged at school. After leaving primary education he went to Roomfield school on the Halifax road and Harry Wilson, one of his masters and later to become a mayor of Todmorden, took a great interest in the young Shackleton's cricketing ability. He helped him into the school first X1 and Derek was soon selected to play for Lancashire schoolboys at Centre Vale park, Todmorden.

Like so many others at that time Derek left school at the age of 14 with just a basic education and obtained work at a local warehouse. He quickly became bored and restless with this undemanding and monotonous work and, after some advice from a friend of his father, he became a semi-skilled worker at a local tinsmiths.

It was natural that Todmorden Cricket Club would soon start showing interest especially as Derek was often seen practising in the local nets. It seems strange that between 1939, when he made his first appearance for Todmorden, and 1948, the year of his Hampshire debut, he made relatively few appearances for his home town club but this was due to his army call up in 1943. He played fairly regularly in 1941 and 1942 but, afterwards on only isolated occasions.

Derek's father encouraged him although did not play himself. It is believed that other Shackletons represented Todmorden and it is quite likely they were relatives but that was well in the past and Derek was carrying the flag for that generation of the family.

Todmorden is the only Yorkshire club playing in the Lancashire

League and stage their home matches at the picturesque Centre Vale, situated as its name would imply in the centre of the town. Lancashire League cricket is tough and uncompromising and Derek would have experienced a stern and probing baptism. Some of the world's most famous cricketers have played in the League with no holds barred - a true testing ground of ability and character.

The young Shackleton's potential was not ill founded when he made two appearances for the second X1 in 1939 at the age of 15 and before his 16th birthday he had made his debut for the first X1. His major contributions came in 1941 and 1942 when he was a regular member, primarily as a batsman.

Derek's life revolved around Todmorden and only on rare occasions did he travel far, although he does remember a family holiday in Skegness. Basically he only travelled to other towns in Lancashire when Todmorden were playing away and other pursuits were simple ones - the local cinema and, a little later, dances on a Saturday night at the Co-operative hall. Quite an innocent but an enjoyable period in his life.

In the splendidly produced 150th anniversary publication of the history of Todmorden Cricket Club there is mention of a match against Bacup in 1941 in which a 16 year old Shackleton scored 95 in a two hour stay at the crease rescuing his side from a 42 for five situation. Todmorden scored 168 for nine and, in reply, Bacup reached 138 for eight with Todmorden using seven bowlers but not Shackleton. In fact he did not bowl at all that season.

In 1942 he played regularly for the first team again and there is now a record of his bowling capabilities. Still only 17 he took 20 wickets at an average of 10.45. When playing at Colne the skipper, Billy Scott asked Derek if he could bowl. Derek grasped the opportunity and, on his bowling debut, took 4-9 and, in the next game against Nelson, took the new ball and, with it, 5 wickets. In hindsight it is perhaps a little odd that he would later sign for Hampshire as a batsman who could bowl leg breaks whereas he had been bowling seamers for Todmorden and would become the finest medium pace seam bowler of his generation. That same year he proved his all round worth scoring 388 runs at an average of 27.71 with a highest score of 113 not out.

However, with the war at a critical stage and as he was now of an age to be called up he joined the army in 1943 and subsequently played few matches for Todmorden. Indeed between 1940 and 1946 he played in a total of only just over fifty games for his home town, a figure which would have been much higher but for his army call up.

It is possible that, with so many young men in the forces at that time, the standard of League cricket was not as high as it had been prior to 1939 and would become again later but Shackleton's figures, bearing in mind he played almost all of his cricket for Todmorden before he was 18 showed his considerable potential.

A statistical record of his days with Todmorden is given below :

TODMORDEN 1939-1946

Second XI										
	Batting					Bowling				
	Inn	NO	R	H	Ave	O	M	R	W	Ave
1939	2	1	24	21	24.00					
First XI										
1940	8	0	87	26	10.87					
1941	22	1	389	95	18.52					
1942	17	3	388	113*	27.71	72.5	16	209	20	10.45
1943	2	0	53	48	26.50					
1944	2	0	7	7	3.50	1.5	0	6	2	3.00
1945	1	0	19	19	19.00					
1946	1	0	8	8	8.00					
Total	53	4	951	113*	19.40	74.2	16	215	22	9.77

As with first class county sides the Northern Leagues experienced heydays between the wars and in the immediate period following the end of the second world war. Each side had its professional and spectators were privileged to see such legends as Learie Constantine, Everton Weekes, Ray Lindwall, Wes Hall, Charlie Griffith, Basil D'Oliveira, Ian Chappell, Sonny Ramadhin amongst many others. It is reputed that when Constantine played at Centre Vale there were over six thousand spectators . In addition two other cricketing giants - Brian Close and Frank Tyson - were professionals at Centre Vale. No bowler, however, struck such fear into League batsmen as did the West Indian, Roy Gilchrist. Gilchrist, a bowler of awesome pace on wickets nowhere near test standard was quite terrifying, to such an extent that, in one match, the Oldham skipper refused to allow his batsmen to face an assault which was likely to result in a serious injury, or worse. In three controversial years Gilchrist, first with Middleton and then with Bacup, took over 400 wickets, many of them by reputation alone.

Todmorden itself produced several players who later graced the county scene, the most famous being Shackleton and Peter Lever, who became England's bowling coach for a brief period in the mid 1990s.

Lever played for his country on seventeen occasions in the 1970s and had a very distinguished career with Lancashire. He made his debut for Todmorden in 1954 as a 13 year old and had two full seasons with the club in 1958 and 1959 before signing for Lancashire. A highly respected aggressive right arm fast bowler he had the ability to produce a quite devastating late out swinger when pitching the ball up. His most successful series for England was on the 1970/1971 tour to Australia when he provided ideal support for John Snow.

Richard Horsfall played for Todmorden just before the war and returned to Centre Vale after playing for Essex between 1947 and 1955 and a handful of games for Glamorgan in 1956. One match Dick Horsfall would undoubtedly have remembered was the game against the immensely powerful Australian side of 1948. He was in the Essex team who, in a single day, conceded a total of 721 with Bradman scoring 187, one of four century makers. Horsfall was his side's second highest scorer with 11 in an Essex reply of 83.

Peter Greenwood made his debut for Lancashire in 1948 and, as an off break bowler, took over 200 wickets for the county but his appearances were limited because of the skills of Roy Tattersall. Greenwood and Derek were close school friends and were born within a month of each other. He was a good friend to have because his father was a butcher and, with meat being scarce, the Shackleton family received a little preferential treatment. Greenwood played his first game for Todmorden in 1940 but, like his schoolfriend, his career was disrupted by the war. He, too, played just over fifty games for Todmorden but, unlike Derek, he was able to have more opportunities to bowl and, in his brief career with Todmorden, took 110 wickets against Derek's 22.

Ken Fiddling, a wicket keeper, was born just down the road at Hebden Bridge and established himself as first choice keeper for Todmorden in 1936. Later, he signed for Yorkshire but had more success with Northamptonshire for whom he signed in 1947 and remained with them until he had to retire, due to a foot injury, in 1953.

Todmorden, as a small town, can be justifiably proud of the fact that there are at least eight players born locally who have played first class cricket. What is unusual is that three represented one county - Hampshire. Apart from Shackleton two others had spells of varying length with the southern county

Walter Herbert Livsey was born in Todmorden in 1893 and had a distinguished career with Hampshire between 1913 and 1929. Initially he had a trial with Surrey Colts in 1912 but failed to make a big enough impression and joined Hampshire the following season and, in 1914, became the first choice wicket keeper. He was good enough to be selected for the MCC tour to South Africa in 1922/1923 but broke a finger early on and did not feature in any of the test matches. He did, though, play a key role in one of the most remarkable county championship matches ever played.

At Edgbaston in 1922 Hampshire were dismissed by Warwickshire for a humiliating total of 15, their lowest ever score, and had a deficit on first innings of 208. Following on, Hampshire were 177 for six still 31 runs behind and defeat looming. A slow turnabout in fortunes began to take place although when Livsey joined George Brown with the score at 274 for eight Hampshire's lead was a very modest 66. However, they put on 177 for the ninth wicket before Brown departed for a magnificent 172 and then Livsey featured in a last wicket stand of 70 with George Boyes - Livsey remaining undefeated on 110. Astonishingly Hampshire won by 155 runs and the events at Edgbaston in June 1922 remain part of the county's folklore. Livsey also shares with Horace Bowell the record tenth wicket partnership for Hampshire of 192 against Worcestershire in 1921.

Harold Dawson, who broke many batting records with Todmorden in the Lancashire League, played a few games for Hampshire in 1947 and 1948. In fact Dawson played in Derek Shackleton's debut match against Cambridge University at Aldershot in June 1948 : thus Todmorden had two home bred lads playing first class cricket together and this was repeated in the following match against the Combined Services.

The Todmorden 'octet' is completed by Derek's son, Julian, who played for Gloucestershire between 1971 and 1978. He is, perhaps, overlooked when compiling a list of Todmorden born players because he has lived virtually all of his life in the south and made no appearances for the town of his birth.

Because he failed an eye test Derek had little option but to join the non combative Pioneer Corps in 1943. A problem in his left eye had been discovered when he was at school and would continue to give him trouble throughout his life. He spent much of his time at Didcot and then Shrewsbury and was able to continue with both his football and cricket. He was selected for various army teams and, at cricket, he continued mainly as a batsman and, when bowling, would turn to leg breaks. No statistical information is available but he remembers being reasonably successful. As a footballer he had been good enough to be on Burnley's books as a goal keeper in 1942/1943 (he played mainly as a full back in the army) although with the ever deteriorating sight in the eye it is difficult to imagine him pursuing a football career with any great success. It would later become one of the great mysteries of the cricket world as to why he could have been so successful with this substantial liability. With the war coming to an end Derek was now looking forward to his demob which would take place in 1947.

During one of his last periods of leave Derek went along to watch Todmorden which coincided with a visit by Sam Staples, the Hampshire coach. Staples had seen Derek in action when he was playing for an army side and had travelled north to see if any talent could be unearthed from the Leagues. This would have been at the beginning of the 1947 season. Harold Sutcliffe, a former secretary and chairman of Todmorden CC introduced Derek to Staples with kind words about the young man's potential. He was offered a trial at the County ground in Southampton but Derek, being home on only a few days leave and with the future very unpredictable following the war sought the advice of his father. Walter Shackleton had no doubts whatsoever that his son should take up the offer and the invitation was accepted. Derek stayed with Sam Staples for a few days and then returned to camp. He had made a good enough impression to be offered a second trial and then, following his demob, signed professional forms for Hampshire in July 1947. A dream had been realised for this quiet likeable young man and was to be the start of a quite extraordinary career spanning the next 20 years.

Great credit must be given to Staples for what was to be either an extremely astute signing or a very fortuitous one. Shackleton had been signed as a batsman with the additional asset of being able to bowl occasional leg breaks. There was not the slightest hint at this stage that he would become one of the finest seam bowlers in the game's history and the most successful of his type in post war cricket. It is almost certain that he would not have had a long career as a batsman as his subsequent figures would show. Admittedly with the sheer quantity of bowling he would be asked to do over the next two decades his batting would have suffered but it is generally accepted that if he had concentrated on batting alone he would have been only moderately successful. In addition he had the virtual lack of sight in his left eye of which the county were totally unaware and something which Derek kept secret for almost twenty years. Lack of total vision would be a severe enough handicap for any player but, for a right handed batsman, the defect in the left, i.e. the 'forward' eye, would appear to create insurmountable difficulties but he somehow managed and scored nearly 10,000 runs in his career with twenty half centuries.

Was Staples simply very lucky with the signing or did he have a sixth sense that here was someone who was going to be special?

Staples, himself, had been a very fine bowler with Nottinghamshire between the wars, largely medium paced cutters on an impeccable length and he could bowl for very long spells - shades of the future 'Shack'. He was the perfect foil to the quicker Nottinghamshire opening attack of Harold Larwood and Bill Voce. An example of his own abilities was in a match against Hampshire at Southampton in May

1932. He had match figures of 36-24-21-10 with Hampshire being dismissed for 57 and 30. He was an astute cricketer, very knowledgeable about the game and a fine coach with Hampshire albeit for only a short period. He soon became very ill and was replaced by Arthur Holt in the spring of 1949. Just over a year later he died, in fact a month before Derek received his first test cap. How delighted he would have been and there is no doubt that the signing of Derek Shackleton was the most significant one he made for the county. He bequeathed Hampshire a wonderful legacy.

Derek remembers playing about six matches for the Hampshire Club and Ground side at the end of the 1947 season and then returned to his parents' home in Todmorden for the winter. The following spring he journeyed to Southampton with great excitement and expectancy. Little did he realise that, almost immediately, he would become the central figure in a decision which was to have such a bearing on his own career and one which was to reap such benefit for his adopted county.

Chapter Three

And So to Bath

The 1948 season dawned with great expectancy partly due to the fond memories of the previous remarkable summer but, perhaps more importantly, to the first post war visit by the all powerful Australians. It would also be the last trip as a player by arguably the finest batsman the game has ever known, Don Bradman, who would receive the first Knighthood bestowed to a cricketer still playing. Statistically no batsmen bear comparison and his feats and reputation were quite awesome. Even in this, his fortieth year, he averaged 73 in the tests and scored nearly 2,500 runs in all on the tour averaging just under 90 with eleven first class centuries.

The weather in April was also very pleasantly warm and, when the Hampshire players returned for pre season training, there was a general feeling of optimism although the problems of an ageing side were still there.

There had been great efforts during the winter to strengthen the side and the county had been close to signing Allan Rae, a left handed opening batsman from Jamaica, who later played fifteen tests for the West Indies. A tall, friendly man, he would have provided much needed reliability and solidity to the batting which, indeed, he later did with great effect when the West Indians toured England in 1950. Whilst the names of Worrell, Weekes and Walcott spring readily to mind it should be remembered that Rae, on that tour, finished second in the test averages with 62.83.

The Hampshire committee were still very concerned about the quality of the bowling and these anxieties resulted in the now famous edict by the chairman, W K Pearce. Summoning the skipper, Desmond Eagar, before one of the practice sessions he commanded that, in view of the lack of any new bowlers, everyone on the staff must bowl fast in the nets to see what hidden talents there may be. This single decision was to have a very direct bearing on the career of one player and on the fortunes of the county during the following twenty years.

Derek Shackleton had spent the winter in the north but was now looking forward, albeit somewhat nervously, to his first season with his adopted county. Having been signed as a batsman he had only bowled occasional innocuous leg breaks in the nets, certainly harmless enough not to cause batsmen undue alarms.

Following the chairman's instructions there were some interesting and humorous attempts at bowling fast in the nets that day. In particular Eagar's mimicry of emulating Bill Voce caused great hilarity. However, what created the most interest and comment was the sight of the young Yorkshireman (although at that time he was considered to be from Lancashire) giving the immediate impression that here was someone who might just solve at least part of the bowling problem. He had bowled very straight with a high natural action and, although not genuinely fast, produced deliveries that were distinctly lively. Derek had bowled seamers for Todmorden some years earlier but not seriously since then and it seemed, that in a few moments, a transformation had taken place which would clinch a long term career for the player and make the biggest individual contribution to the county's fortunes over the coming years. It was an extraordinary natural ability. He was uncoached, unspoilt and now unmasked and the chairman and captain decided, there and then, that Shackleton should forget the leg spin and concentrate on seam.

Established players at that time such as Leo Harrison, Neville Rogers, Gerry Hill and Charles Knott all remember that day clearly and were sufficiently impressed to know that here was someone quite special. Rogers recalls the first match that Shackleton bowled seamers for the county. It was at the beginning of the 1948 season in a second X1 game against Wiltshire at Bournemouth. He took 8 wickets in that match and reports of his performance were quickly relayed to the chairman and those involved in the selection of the first X1.

It was quite apparent that it would not be too long before he would be seriously considered for the first team and his opportunity came on June 12th 1948 at the start of a cricket week at the Services ground in Aldershot.

The first of two matches was against a strong Cambridge University side which included John Dewes, Hubert Doggart, Trevor Bailey and Doug Insole. Bailey, of course, went on to play sixty one times for England and the other three all represented their country. The quality of the opposition, and certainly the batting, was high and would prove a good test. Although George Heath was the senior bowler the opening attack was shared by Shackleton and Major A N E Waldron whose only two appearances for Hampshire were during that week at Aldershot. Heath took 6-63 in the University's first innings but the debutant took 3-47 off 23.4 overs including the wicket of Dewes. The later renowned accuracy and meanness was immediately evident - just 2 runs per over conceded.

Harrison kept wicket in that match and two dismissals "caught Harrison bowled Shackleton" were the forerunner of a very familiar pattern over many subsequent seasons. Harrison had made his own debut at the age of 17 in 1939 and was another player who had lost six years to the war. A shrewd reader of the game he was to become best placed of anyone to analyse and appreciate this particular bowler and who, later, would give very thoughtful views on the reasons behind the success of his colleague.

The second game at Aldershot was against the Combined Services, a match in which 'Writer' P B H May played for the opposition and Jimmy Gray made his debut for Hampshire. Shackleton did not take any wickets but conceded only 9 runs in 8 overs. Hampshire won by an innings margin but only after a disastrous start to their innings. Losing 4 wickets for 15 they recovered to reach 269 due to fine efforts from the middle and late order batsmen including an eighth wicket stand of 99 between Gray and Shackleton, the latter making 63, the highest individual score of the match. The Combined Services, on a drying pitch, were twice dismissed cheaply largely due to the off spin of Hill who had match figures of 12-94.

During that week in June 1948 two highly significant debuts had been made, players who would prove to be so important to the county over the next two decades.

Gray later recalled that "Shack and I were lucky because we had come on the scene when there were opportunities. Hampshire were desperate for young players at that time and there were lots of places available in 1948". He expands on the good fortune of the timing of their entries into the first class game. "There was, and still is," says Gray "a huge gap between second X1 and first X1 cricket and, if the senior side is settled and playing well, there is very little opportunity, and indeed sometimes a great reluctance to risk blooding a young untried player simply on success achieved in a second X1. In 1948, however, the county had to seriously consider younger players".

During the Aldershot week Field Marshal Montgomery of Alamein met the players during one of the lunch breaks. Neville Rogers remembers the visit and, on hearing that the Field Marshal was in attendance the players "prepared for inspection of kit. Pads were placed upright with bats down". He had a propensity for signing his autograph - on anything within reach. Jim Bailey, the slightly portly, good humoured and highly thoughtful cricketer had just purchased a new bat. On seeing the bat in the corner of the dressing room the Field Marshal approached it with some relish. Bailey, on seeing the likely outcome, quickly removed the bat politely explaining that he wanted to use it shortly and did not want it marked in any way. Undeterred the eminent general obviously wanted to make his presence felt. He was known not to be a great enthusiast of county cricket but showed sufficient interest that day to point out the dangers of the elderly make up of the side. "You've too many old 'uns" he perceived, "I sacked all my older generals, replaced them with younger ones. I suggest you do the same". Ironically it was during that week that the first very positive action was taken to bring in younger, skilful players with the introduction of Shackleton and Gray.

Derek had shown enough promise and achieved sufficient success at Aldershot to warrant selection for his first county championship match at Bath against Somerset. Although he had taken only 4 wickets in the two games he had bowled extremely accurately and appeared to have a very wise experienced head on young shoulders.

He was, nevertheless, surprised to be selected as the established bowlers - Herman, Knott and particularly Bailey were having good seasons. It was in the dressing room during the late Friday afternoon at Aldershot that he heard the news. "Shack, we're taking you to Bath". It was a simple short sentence from the skipper but took Derek totally unawares. He had to explain that he had no change of clothing with which to go straight down to the West Country but a message was relayed to Southampton and additional kit was made available.

Even at this early stage in his career "Shack" was the name affectionately given to him and which would be widely used, not just by his colleagues but opponents alike.

The match was a good one for Hampshire. Not only did they win by 36 runs but it set them on a profitable run of nine matches of which they won six and drew two taking them to the dizzy heights of fifth position at the end of July. For Derek it had been a highly satisfactory, if unspectacular championship debut. He didn't take a wicket - indeed he was given only 2 overs in the Somerset first innings - but in his match total of 11 overs he only conceded 15 runs. What makes this mean economy rate even more impressive is because he bowled several overs to Harold Gimblett, one of the most experienced and certainly one of the hardest hitting batsmen in the country. On his own county championship debut in 1935 he caused a sensation by treating the Essex attack with total disdain hitting 123 in eighty minutes. In another game he hit 3 sixes in an over during which his partner appealed against the light.

Derek did not play in the next two games against Surrey and Northamptonshire but returned for the match against Leicestershire at Southampton when Gray made his championship debut. Once again he was wicketless and then didn't even bowl during the first of two consecutive matches against Sussex. He now feels that, during that early period, whilst the county were anxious to inject new blood into the side the fact that so many players had been together for so long there was a natural and understandable tendency to stick together and, for a while, he felt he was an outsider. Nothing particularly unfriendly or resentful but perhaps the realisation had now hit them that their own careers were coming to an end and Shackleton was one of the natural replacements. He had been given only short bursts of bowling and, for a man who was to thrive on extremely lengthy spells, his output of just 27 overs in his first three championship matches would not have brought about the slightest hint of a sweat nor indeed, as he was later to prove, would 27 overs in one innings alone.

In the second Sussex game at Portsmouth he took his first championship wickets, those of John Langridge and Hubert Doggart both of whom were caught behind by Harrison. He then played in the second of the Portsmouth Festival matches and although strangely given only 8 overs took the important wicket of Reg Simpson.

Shackleton's selection was still not automatic and, when he did play, he was greatly underbowled. Herman, Knott and Bailey were doing the lion's share of the work and Bailey was having a marvellous year in the autumn of his career. Not only did he achieve the double of 1000 runs and 100 wickets he also scored more runs and took more wickets than any other Hampshire player. To further underline his dominance he headed both the batting and bowling averages. A portent of his season to come came in the first championship match of the summer against the powerful Middlesex side at Lord's. In the first innings Bailey took 5-26 in 22 overs and his victims were no less than Robertson, Edrich, Compton, Mann and Fairbairn. Another interesting fact about Bailey's season was that, although he scored most runs and topped the averages, he did not hit one century. He was consistency personified and he very rarely failed that summer.

Hampshire had experienced an encouraging season even though they had slipped from fifth at the end of July to their final ninth position. It had been a great improvement on 1947 and was their most successful year since 1932. Plans for the future development of the playing staff were well under way with the introduction of Shackleton and Gray, the re-emergence of Harrison, the consistency of Rogers and the promise of Burden who was away doing his National Service. In addition there was, of course, the enthusiastic captaincy of Eagar.

There was encouragement that year for the more modest counties when an unfashionable side, Glamorgan, won the championship for the first time. A team of no apparent stars they were welded together under the strong leadership of Wilfred Wooller. The result was a side who knew their limitations but played to their strengths which basically were good, if unspectacular, all round performances from individuals who enjoyed a great team spirit due to playing together so frequently. Ten of their players played in at least twenty two of the twenty six matches and this bears out the theory that, in most sports, a team has an increased chance of success if there are as few changes as possible. The championship was actually clinched at Bournemouth on August 24th. When J C Clay appealed for lbw against Knott the Welsh umpire Dai Davies' finger went up - "That's out and the championship's ours !"

Although Derek did not play against the invincible Australians mention should be made of Hampshire's fighting performance against the tourists at Southampton. In a low scoring match on a difficult wicket Hampshire led the Australians on first innings - the only county side to do so during the whole tour. Charles Knott took 5-57, figures which were slightly dented when Keith Miller hit him for 3 successive sixes. Knott was disappointed that Bradman didn't play because he would have loved to have had the chance of bowling to the world's greatest batsman on a wicket giving the bowlers some assistance. Knott met Bill Brown a few years ago and the Australian opener remembers the game as it was one of those very rare occasions on the tour when there was a distinct possibility they could lose. In the end the tourists won by 8 wickets. So dominant were the 1948 Australians that they won twenty three and drew eight of their thirty one matches and easily retained the 'Ashes' with a 4-0 margin of victory. All five Wisden Cricketers of the Year were Australian.

When the season ended Derek went back to Todmorden to stay with his parents for the winter. Earlier that year when he had joined the players for pre season training he was expecting to play mainly in the second X1 as a batsman. That he should finish the season as a fast medium bowler, and likely to become the first choice opener, both surprised and delighted him.

By this time Derek had met, and was dating, a pretty, fair haired girl from Todmorden. Kathy, like Derek, was an only child and her father had died when she was very young. Also, like Derek, she came from a humble but comfortable background although , as she proudly points out, her mother's terraced house had the luxury of an indoor bathroom which was not too common in those days! Derek and Kathy met at a Saturday night dance just before Christmas in 1947. When asked about the precise venue Derek was certain it was the Co-operative Hall, Kathy was equally adamant it was at the Town Hall. "Ah, yes, I remember it well !" Derek later conceded that Kathy was right.

Life was simple, but happy and uncomplicated; they enjoyed the usual pursuits of going to the cinema, to local dances and also walking in the hills and on the moors surrounding Todmorden.

On returning to Southampton in the spring of 1949 the Hampshire

Committee decided to send Derek to Alf Gover's cricket school in London. This would be the first time he had received any formal coaching and, being such a truly natural bowler, there was not much he had to learn. His silky smooth run up, high action and beautifully co-ordinated arm and wrist movement could not be improved upon nor, of course, even at this early stage of his career could his accuracy. Derek, with Kathy, stayed with Vic Ransom and his wife Margaret during this particular week and, according to Ransom, Shack already had everything and he didn't necessarily gain anything from going to the school. This perhaps is not entirely true. Generally his main deliveries were in swingers but during the week of coaching he began to develop the out swinger and this he would use to great effect a little later in his career but, for some years, the stock delivery would be the ball coming into the right hander.

Of even more importance from this stay in London was Derek's proposal of marriage. The engagement ring was purchased in Clapham and he and Kathy were to be wed within eighteen months.

Before the start of the 1949 season Hampshire made two signings under the Special Registration Rule which applied that year.

Cliff Walker had played just a handful of games for Yorkshire in 1947 and 1948 and, on his debut at Bradford (against Hampshire), had a match aggregate of 112 for once out. His opportunities for Yorkshire, with their immensely strong batting line up, were limited, however, and he grasped the opportunity to travel south.

Alan Rayment was similarly placed at Middlesex. A highly promising, attractive batsman and brilliant fielder he had played a few times for Middlesex second X1 and had made a favourable impression in a match against Hampshire's second string at Bournemouth. He would have loved to have established himself at Lord's but realistically knew that his opportunities there would be sparse. At Hampshire there were a large number of 'due to be retired' players and he decided it would be more sensible to take his chances with them.

In addition to Walker and Rayment Hampshire signed Dick Carty, a fast medium bowler who had been playing Southampton Parks cricket and Reg Dare, a slow left arm bowler who, it was hoped, would be the natural successor to Jim Bailey.

Following the promising start he had made the previous season Derek was looking forward with some relish to the beginning of the 1949 campaign. Any initial excitement was blunted when, inexplicably, he was not picked for the first two games against Glamorgan and Surrey. Perhaps the committee felt that, of all the new signings, he was the one with most potential and that on no account must he become over confident or cock-sure. If they had fully understood the nature of the man they would have realised that he was probably the last person to be adversely affected with any success which came his way. He had the ideal temperament to overcome any difficulties he might encounter. Throughout his whole career he very rarely showed any emotion but not being selected for those two matches still rankles.

The Hampshire bowling attack against Glamorgan consisted of Walker, signed as a batsman and whose 11 wickets in 1949 would cost 73 apiece, and Heath, Knott, Bailey and Hill whose average age was 37 ! In the next match at the Oval Ransom was selected ahead of Shackleton. Ransom had enjoyed some success in 1947 but the next year his availability, as an amateur, limited him to eight matches and his 19 wickets cost 40.52. It was already known that, because of his business interests he would only be available for a few games in 1949. Hampshire's five bowlers at the Oval were aged between 31 and 41 and Surrey won comfortably by an innings and 58 runs.

The selection committee then came to their senses and Shack was picked for the next match against Nottinghamshire at Southampton and, until he retired, would only miss games because of injury - which was extremely rare - or because of test calls and other representative matches.

The next four games saw him greatly under-used, certainly in three of them, bowling only 5,11 and 15 overs against Nottinghamshire, Gloucestershire and Kent respectively. Admittedly these games were on wickets favouring spin but generally, as he was to prove, Derek could also make full use of a turning wicket. Again it appeared the county were being over protective.

He did, though, have a good long bowl at Taunton where, once more, he pitted his wits against Gimblett. The Somerset farmer had an outstanding match scoring a century in each innings for the first time. Probably the fastest scoring opening batsman of his generation he could destroy attacks with ease but Derek did not buckle under the onslaught and his match figures of 5-129 off 48 overs were very commendable in the circumstances. In the first innings he conceded only 45 runs off 21 overs and Gimblett was uncharacteristically restrained.

The return match against Somerset at Portsmouth was an important milestone for Shackleton. The United Services ground was, and to a certain extent still is, a wicket which generally favoured the seamers. For Derek it would become his 'killing fields' and he would take more wickets there than on any other ground. In this game he took 5 wickets in an innings for the first time - just the first of 194 occasions he would achieve this feat. His analysis of 31.4-8-69-6 would become typical in the years ahead. It proved to the county that here was a young bowler who could bowl for long spells without losing his rhythm or line and length and who could give some relief to the older players who could not be expected to put in so much work. After that performance he became first choice to open the bowling and could be relied upon totally - already his skipper and colleagues knew that a loose delivery would be almost unheard of.

However, Hampshire were not enjoying a great amount of success and, until early July, had won only one game - even Oxford University beat them. They then comfortably defeated Derbyshire with Shackleton taking 7-90 in the second innings and Dick Carty, who made his debut a few weeks earlier, taking 5-43 in the first innings. It seemed probable at the time that Carty would become Derek's first regular opening partner. He had a distinctly lively brisk pace and, together with a natural confidence in his own ability, there was cautious optimism that the county had an opening attack of some genuine promise and substance. Both were in their mid twenties, working well in harness and taking wickets. Carty, though, was already experiencing injury problems which were to blight his short career and recurring ankle injuries reduced his appearances in 1949 to just nine.

In the next match at Portsmouth against Gloucestershire Derek took 10 wickets in a game for the first time. He had final figures of 12-214 in 57 overs and dismissed Tom Graveney twice - for 0 and 38, the second innings knock being a majestic little cameo with Gloucestershire going for quick runs. There were nine flowing boundaries, mainly drives off the front foot.

Graveney, like Shackleton, was in his first full season in county cricket and he became one of the most stylish of all post war batsmen. Tall and elegant he scored nearly 48,000 runs during his distinguished career, none in an ugly fashion and the majority with true grace and panache. He was always a joy to watch and scored 4882 runs for England at an average of 44.38, a very high quality batsman indeed. He was a front foot player and, as so many batsmen were to discover over the next twenty years, it was the only way to combat Shackleton.

Graveney has admitted that he was never at ease against him. For a man who scored so many runs throughout his career with 122 centuries to his name his record against Hampshire, at least when he was with Gloucestershire, was quite modest. His 33 innings in matches between the counties when Shackleton was playing produced just 728 runs at an average of 22.75. Derek, surprisingly, does not remember dismissing Graveney too often but actually claimed his wicket on eight occasions when Graveney was playing for Gloucestershire and a further five times after he moved to Worcestershire.

"I never relished playing against Hampshire" Graveney recalls, "certainly when I was with Gloucestershire. You were aware that you were facing a bowler, so skilled, that there was absolutely no room for error. I played him off the front foot which was the only way but if you made a mistake you knew the chances were you would be back in the pavilion".

He remembers he experienced a great sense of relief when Eagar or, in later years, Ingleby-Mackenzie gave Shack a rest, which was not often. This did not necessarily ease the problems he was experiencing against Hampshire at the time. "Perhaps I then relaxed too much because, as he enjoys reminding me to this day, Jimmy Gray would often dismiss me with his gentle, but deceptive in duckers".

Graveney was just one of a whole line of batsmen of the very highest quality who greatly admired and respected Hampshire's adopted Yorkshireman. "I rate Derek very highly, probably the finest of his type in post war cricket. There have been a large number of average medium pace bowlers who, certainly when wickets were uncovered, exploited English conditions. Shack, however, was in a class of his own and only Tom Cartwright bears comparison".

With the 1949 season in mid stream Derek was now enjoying lengthy spells of bowling for which he would become so renowned, apart from very occasional matches when the wicket was a real turner. Even in those conditions he was able to cut the ball back sharply off the seam and it was this full use of the seam which made the ball do 'magical things' as one former player remarked.

Hampshire were now relying on Shackleton as the spearhead of their attack and the timing of his success could not have been more opportune. Lofty Herman had already retired and George Heath played only four times in 1949 before gracefully bowing out of the game. Jim Bailey who had been such a tower of strength, particularly in the immediate post war years, finally succumbed to 'anno domini' and retired, although he returned for one match in 1952. In that last full season, at the age of 41, he once again scored over 1000 runs and took 82 wickets. Only Knott of the regular older quartet of bowlers would remain for a further few seasons.

The county's results were not improving, however, and a defeat by Middlesex at Bournemouth was the first of five successive reverses. This was Derek's first encounter with Edrich and Compton and honours were even. In the Middlesex first innings Compton was bowled by Shackleton for 2 but Edrich scored 182 and, in the second innings, he dismissed Edrich for 4 but Compton hit a fine 102 not out.

It was, though, the batting performance of Jack Robertson that Derek remembers more clearly. Batting faultlessly in the first innings he scored 123 in just over three hours and followed this with 42 in the second. When asked, in later years, who he considered were the finest batsmen he played against the name of Robertson was always mentioned. "I would have gladly given Jack 50 runs to stay in the pavilion". Generous words from someone who loathed giving runs away but was an indicator of how much he admired such a gifted but under-rated batsman. When the illustrious Middlesex 'twins' were breaking records, daily it seemed, in 1947 it is sometimes overlooked that Robertson scored 2760 runs and, like Graveney, with true elegance and fluency.

Middlesex shared the championship that year with Yorkshire who provided the opposition for the fifth match in this depressing sequence of results. A not too cleverly worked out fixture list meant that the players had to travel overnight from Portsmouth to Hull where they arrived, exhausted, at 3 a.m. There was to be a similar occurrence the following year.

After the defeat by Yorkshire, Hampshire ended the season on a better note winning three of their last six matches and this relative period of success was sufficient to avoid them finishing bottom of the championship table. Their two earlier victories against the bottom county, Leicestershire, proved to be crucial.

The final match of the 1949 season was of personal significance to Derek. Hampshire beat Sussex convincingly and, although he only took 2 wickets, the second, which dismissed S C Griffith, was his 100th of the season. A considerable achievement for someone in his first full season. As Eagar was to observe "opposing batsmen found they had a new problem to tackle in Derek Shackleton". He added, "his rapid advance was the best thing that has happened to Hampshire cricket since the war". He was awarded his county cap which meant, importantly, his wages rose from a meagre £5 per week to £7.13.10.

Even though Derek had largely been something of an unknown quantity in 1949 batsmen treated him with great caution and on only a very few occasions during his career would there be any attempt to 'take him apart'. There was, however, one example that year and was spectacularly successful.

The New Zealand tourists came to Southampton in June and, Hampshire, after a deficit of 301 on first innings, fought back magnificently to leave the opposition with a target of 109 runs in thirty five minutes. When the Hampshire second innings closed on 409 Eagar went across to the New Zealand captain, Hadlee. "Walter, we had better call it a day". "No, Desmond" was the reply. "We are going for them".

Bert Sutcliffe and Martin Donnelly attacked Ransom and Shackleton from the start and, extraordinarily, 50 runs were on the board in ten minutes. Northlands Road has rarely, if ever, been so peppered with both bowlers being dispatched to all parts. Ransom remembers his younger colleague being uncharacteristically rattled. "Vic, what the bloody hell's going on out here ?" He had been taken quite unawares by this quite savage onslaught to which he was certainly not accustomed.

It was, to a large extent, an artificial finish. The New Zealand players were padded up in front of the pavilion and the incoming and outgoing batsmen ran to and from the wicket. In addition, the Hampshire fielders ran across after each over. The winning runs came with five minutes to spare and Shackleton had been hit for 56 in 5.5 overs. Virtually 12 overs in half an hour with inevitable delays caused by retrieving the ball after so many sixes plus the time taken when each of the 3 wickets fell would be unthinkable now. Even in those days a captain would not have been so generous if the outcome had involved crucial championship points. It did, though, make great entertainment - except for the two bowlers !

During this fine first full season it should be remembered that Derek originally signed for Hampshire as a batsman and he came close, in that early period, to being classed as a genuine all rounder. In 1949 he came near to achieving the double of 1000 runs and 100 wickets. He has two disappointments with his batting - that he didn't reach 1000 runs in a season and that he never scored a century. He was very close to both that year.

His two highest ever scores occurred in 1949, both at Bournemouth. In July he hit 84 in a sixth wicket stand of 138 which helped to save the game against Glamorgan. Just over one month later he bettered this with 87 not out against Essex with his first 50 coming in under an hour. He would never again get so close to three figures and his solitary century for Todmorden in 1942 remains the only occasion he scored a 100 in any form of cricket.

At the start of the final match of the season he had scored 910 runs and the skipper, thoughtfully, put him up in the batting order to number five to give him more opportunity of scoring the required 90. Unfortunately, he was dismissed for 4 and, with Hampshire winning by an innings, he had no second opportunity.

His batting technique was straightforward. Standing face on to the bowler (partly because of the problem in his left eye) his main area for runs was the arc between long on and long off and the lofted on drive was probably his most lucrative shot. It was not too long before the opposition learned to always have at least two men deep behind the bowler.

Although he was close to the double that year he could not really be considered a true all rounder but he was good enough to score twenty half centuries during his career and top scored for England on his test debut. Inevitably his batting would suffer the more bowling he was asked to do over subsequent years. He favoured the number eight spot from where he would make some very useful, late order, contributions.

A thoroughly successful first full season saw him established as Hampshire's premier seam bowler but the true test of his ability and character would follow.

Chapter Four

Trent Bridge and A Meeting with Frank

Derek was a relatively unknown quantity at the beginning of the 1949 season and some batsmen did not, initially, take him too seriously. They would soon learn. The county circuit is like the bush telegraph and the word was soon passing around that here was someone who had to be treated with respect. It was generally agreed that, with his uncanny accuracy and late in swing, the most successful method to combat him was to play forward. No one was more qualified to confirm this judgment than Leo Harrison. "When we saw a batsman go on to the back foot we just knew it wouldn't be long before he would be in serious trouble".

However skilful and gifted a batsman may be he will also want to add to his armoury by noting the strengths and weaknesses of opposition bowlers. If a fresh face emerges, and certainly if he shows immediate promise, an intelligent, experienced player will do his utmost to find any flaws. There are many examples, throughout the game's history, of a young player being 'found out' after a good first season and who turned out to be a one year wonder. Not so with Derek.

His true test would undoubtedly come in 1950 but he had a very equable temperament and took everything in his stride. Initially his main asset was his accuracy, which was taken almost to the point of extreme, and the ability to frequently hit the seam. Of his 100 wickets in 1949 71 had been bowled, trapped lbw or caught behind. This is an exceptionally high ratio and many of the remaining dismissals were as a result of catches close to the wicket particularly in the leg trap - there were no restrictions in those days to the number of fielders on the leg side. Derek's simple theory was that, by bowling straight, you immediately had two possibilities of getting a batsman out - bowled or lbw. Why waste unnecessary energy and also why give a batsman early easy opportunities to score runs and ease the pressure ?

The new, and indeed any subsequent, season would not find him out and in fact he became an even more difficult proposition. To give him some assistance the county made another important signing which enabled them to have one of the best seam attacks in the country.

Vic Cannings was born in the village of Bighton situated amongst the lovely rolling downs of central Hampshire. He first played cricket for Preston Candover against other local village sides and then in Surrey when his family, who were farm workers, moved to Farnham. The owner of the 'Big House' recommended the 16 year old Cannings to the captain of Surrey's second X1 who also lived in Farnham. He was soon selected for the 'Young players of Surrey' meeting the Bedser twins and Stuart Surridge.

In 1938 Cannings joined the Palestine police and enjoyed the luxury of four or five matches a week. When the war started he still continued his cricket and played alongside people such as Lindsay Hassett, Norman Yardley, Jim Laker, Bob Appleyard and Peter Smith. He also played a lot of football (it seems that in the 1950s Hampshire could have put out a very useful football team) and life, at first, was very enjoyable.

After coming home in 1946 Cannings had trials with Hampshire, Middlesex and Glamorgan, all of whom hinted that they may be able to take him on the following season. However, in the meantime, he had been recommended to Warwickshire by Jack Marshall, a master at Warwick School, and someone he knew from his Palestine days. After a successful trial he signed for the Midlands county on Paddington station with wages of £5 per week.

Cannings had a reasonably successful season in 1947 taking 61 wickets and making a good, and obviously a lasting, impression in a match against Hampshire - a mental note had been duly made by Desmond Eagar. His opportunities then became limited especially as Warwickshire had a very large playing staff and, at the end of the 1949 season, he had a conversation with Johnny Arnold and Neil McCorkell when Hampshire visited Edgbaston. They confirmed that Hampshire were still looking for new bowlers as Heath and Herman had, by then, retired. Eagar also spoke to him and said that if he could get his release from Warwickshire Hampshire would take him on notwithstanding he would be 30 at the start of the 1950 season. The release was obtained and a very astute signing was made because 'Shack and Vic' became, during the next decade, one of the most feared opening attacks in the country.

A cheerful man who took his cricket very seriously Cannings' career really blossomed with his home county. It is worth recalling that he had an immense confidence in his ability as a batsman although his career average of 10.85 does not really bear this out. It was while he was with Warwickshire that he hit his highest ever score of 61 against

Nottinghamshire. He clearly remembers the innings because he admits he was dropped at least six times - mainly off the hard working Harold Butler who, eventually, was absolutely seething. Finally Charlie Harris caught him and, clutching the ball tightly, ran half way round the ground shouting "I got him, I got him". To add to Butler's despair it was Arthur Jepson who took Cannings' wicket .

There was a widely held and justified belief that the skipper would 'wind Shack up at the end of April and he would just keep going until mid September'. There were a few seasons when it would take slightly longer for everything to be running smoothly. He always loved the warm sun on his back and did not enjoy those occasions when April and May turned out to be a continuation of the winter. The start of the 1950 season was a case in point.

It did not augur well when a friendly match against Sussex was abandoned because of snow. Shackleton then took only 9 wickets in his first three matches (although some bowlers would have been reasonably content) but in the next game he produced a devastating performance against Leicestershire at Portsmouth. In the first innings he took 8-39, the best performance of his career to date, and followed this with 4-43. He bowled 54 overs in the match and conceded just 82 runs. He was proving that his successes in 1949 were not a flash in the pan and batsmen were going to continue to have problems. Shack himself was building up his own knowledge of opposing batsmen to use to his advantage in the years ahead.

Cannings was by now his regular opening partner as the unlucky Carty's appearances were still being restricted by injury. He made his debut at Lord's against Middlesex in a match played under a one day rule because rain prevented any play until lunch on the third day. Cannings dismissed both the Compton brothers and Robertson and Shackleton's 3 wicket haul comprised of Edrich, Brown and Robins. This was the first occasion they had bowled in tandem and had made a very impressive start.

The two seamers were complementing each other with their own particular styles. At that time Shackleton generally bowled the in swinger and Cannings' stock ball was the one moving away from the right hander. There was never any problem between them as to which end they would take. The choice would often depend on wind direction to assist each individual's swing.

What was also giving the bowlers tremendous encouragement was the fine fielding, especially the close to the wicket catching. The benefits from reducing the average age to 29 from 33 in 1946 were very apparent. A bowler's confidence can be dramatically boosted in the knowledge that snicks and edges will 'stick' but he can be quickly demoralised if catches are frequently put down. At that time Eagar,

Rogers, Dare and Gray were fine close catchers and Rayment quite brilliant in the covers. The fielding would reach even greater heights in subsequent years.

The county's policy of giving the younger players more opportunities was reaping rewards because they suffered only one defeat in their first eight matches. In addition, Arnold, McCorkell, Hill and Knott from pre-war days were still playing regularly and providing invaluable experience.

Hampshire were involved in their second tied match within three years when they met Kent in the usual Whitsun Bank Holiday fixture at Southampton. It was a consistently even game throughout with each of the four innings totals ranging between 152 and 180. On a wicket taking spin Doug Wright of Kent and Knott had a particularly good match and Knott's batting was needed to inch Hampshire towards their second innings target of 153. When the ninth wicket fell 22 runs were still required and the two batsmen at the crease were, ultimately, to have career batting averages for Hampshire in single figures. The odds were very much on a Kent victory. However, Cannings with immense confidence produced several lucrative 'dabs' and these, together with four leg byes and a majestic off drive for 4 by Knott took them to within three of the target. Knott, confidence high, then lashed out for an edged 2 but, repeating the shot, was caught by Arthur Fagg.

Hampshire comfortably beat Sussex at Portsmouth with Shackleton taking a 'customary' haul of 9 wickets but the next championship match against Nottinghamshire at Trent Bridge resulted in a high scoring draw after the home side had been dealt some early shocks. Cannings and Carty sent the first four Notts batsmen back to the pavilion with a combined score of six but they reached a total of 401 due to an obdurate innings of 239 not out by the opener, Charlie Harris. Harris was one of the relatively few batsmen who seemed to tackle Shackleton more effectively than most and made many useful scores against Hampshire. This turned out to be his highest score in first class cricket but sadly he was soon to be troubled by ill health and died at the tragically young age of 45. McCorkell, Rogers and Arnold all scored hundreds for Hampshire in reply and the match meandered towards a meaningless draw.

Don Kenyon of Worcestershire was a regular thorn in Hampshire's side and, for a period at least, probably played Shackleton with more confidence than any other player. He was the main reason why, in the next match at Southampton, Worcestershire won by 8 wickets with Kenyon scoring 109 and then 67 in thirty five minutes. In that second innings Shackleton and Cannings had very uncharacteristic figures of 10-0-72-0 and 7-0-52-0 respectively.

Kenyon had a very fine record against Hampshire and in games in which he and Shack were in direct opposition he had an overall average of just under 46.

Inn	NO	Runs	Hst	Ave	100s	Dismissed by Shackleton
51	5	2113	229	45.93	6	10

However, there is a distinct contrast in Kenyon's figures up to the end of 1959 and those from 1960-1967, and bears out Derek's comment that "I finally sussed Don, although he did really well against me for some time". The earlier figures can be split as follows:

	Inn	NO	Runs	Hst	Ave	100s	Dismissed by Shackleton
1948-59	36	4	1800	229	56.25	6	3
1960-67	15	1	313	73	22.35	-	7

Here were two shrewd cricketing brains each respecting the other's skills, and honours overall coming out just about even.

Derek, throughout his long career, bowled to many more naturally gifted batsmen than Kenyon, but of those players who faced him on more than a handful of occasions, i.e, not including batsmen who may have achieved a freak average after say just two or three innings - only Peter May had a higher average when playing against a Shackleton led Hampshire attack.

Another defeat followed at the hands of Somerset at Taunton within two days notwithstanding fine bowling by Shackleton and Cannings in the first innings and Knott and Dare in the second. Generally, though, the fortunes of the county were encouraging and they remained unbeaten for the next five matches and, until mid July, held a position in the county table no lower than sixth.

July 1950 was an exciting month for Derek and the start of a period which would bring him much personal happiness.

The West Indian tourists were proving to be almost as powerful as the 1948 Australians and outplayed England in three test matches to win the series by a 3 to 1 margin. Their considerable strengths lay in their formidable batting and, surprisingly at the time, with their two spinners, Ramadhin and Valentine. Strangely, in view of what would occur in subsequent tours, the pace bowlers in their party made little impression.

They came to Southampton at the beginning of July and treated the crowd of 10,000 on the Saturday to a marvellous exhibition of batsmanship reaching 539 for four declared. With McCorkell keeping wicket Harrison was fielding in the deep, and quite brilliantly. He recalls that, in hindsight, it was a mistake dismissing Allan Rae so early - he was a more patient batsman than his more flamboyant colleagues - and with Trestrail gone "this simply brought Weekes to the wicket to join Roy Marshall. He (Weekes), in an innings of 246 not out in just over four hours did not hit the ball in the air once". Records show that there were no sixes in his innings but, with a whole armoury of attacking strokes on both sides of the wicket, he drove, cut and caressed 35 fours . Derek himself remembers that bowling to Weekes was like bowling against a barn door so wide did the bat appear to be.

To Hampshire's credit they fielded magnificently all day and, although 539 runs were scored, they did bowl 142 overs so that the run rate was actually less than 4 an over. Marshall also batted superbly and had made such an impression that it was not too long before the county signed him.

Unfortunately the match was spoiled due to rain on the Monday but on the final day Rogers scored a century before lunch in two and a half hours - play started early that morning. It was the only occasion in his career that he got off the mark with a six.

Although Derek took only one wicket - that of his future Hampshire colleague - he was enjoying a fine season, bowling consistently well and hardly a game passed without him taking a clutch of wickets. He was very much in the England selectors' minds and he was picked for the third test at Trent Bridge.

John Arnold was the last Hampshire player to be picked for his country - way back in 1931 when he played in the Lord's test against New Zealand. He scored 0 and 34 and was never selected again. A double International at soccer and cricket (he had played football for Southampton and Fulham) Arnold was a marvellous team man in a career spanning twenty years, and also a very dependable and attractive batsman. Hampshire were an unfashionable county and did not often expect their players to 'get the call' from Lord's. In truth, during the 1930s and 1940s, Hampshire didn't really have anyone, except perhaps Arnold, with strong claims to be picked for England. Although Kennedy and Mead were still playing in the first of those two decades they were, by then, well into their forties and could not seriously be considered for test selection.

The 'call' did, however, come to Derek during the weekend of July 15th and 16th and there was an irony in the timing of the selection. He heard the good news the day after Arnold was completing his last game for Hampshire. Even at the age of 42 he was enjoying one of his finest seasons and would finish top of the batting averages at 43.34. He was, though, being dogged by ill health and he didn't play again that, or any subsequent, season.

For Derek it was a dream come true. The first Todmorden man to represent his country and, remarkably, he was still only in the middle of his second full season and had been bowling seamers seriously for little more than two years.

Although England had won the first test comfortably at Old Trafford they were totally outplayed at Lord's, losing by the huge margin of 326 runs. This was much to the great delight of the new immigrants from the Caribbean who were making Britain, and particularly London at that time, their new home. The victory brought forth the sight of impromptu calypso groups invading the hallowed turf. "Those little friends of mine, Ramadhin and Valentine". The two spinners had wrought havoc, bowling 231 overs between them and taking 18 of the 20 wickets. Thursday 29th June 1950 was a day of ignominy for English sport because not only were the cricketers well beaten (this test had started on a Saturday) but several thousands of miles away the England football team were beaten 1-0 in Brazil - not by the Brazilians but by the U.S.A.

Several changes were made for Trent Bridge, some enforced due to injury, and Shackleton was brought in to open the attack with Bedser. In those early post-war years England's bowling, with the shining exception of the Surrey man, was simply not up to normal test match standard. There was nobody of real pace and certainly no spinners at the time to match Ramadhin and Valentine. Derek was, therefore, looking forward to the chance being offered but success, in this his first test, came in a slightly unexpected manner.

Norman Yardley won the toss for England and, after some considerable deliberation, decided to bat. The match was really won and lost on that first morning because, on a green wicket which Derek would have loved to have used, England lost 4 wickets for 25 runs to the opening attack of Worrell and Johnson. The wicket eased during the day but the damage had been done and the West Indies took full control. At the fall of the sixth wicket with the score at 105 Shackleton joined Godfrey Evans.

Although he would never again reach the peak of his batting performance of 1949 he would remain a useful late order batsman and, earlier in 1950, he had hit a fine 73 against Sussex at Portsmouth and an even better 67 off the Surrey attack at Guildford when Laker took 6-72. In the last match before the test he hit 41 at Derby so he was quite capable of putting together some very useful innings.

He admits he was feeling nervous when he walked to the crease and recalled "when I took guard I couldn't keep my right leg still, it was shaking like jelly". Evans, who at Old Trafford that year had scored his first test century, gave Derek great encouragement - "Just play your own game, Shack, just play your own game". Ramadhin and Valentine were bowling at the time. He remembers that he did not have too many problems with Valentine but had difficulty in 'reading' Ramadhin although he was certainly not alone in this respect. The first ball he received from him resulted in a loud appeal for a stumping which umpire Frank Chester gave not out. After this let off Derek hit Ramadhin back over his head for 2 and relaxed a little. His score began to tick along quite nicely so much so that the spinners were taken off, something which did not happen too often that summer.

Worrell and Johnson returned to the attack and, after hitting Worrell through the covers for 4, Derek, perhaps now relaxing a little too much as he was within sight of 50, was bowled by a ball which nipped back sharply. He had, in his first test, made the highest score of the England innings. The crowd appreciated the fightback by the late order batsmen and Derek's performance in particular. Even though it was a relatively modest score he was given a standing ovation and admits to having 'goose bumps' during his walk back to the pavilion. His 42 had taken only seventy minutes.

The wicket was much easier when it was the West Indies turn to bat and Bedser and Shackleton did not have the opportunity to exploit the earlier green conditions. After a solid start by Rae and Stollmeyer, Weekes joined Worrell at the fall of the third wicket and, together, produced a scintillating partnership of 283. Derek rates Worrell's innings as one of the finest he ever saw. He had batted with a nonchalant ease, almost casual, but how the ball sped to the boundary ! His 261 had been scored in just over five and a half hours and included 2 sixes and 35 fours. The crowd had been treated to a truly majestic performance.

Not only was Worrell a great batsman he would become a highly respected captain in later years. His calm temperament would defuse any potential volatile situation before it could develop. He was a thoroughly nice man but one with strong convictions. When he died of leukaemia at the age of 43 the West Indies were robbed of an exemplary ambassador for their cricket and someone who, almost certainly, would have become a true statesman in world affairs. He thoroughly deserved the Knighthood he received in the New Year's Honours list of 1964.

Derek did not realise it at the time but, within a few months, he and Worrell would be playing together.

Weekes had also batted magnificently but, for once, had been largely overshadowed by Worrell. He was also a free scoring batsman but, as Shackleton had discovered earlier in the month, he was a most difficult player to dismiss. He attacked bowlers unmercifully but, like Bradman, would always be looking to eliminate error and had a great defensive technique. He probably hit the ball along the ground more than any other batsman of his generation, only rarely lofting the ball. It is rumoured that he once hit a six in a test match but it is only a rumour!

Derek claimed the wicket of Christiani in the first innings but this was his only success, although he had some consolation that he wasn't the only bowler to suffer. Even Bedser's 5 wickets cost 162 runs.

The West Indies had won comfortably by 10 wickets and the England selectors' response was to retain just three players for the fourth and final test at the Oval - Simpson, Dewes and Bedser. Some changes were unavoidable because of injury but there seemed to be little logic in dropping a player after one match, which was the case with the Hampshire seamer, especially as he had not bowled badly in the face of the Weekes/Worrell onslaught. Cricket, and most sports for that matter, have the occasional and seemingly insignificant momentary flashes of inspiration or misfortune which can greatly alter the course of a game and the reputation of an individual. One such moment happened to Derek during the West Indies first innings. Soon after Weekes came to the crease he produced an almost unplayable delivery - a stock Shack ball - one which pitched outside leg stump and went a fraction of an inch over the off. He remembers it clearly, so close was the delivery to getting one of the world's greatest batsmen out. Who knows what might have happened if a wicket had fallen then - his final analysis could have been so different. He could well have taken further wickets, been selected for the final test and then would have had a good chance of being picked for the winter tour to Australia.

Kathy had joined Derek for part of the test match but she admits she wasn't a great cricket watcher as some wives were but obviously kept a close interest in her future husband's career. She was a very sociable person and enjoyed the parties and functions which cricketers were expected to attend. Kathy felt strongly, and rightly so, that it was important for the wives to be invited to these events, something she later raised quite forcibly with Desmond Eagar. She did spend part of the time at the test but also took the opportunity of watching some tennis nearby as the great Fred Perry was playing.

Derek came away from Trent Bridge a far more experienced cricketer and one who had sampled the unique atmosphere of the big occasion. He had bowled well without luck, had not let the side down in any way and with the added bonus of being England's top scorer in the first innings.

He was then picked for the 'Players' in the annual fixture against the 'Gentlemen'. Unusually for him at Lord's he did not take any wickets and was fairly expensive with Reg Simpson being particularly severe on him. Probably tiredness played its part after his endeavours at Trent Bridge. The game produced several fine individual performances including one by Derek's Hampshire colleague, Charlie Knott who was playing for the 'Gentlemen'. His 5 wicket second innings haul included a hat-trick and Shack was one of the unfortunate trio. When he came to the crease the skipper, Freddie Brown, came up to Knott and said "you should know how to get this fellow out, what field would you like ?" Knott immediately asked for two men back on the long on boundary. Doug Insole was one of those placed in the deep and Derek duly obliged by hitting the ball straight to him.

Returning to the county after two matches playing with, and against, some of the world's finest players may have proved to be something of an anti-climax but Derek was already a model professional and would always give his best for Hampshire. They were paying his wages and he knew that continued good performances for them would keep him in the minds of the test selectors and more tangible rewards. He was now a well known name but his income was no more than the average man in the street. Also, at that time the top footballers were restricted by the maximum wage system.

The season was drawing to a close but certain events took place during the middle of August which were of some 'considerable importance' to him.

On his 26th birthday he produced a quite devastating performance at Leicester. In the late afternoon the home county slumped from 186 for two to 186 for seven in little over ten minutes. Shackleton had taken 5 wickets in nine deliveries - 4 victims were bowled and the other was caught at the wicket. The next match was significant for a different reason and he would hear news which would totally change his plans for the winter ahead.

Hampshire's opponents at Bournemouth were Lancashire and, during the game, Cyril Washbrook, their skipper, received a phone call from George Duckworth who, the previous winter, had managed a Commonwealth tour of India. Derek was asked if he would be available for a similar tour during the coming winter and Duckworth needed an immediate answer. This was on the Thursday 17th August and he had to explain that he was getting married on Saturday and the decision would have to wait until then. This was turning out to be quite a week but he had plenty of time to think during the Lancashire game because he was only required to bowl 8 overs and, batting, scored 0 and 2.

On the Friday evening he travelled by train to Manchester and was met on the station by Kathy who was still living with her mother in Todmorden. Somewhat nervously he told her that he had been asked to go to India for six months and this would mean leaving within a few weeks. It could not have been an easy statement to make on the eve of the wedding but she was understanding and, in Derek's own words "it worked out fine".

The young, and very good looking, couple were married on Saturday 19th August 1950 at St. Mary's Church in Todmorden. With neither Derek's nor Kathy's families being large ones it was inevitably a relatively small wedding followed by a brief honeymoon in Bournemouth. Immediately after the ceremony they travelled south by train but by missing rail connections they arrived at their hotel in the early hours of the morning and were almost locked out. Staying at the same hotel was Deryck Guyler, the radio comedian and personality who had already made a name for himself as 'Frisby Dyke' of Tommy Handley's ITMA fame.

Getting married during the cricket season the couple realised that the county would want their main bowler back as soon as possible - in fact they had been generous in allowing him to miss one match.

Just four days after his wedding Derek took 6-58 in the first innings against Sussex at Eastbourne. Hampshire won a remarkable game with Sussex being dismissed second time around for a paltry 38, the lowest total of the season, having been required to score only 98 for victory. Knott had taken 5-5 in 7 overs in the second innings. This turned out to be Hampshire's final win of 1950 because they were beaten comprehensively by Yorkshire and Gloucestershire and rain ruined the game against Glamorgan.

A slightly disappointing end to the season, therefore, but the county had risen, modestly, from sixteenth to twelfth in the championship table and the younger players were beginning to make quite an impression.

Shackleton had proved that 1949 was no fluke and that he was a very formidable bowler. Other batsmen had not 'found him out' and, although good players realised that generally they would have to play forward to him, few did so with any great confidence. Hardly anyone had the courage to take the initiative and attack him and, if they did, their stay at the wicket was, often, not too prolonged. Apart from Worrell's magnificent innings for the West Indies, which was in a class of its own, only two batsmen that summer had success by attacking him - Don Kenyon for Worcestershire and Reg Simpson for the 'Gentlemen'. Maurice Tompkin scored a fine century for Leicestershire but this was a more cautious, restrained innings - he had watched helplessly from the non-striker's end Derek's 5 wickets in nine deliveries. There was also the small matter of Harris's 239 for Nottinghamshire. However, to find just a few instances of batsmen dominating simply emphasises Shackleton's own steadily increasing controlling influence.

He was an even meaner bowler than in 1949 and in this following year he conceded just 2.51 runs per over, a ratio which would steadily reduce over the seasons ahead. He was proving his theory that time and effort were wasted if you do not bowl straight. Of his 111 wickets 77 were bowled, lbw or caught behind. As before, a considerable number of the remainder were edges to the close catchers and, from available records, it seems that there were hardly any dismissals as a result of a loose ball being hit into the deep.

Mention should also be made of the part played by Vic Cannings. He wasn't giving any light relief at the other end and, with Knott enjoying one of his finest seasons, very few big totals were made against Hampshire. Unfortunately, the batting was disappointing, with Rogers and Arnold the exceptions but the latter's season and career ended in July. Although McCorkell and Walker each scored over 1000 runs their averages were only in the twenties and Gray and Rayment were still in the 'promising' stages of their careers.

For Derek 1950 had been a very good year. Now firmly established as Hampshire's premier bowler, he had made his test debut, was selected for a tour to India and there was personal happiness following his marriage.

Chapter Five

Calcutta to The Raj

After just a few days following the end of the 1950 season in England Derek departed from Tilbury on the SS Chusan. Kathy went back to spend the winter with her mother in Todmorden and being apart for the next six months wasn't what she and Derek had anticipated. Nevertheless it was important for his blossoming career and Derek was both excited and expectant, not only about a first overseas tour, but actually going abroad at all. He didn't realise it at the time but it would be the first of two successive trips to the subcontinent.

India, and what was to become the separate state of Pakistan, were anxious for a quality touring side to visit their vast land such was the enthusiasm for the game there. There was a burgeoning appetite for test cricket and the general standard of the game was steadily rising.

Douglas Jardine had taken a side there in 1933/1934 and England had agreed to tour in 1939/1940 and the players had been selected but somewhat more important events elsewhere decreed the cancellation of the visit. Up to that time India had only played test cricket against England and seven tests in the 1930s resulted in five defeats and two draws but after the war younger talented players were emerging and were hungry to obtain the required experience at test level.

In the absence of a test playing nation to tour during the winter of 1949/1950 the Indians had been delighted to receive a Commonwealth X1 managed by George Duckworth and the whole party comprised of nine Australians, five from England, and two West Indians. Following the success of that tour a second Commonwealth trip was arranged for 1950/1951.

The format this time meant there were more English players but Worrell and Ramadhin (West Indies) and Bruce Dooland, George Tribe and Ken Grieves (Australia) provided additional strength. The three Australians would actually play most of their cricket in England in later years and Grieves was a good enough footballer to keep goal for Bury,

Bolton and Stockport. The English contingent was largely made up of several players who had made a few appearances for their country and had been playing pre-war, and younger ones on the fringe of the test side. These included Shackleton, Laker, Fred Ridgway - the Kent fast bowler, and the Lancashire batsman Jack Ikin who was to have an outstanding tour.

The side was, once again, managed by Duckworth who, in the 1920s and 1930s, had kept wicket for Lancashire and England. A small man in size he was a very fine keeper who made twenty four test appearances and, in addition, was one of the great characters between the wars. A vociferous and demonstrative man it has been said there was only one greater appealer than Duckworth - Dr. Barnardo ! Captaining the side was another former England wicket keeper, Leslie Ames, but his tour was disrupted by back trouble and Worrell skippered the team on many occasions.

The tour would prove to be a wonderful learning experience for Derek, not only by visiting a country of astounding complexities and beauty going through a period of great transition in its history, but also from the benefits he would gain being in such illustrious cricketing company.

The sea trip took about two weeks and, after the long English season, Derek found the journey very relaxing. The break was particularly important in view of the long arduous tour ahead. He would also find playing conditions quite different to those he was used to in England.

As well as the unrelenting heat he also had to get used to the brighter light. Most of all, however, he would have to adapt to bowling on matting wickets. Again his equable temperament would help him overcome any difficulties and with his natural caution he quickly decided he would not change his method of bowling. He would simply continue to bowl very straight and would rely on any breeze and humidity to help his swing.

Coir and coconut matting were used extensively in India at that time and some of the bowlers did experience trouble bowling on these surfaces especially with the final delivery stride. Shackleton did not have any such problems, his very light, smooth run up gave him this advantage - he was so light on his feet that, on occasions in England, no footmarks could be seen and he could have been bowling in plimsoles.

The tour was extremely successful and the Commonwealth team emerged undefeated winning thirteen of the twenty seven matches. They also won the unofficial test series by two games to nil.

Most of the touring party made very positive contributions but none more so than Frank Worrell. He played in twenty three matches, scored nearly 2000 runs and bowled almost 600 overs. He was in the middle of one of the most exhausting periods of cricket any player could have been expected to endure. He had made a similar tour twelve months earlier which was immediately followed by the West Indies tour of England when, again, he played in most matches. The West Indies had a tour of Australia lined up for 1951/1952 so there would be no respite. Travelling in such a vast country as India was, in itself, wearisome. Incredibly he maintained his form throughout all these tours. A gentleman and diplomat he never bemoaned these pressures and, unlike in later generations , he didn't receive great financial rewards.

Derek also had a good tour taking 49 wickets at 25.67 and, making useful contributions with the bat , finished with an average of just under 20. For the first half of the tour his figures were not startling but he was certainly accurate and batsmen were having difficulties scoring off him. He played in three of the unofficial tests and it was the match at Madras which brought him most success. He played in the first test at New Delhi and had match figures of 1-59 off 22 overs. It was the spin attack, led by Ramadhin, which did most of the damage there. Shackleton wasn't picked for the second and third tests but bowled very well against the Madras Governor's X1 with match figures of 10-111 and this clinched his place for the next test on the same ground.

He had two very lengthy spells at Madras, in particular in the second innings when he bowled 51 overs mainly in tandem with Worrell. The wicket favoured the batsmen throughout and, whilst Merchant, Umrigar and Hazare made good scores and were players of genuine test quality Shackleton dismissed them all, the latter two in both innings. It was hard work in extreme heat and his 7 wickets in 89 overs were well earned.

In that match Jack Ikin scored 110 and 86 continuing the fine form he displayed throughout the whole tour. A player of courage his performances for England were both unlucky and disappointing. As a very inexperienced player he went on two tough overseas tours - to Australia in 1946/1947 and to the West Indies in 1947/1948 - when England were well beaten on both occasions. He was a much better batsman than his final test record would indicate and he was outstanding on the Commonwealth tour, finishing top of the test batting averages with 625 runs at 89.28.

Derek was thoroughly enjoying the tour, the only drawback being that he had left his young wife at home after just a few weeks of marriage.

He had quickly learned to look after himself in a totally different environment. Stamina, even in the extreme heat was not a problem. In any case Derek has always liked hot weather. The easy smooth run up was to prove a great advantage and even in the heat he rarely raised a sweat.

Tours to India are notorious for problems which can result from a change of diet. Derek had a very straightforward approach - he just lived on egg and chips, as did Fred Ridgway. He hasn't said if eating so many eggs created other problems ! George Duckworth could not understand Derek's reluctance to try the local dishes. At the head of the table one evening Duckworth noticed the now routine plate of egg and chips. "Shack, you want to get some of this (i.e. curry) down you. It'll do you the world of good".

"George, you eat what you want to eat and I'll eat what I want" was the reply. He certainly wasn't going to change his eating habits. Lying on his bed at night he would often hear other players rushing to and from the bathroom, something he never had to do. He kept to a basic routine and did not suffer from stomach complaints or the dreaded 'Delhi Belly'.

Partly because of these potential problems many England players made themselves unavailable for early post war tours to India and the MCC did not put them under any undue pressure believing that a second string team would prove more than adequate to beat a side not really considered true test material. However, the party led by Nigel Howard in 1951/1952 could only draw the series and Ted Dexter's almost full strength team (Cowdrey, Trueman and Statham chose not to go) ten years later were soundly beaten. As the 1970s unfolded England were in no position to underestimate any test playing nation.

On the Commonwealth tour Derek had the pleasure of meeting one of the characters of pre-war cricket, Eddie Paynter. Paynter was a small gutsy player and a late developer, not gaining a regular place for Lancashire until he was 30. He made twenty test appearances in the 1930s with a remarkable average of 59.23 - for England only Herbert Sutcliffe has a higher one. He was in India coaching and told Derek that he had turned down an opportunity to tour India with Jardine's party in 1933/1934. Because of injuries and illness at one stage on the Commonwealth tour Paynter was called up to fill the breach and made two appearances at the age of 49. In a game against the Bombay Governor's X1 he scored 75 not out sharing in a sixth wicket partnership with Derek who hit 55 not out, his highest score of the tour.

The unluckiest players were Laker and Dick Spooner, both of whom had to return home early. Derek recalls that Laker had a very fine tour until it was cut short due to sinus trouble. He played in only one test but took 8 wickets at an average of just 15. Most of the internal travel on the tour was by air but neither Laker nor Spooner would fly and the long, and not particularly comfortable, train journeys added to their discomfort. The flights would take only a few hours but the rail trip could last two days with innumerable stops. When Laker and Spooner finally arrived at their destinations they looked haggard with a good growth of stubble.

Derek had a very high regard for Laker who he considers the finest off spinner he ever saw and one of the most intelligent 'readers' of the game. Many of Laker's attributes could equally apply to the Hampshire seamer. He has been described as : "Perhaps the best of all off spinners, with a high model action, sharp spin, great accuracy, flight and the intelligence to think batsmen out. A Yorkshireman of few words, his approach to cricket and to life was independent, detached, cool. His figures did his talking for him". Apart from the references to 'off spinner' and 'sharp spin' this tribute could be an ideal testament to Shackleton. What a Yorkshire attack there could have been in the 1950s with Trueman, Shackleton, Appleyard, Laker and Illingworth. It wasn't bad anyway as Wardle shouldn't be overlooked.

After two matches in Colombo the tour ended in a high scoring draw against the Prime Minister's X1 in Bombay. Fishlock and Ames both hit centuries for the tourists but batting honours went to Imtiaz Ahmed who, later, would make forty one test appearances for Pakistan. In this game he hit 300 not out which was to prove his highest ever score. He was a member of Pakistan's first touring side to England in 1954 and, in their famous victory at the Oval he held seven catches as wicket keeper.

A memorable but tiring trip had come to an end. As with his first two full seasons in county cricket Derek could, justifiably, be pleased with his performance and proved he could be successful on slower wickets which normally assisted the spinners. His maxim of bowling straight could not be faulted and was such an asset in the particular conditions he encountered. The experience gained by playing alongside players such as Laker, Worrell and Ramadhin was invaluable.

He has very fond memories of that first tour and saw, as he put it, 'how the other half lived'. He had been brought up in a town which had been greatly affected by the Great Depression but he had not seen poverty on the scale of cities like Calcutta. At the other end of the spectrum he had also witnessed the life of the Maharajah and the luxury and opulent lifestyle of those enjoying the last days of the British Raj. The contrast was extreme and something he always remembers but everywhere he went and everyone he met Derek has only pleasant recollections and the hospitality was genuine and sincere.

Returning home from India towards the end of March there was little time before the start of the 1951 season in England. Derek, initially went back to Todmorden but, after a few days, he and Kathy travelled down to Southampton. By now Derek was reasonably comfortable living in the south. He had spent most of his army days there and had been based in Southampton during the two previous summers. Kathy did not find it quite so easy. This would now be her first prolonged absence away from Todmorden and she immediately found southerners more reserved and less openly friendly, and she took much longer to settle. They were indebted to Ernie and Bella Knights, both Geordies, who showed a lot of kindness and warmth and greatly helped Kathy, in particular, feel more at home. Ernie had been appointed head groundsman at the county ground in Southampton in 1949. Derek and Kathy found a small flat in the Portswood district of Southampton where they would live for about six months.

There was very little change to the Hampshire playing staff although professional contracts had been offered to, and accepted by, Mervyn Burden, Malcolm Heath (no relation to George) and Peter Sainsbury. Due to National Service their debuts were delayed for at least two years.

Hampshire - and Shackleton - made an excellent start to the season. After four games they led the championship table with three victories, albeit by very narrow margins.

Unlike in some later seasons Derek showed impressive form right from the start almost certainly due to the fact that he had been bowling non stop for twelve months and the machine had not been switched off. This continuous bowling would have adversely affected many other players. For example, Alec Bedser, strong and big hearted as he was, suffered from bearing the brunt of England's bowling on overseas tours. Shackleton's reserves of stamina were huge and he revelled in long spells of bowling. With another winter tour coming up he was to bowl virtually without a break from April 1950 until September 1952 - thirty consecutive months during which he bowled, incredibly, over 4,300 overs. He had not changed his basic formula - he just nagged and nagged away with an impeccable line and length with movement through the air and off the wicket. He was totally confident this recipe would always bring him wickets. Being a tall, slim man he could have been quicker than he was, although he was deceptively nippy, but this would have meant more exertion and a possible loss of accuracy. He would then have been unable to bowl for such long periods and there might have been a greater risk of injury, something throughout his whole career he was to suffer on only a very few isolated occasions.

The only rest he had during this period was when he was on board ship !

The first four matches of the 1951 season were tight affairs indeed.

Hampshire were unlucky not to win the first match against Northamptonshire at Peterborough needing four runs to win when they ran out of time. The next two games resulted in victories over Kent (Shackleton dismissing an eighteen year old Cowdrey) and Nottinghamshire by 36 runs and 16 runs respectively. In three matches the combination of Shackleton and Cannings had accounted for 49 of the 58 wickets to fall and there was not a better opening attack in the country.

On a damp wicket at Lord's - the Festival of Britain year was to prove to be not one of the best summers - Hampshire won an exciting match against Middlesex by 43 runs and brilliant fielding played a major part. Set 221 to win Middlesex started magnificently with an opening stand of over 100 by Robertson and Brown and seemed to be cruising to victory. However, three run outs accounted for Robertson, Denis Compton and Thompson and a superb catch in the deep by Rogers to dismiss Leslie Compton meant that Shackleton and Cannings could wrap up the tail.

This win took Hampshire to the top of the table but such was the closeness of these early results that just a little misfortune could have meant three defeats and, perhaps, bottom place. Often the difference between success and failure is very slight.

The early victories were followed by six consecutive draws and then a defeat by Sussex and this sequence meant they soon lost top position. One of the drawn games was against Surrey at Southampton during which Shackleton came in for some unexpected punishment. G.J. Whittaker, batting at number six had the temerity to hook him for 3 sixes. Whittaker, although playing in most of Surrey's matches that year, was not a regular player for very long. According to 'Wisden' he hit 32 sixes in 1951 "yet one felt he could do better with only a little discretion". His performances over the next two seasons deteriorated and he drifted out of the game at the end of 1953.

Jimmy Gray remembers Whittaker's brief onslaught and agreed he was a really good 'hitter' but he didn't 'bat' Shackleton. On the other hand he remembers Maurice Tremlett of Somerset batting as well as anyone against Derek that year. "Tremlett was a fine driver and drove him powerfully in an innings of 107 at Southampton. The ball wasn't swinging much that day but it was an exceptionally fine piece of attacking cricket". Tremlett also scored 59 in the second innings and, to complete a fine season against Hampshire, he hit 83 and 72 at Bath. He had top scored for Somerset in each of those four innings.

This treatment, being so isolated, would have surprised Derek but would not have upset him greatly. Indeed he was a very generous opponent and would often applaud a fine shot. He was perfectly happy with his bowling performances and if he was occasionally hit he took it gracefully. He knew that, generally, he would get the upper hand.

The last sixteen championship matches produced only one win with nine draws and six defeats which included a game against Lancashire at Liverpool vividly recalled by Gerry Hill because of the wearisome journeys which have to be undertaken by counties situated at the farthest ends of the country. After a long drawn out game against Worcestershire at Southampton which went the full distance Hampshire had to travel overnight to Liverpool where they arrived, exhausted, in the early hours of the morning. It was little wonder, therefore, that Hampshire gave a mediocre performance but again Shackleton showed his depths of stamina by bowling 50 overs and taking 5 wickets in the only Lancashire innings. The Todmorden born off spinner, Peter Greenwood, had match figures for Lancashire of 8-52. Hill, at the age of 38 and still making very valuable contributions, also showed remarkable resilience by bowling 58 overs.

Travelling was tiring in those pre motorway days. Train journeys were often undertaken at night and involved connections when the timings did not necessarily relate to the official timetable. Sometimes old RAF Bedford coaches were used but these were extremely uncomfortable with very hard seats and the players would arrive at their destination stiff and tired and it took some while before limbs and muscles were in complete harmony. It would be a little while before cars were used regularly. Alan Rayment recalls that, at that time, only Eagar, Knott and Walker had 'respectable' cars whilst Jimmy Gray owned an old Morris 12 and Reg Dare an old Hillman van.

In the midst of the disappointing sequence of results came the excellent news that Shack had been selected for the fifth and final test at the Oval against South Africa. In addition his Hampshire compatriot Neville Rogers was picked as twelfth man. In those days the eleven were chosen knowing they would definitely play and the twelfth man knew he would not be involved in a playing capacity unless an injury occurred.

Rogers was enjoying his finest season for Hampshire and many believed this recognition was long overdue. For some years Hutton and Washbrook had been England's automatic opening pair but Washbrook was now 37 and had averaged only 17 in the winter series in Australia, although with the notable exception of Hutton, no batsman distinguished himself on that tour. Ikin and Frank Lowson partnered Hutton in 1951 each with only modest success.

This was the closest Rogers came to winning a test cap. The game is littered with players who either played just a handful of games for their country or who missed out altogether. Those who consistently scored 2,000 runs in a season or took 100 wickets but who were never given an extended opportunity at test level. Shackleton, of course, comes into this category but, as an opening batsman, Rogers was one of the very finest not given the opportunity ; certainly less talented players have represented England.

The 1951 South Africans did not enjoy the weather which shone so brightly on their 1947 counterparts. Of their thirty first class matches only five were won with no less than twenty draws. The weather played its part in so many indecisive results but the batting throughout the tour, Eric Rowan apart, was only average and the bowling lacked penetration. However, although they lost the test series 3-1 they came close to winning at the Oval which, if they had, would have meant a drawn series.

The fifth test was considered to be the best match of the series although slow scoring dominated throughout and the highest individual score was only 73. South Africa won the toss and, taking no risks on a turning wicket, reached 202 from 106 overs. Whilst Laker did most damage Shackleton tied the batsman down so completely he conceded only 20 runs from his 15 overs. His solitary wicket was that of Michael Melle whose father had played for Hampshire just before, and immediately after, the first world war.

In England's reply Compton played a memorable, if quite uncharacteristic, innings of 73 which took him 220 minutes. For such a great player he had experienced a nightmare series in Australia in 1950/1951 and the infamous knee was becoming a persistent and painful handicap. He had actually started the season in fine fettle perhaps sensing that South Africa, his favourite country, would inspire him yet again. Whilst it was a mutual love affair the South Africans may have preferred him not to have indulged himself so frequently. Of his seventeen test centuries seven were against South Africa and his only failures against them occurred in his final tour of 1956/1957 when his knee was far too much of a liability. In May 1951 he was back to the form of earlier years scoring 909 runs including five centuries but the knee was restricting his natural freedom and, although he finished the series with an average of 52, it was not the joyous Compton of old. His innings at the Oval was a great tribute, not only to his extraordinary skills but also to his courage. He was last out and Shackleton had made a useful contribution of 14 in a seventh wicket stand of 28, important in such a low scoring match.

South Africa had a small lead of 8 on first innings and, struggling once more against Laker, were dismissed in their second innings for 154 leaving England with a target of 163. Shackleton had again been economical conceding only 19 runs in 10 overs.

England started well in reply but slipped from 53 for none to 90 for four and, when Derek joined Laker with the score at 151 for six , 12 runs were still needed. A slightly nervous time in a low scoring battle. Wickets had fallen regularly throughout the match and the South Africans had certainly not given up hope. He remained calm, however, and stayed with Laker to enable him to score the winning runs.

Returning to the county side Shackleton and Rogers were once again in opposition to the tourists. Another tight game ended in a creditable draw with Shackleton, Cannings and Knott all taking 5 wickets and Rogers, if he had to prove a point, doing it most decisively with scores of 37 and 118.

Hampshire were reasonably pleased with their progress rising three places to ninth. However, only five of their twenty eight matches resulted in wins and it was a season with a preponderance of drawn games - sixteen ending without a definite result.

Shackleton's advance continued relentlessly. He took more wickets - 130 - than ever before and at a lower average. Again a high percentage of his wickets were bowled, lbw or caught at the wicket. He was, though, the first to acknowledge the very positive help provided at the other end by Vic Cannings who also took 100 wickets in all games. They were now doing the lion's share of the bowling and the only really effective assistance was coming from Knott. The batting had been encouraging with more consistent support for Rogers. Gray and Harrison both reached 1,000 runs as did McCorkell in his last season before taking up a coaching position in South Africa. Fittingly he hit the only double century of his career in the match against Gloucestershire in June.

For Derek there was to be no rest. It was never ending cricket as he had been selected for the MCC tour to India, Pakistan and Ceylon and, for the second year running, would be travelling by boat within days of the English season finishing.

They vacated their flat in Portswood and Kathy would once again spend the winter with her mother in Todmorden. It was not an easy time for her or indeed for either of them. Twelve months earlier they had been separated for a long period just weeks after their marriage. This time Kathy was pregnant with the baby due in January, right in the middle of the tour. Another anxious time for them both but they were grateful that she would be able to stay with her mother and be with other friends and relations.

Derek departed from Tilbury, once again on the SS Chusan excited by the prospect of the tour but naturally worried about his wife. He was joined by two of his colleagues from the previous winter's Commonwealth tour - Fred Ridgway and Dick Spooner. Spooner was quite prepared to go to India again notwithstanding the illness which had laid him low cutting his tour short. Happily he came through the new trip unscathed.

The tour party was in no way a first choice England side but such was (and is) the enthusiasm for cricket in India that this did not concern either the cricket authorities or the public. In their eyes the selected team was the full strength England. Opportunities were given to the younger, promising players added to which were more experienced stalwarts such as Robertson, Spooner and 'Dusty' Rhodes, the Derbyshire leg break bowler. Most of the others were under thirty and on the fringe of the full test side.

The sea trip was not only relaxing it enabled the team to get to know one another. Although it added to the time being away from home travelling by sea (as opposed to flying from Heathrow and arriving in half a day) seemed a more pleasant way to start a tour provided, of course, the weather was clement. The cabins were arranged in a way that sharing was allocated on an alphabetical basis and Derek's cabin mate was Brian Statham, still only twenty one but already thought highly enough to have been flown out the previous winter to join the injury hit tourists in Australia.

When they arrived in Bombay the players were treated like film stars being showered with garlands and mobbed by large crowds. This enthusiasm would follow them everywhere.

The first match was played at the magnificent Brabourne Stadium in Bombay in extremely hot and humid conditions. It was a somewhat lacklustre game but Graveney immediately found his form with a fine century proving that even on the slower wickets quality attacking batting would thrive. The highest score for the Universities of India side was made by Pankaj Roy who was already regarded as a future test batsman. He was to have an outstanding series that winter but a nightmare one in England the following summer when he suffered five 'ducks' in seven innings. The pace of Trueman was too much for him but, to his credit, he fought back in later years to finish with nearly 2,500 test runs at an average of just under 33.

The next match resulted in an exciting 2 wickets win against Western India on coir matting at Ahmedabad. Batting was not easy on this surface with the spinners getting a lot of sharp turn and the seamers cutting it back alarmingly. Shackleton had a good game with figures of 5-54 in 25.1 overs.

The players had to quickly learn to adapt to all types of conditions. The next game at Indore was on jute matting which took spin but less dramatically than on coir, and then at Amritsar they were back on turf. Play started late there with allegations of sabotage due to over zealous watering. It was agreed that a new wicket would be laid but after about an hour of near chaos due to so many helpers it was then discovered that the two sets of stumps were not parallel. The same procedure had to be repeated and play didn't start until well after lunch by which time the crowd, in unrelenting heat, were understandably restless.

After the early win at Ahmedabad there was a long sequence of drawn games, in fact it was two and a half months before they registered their next victory beating Bengal by an innings in Calcutta. In the meantime they had lost to Pakistan in Karachi where they first encountered Hanif Mohammed, then only sixteen. In those more gentlemanly days Statham, who was already genuinely quick, and Shackleton, a brisk medium pacer, did not immediately pull out all the stops and bowl flat out at this young lad. After a few overs they realised that Hanif was defensively very sound and mature well beyond his years and so the bowlers reverted to full pace, still not troubling him in the slightest. Hanif made scores of 26, 71, 2 and 64 against the MCC and later would hit nearly 4,000 runs for his country at an average of 44.

Pakistan won a close match by four wickets but there was a certain unease about the umpiring even then, perhaps a fore-runner of the distrust between the two countries which was prevalent certainly in the 1980s and culminating in the furious row between Mike Gatting and the Pakistan umpire, Shakoor Rana, during the 1987/1988 tour. In the 1951 match in Karachi there were over thirty appeals for lbw made by the MCC bowlers, mostly by Statham and Shackleton, and all were turned down. As 'Wisden' tactfully put it the MCC were "surprised" especially as the two main bowlers were two of the most accurate in the world and neither was noted as being 'over enthusiastic' with their appealing. This should not take anything away from the young Pakistani team who played some enterprising cricket. The MCC batsmen struggled against the leg cutters of Fazal Mahmood and the pace of Khan Mohammed although Graveney batted beautifully in the second innings but with little support.

England had, by this time, drawn the first test against India in New Delhi. Although they were handicapped by the absence of Graveney it was, nevertheless, disappointing to total only 203 in the first innings and, in reply, India amassed 418 before declaring. The wicket and the run rates were slow and the England bowlers all struggled including Shackleton who took 1-76 off 29 overs. With two run outs only four wickets fell to bowlers.

England did, however, claw back from the clutches of defeat to gain an honourable draw due mainly to the Glamorgan all rounder Allan Watkins playing the innings of his life. Undefeated on 138 he batted for well over a day and a half and was ably assisted by Lowson and Carr. Shackleton was Watkins' final partner and, together, they put on 59 in an unbroken seventh wicket stand.

During this test the players encountered typical enthusiasm from the spectators. Mostly high spirited but occasionally frightening. Various landmarks were celebrated by letting off fireworks, especially when English wickets fell and when, in this match, Merchant and Hazare, who both made big centuries, passed their 50s and then 100s and probably when they reached 150. Fielding in the deep was not always a comfortable place to be as quite an area inside the boundary was strewn with bottles and other missiles. It all added up to quite new experiences for the players.

The second and third tests at Bombay and Calcutta were also drawn but England were much more impressive. Shackleton was yet again unlucky to be left out because no bowler had reaped any reward on the slow wicket at Delhi. It was now becoming a habit for the England selectors to drop him after just one game. Graveney's return, however, greatly strengthened the batting and he played a vital, if restrained, innings scoring 175 in over eight hours in Bombay. There was also little chance of a result at Calcutta where the wicket was lifeless and, throughout the series, the run rate for both sides was little more than 2 an over.

Derek had enjoyed a little bit of a rest after the short Pakistan part of the tour. He sat out the game against Bombay and, by missing the second test against India, he didn't play for three weeks.

A somewhat dull draw followed against Maharashtra in Poona with Derek, one of five MCC batsmen to hit half centuries. His score of 66 was his highest of the tour. The general monotony was relieved in somewhat unusual fashion.

At that time a monkey by the name of Jacko was well known in Poona and would often appear at the cricket ground. During the Maharashtra first innings, which was progressing at snail's pace, the monkey, in an effort to enliven matters, ran across the ground trying to make friends with the MCC fieldsmen. They probably welcomed the diversion and invited him to field in the slips. The problem was that he wouldn't keep still and with frequent stoppages of play the joke, and Jacko's antics, were wearing a bit thin. An enterprising young man drove him off with a stick but not before he had taken a liking to the square leg umpire's coat. The next day, during the MCC innings, he decided his place was in the gully but he seemed to become bored more quickly and retired to watch the game from the pavilion roof.

England won the fourth test at Kanpur in a low scoring game. The wicket turned almost from the start and the English spinners took 19 of the 20 wickets - the other being a run out. Watkins top scored with 66 in the first innings and Graveney, batting elegantly as usual, ensured victory with 48 not out in the second. There was a large police presence at Kanpur because of trouble which had occurred during the Commonwealth tour twelve months earlier. Students had been blamed for near riots and the trouble had apparently arisen because they were waiting to see an Indian film actress. There is even more enthusiasm for Indian cinema than for cricket. However, there was to be no such repeat incident.

After the fourth test Derek was picked for the next three games against Central Zone, Hyderabad and South Zone and welcomed this activity as his mind was obviously now very much focused on the impending birth of their first child. By this time - January 1952 - the baby was due any day and, being so far away, he must have felt quite helpless. He bowled a lot of overs during this period which kept his mind occupied.

After the game at Hyderabad came the news that Kathy had given birth to a boy - Julian - but the telegram which had been sent from Todmorden was not received by Derek for several days. It had been chasing him around on his travels. The tour still had four weeks to run and Derek was enjoying his cricket but, on this occasion, he couldn't wait to get home again.

Whilst he continued to take wickets regularly the selectors were not keen to make changes to the side that won at Kanpur and the team for the fifth and final test at Madras would have been unchanged but for the fact that Howard had to withdraw because of pleurisy. England were soundly beaten by an innings and 8 runs and India, at last, had recorded their first test victory and emphatically so. It had been a genuine all round team effort but three players deserve special mention - Roy who scored 111, Umrigar with 130 not out and, in particular, Vinoo Mankad with match bowling figures of 12-108.

Once again Derek had enjoyed a long, but very rewarding, trip to India, Pakistan and Ceylon and it does not seem logical that he played in only one of the tests. The selectors did not consider him to be an automatic choice but their persistence in sticking to the two quickest bowlers did not make sense and not just with hindsight. It has never been easy for pacemen to achieve a great deal on the slower wickets encountered in that part of the world and, until Kapil Dev came along a quarter of a century later, India's own attack was based on two medium pacers and two or three quality spinners. Both Statham and Ridgway struggled in the tests and Ridgway, especially, was lucky to keep his place as his 7 wickets in five tests cost 54 runs each. It is certain that Shackleton would have been more of a problem for the Indian batsmen with his slightly slower pace and the movement he could generate through the air and off the seam. He should have been given more opportunities.

Many years later some 'experts' would argue that Shackleton would not have been successful on overseas wickets, that he was strictly a bowler for typical English conditions. Yet on two consecutive tours to India and Pakistan he claimed a total of 100 wickets at an average of 24.43. It is also likely that he would have caused similar problems in South Africa and especially New Zealand where the wickets are greener. Possibly he may not have had the additional pace necessary on the faster, bouncier wickets of Australia and the West Indies but because of his great accuracy and the movement off the seam , even if not so pronounced as in England, he would still have given batsmen a lot to think about. In more recent years Angus Fraser has enjoyed three highly successful tours to the Caribbean simply by bowling a good line and length .

It was now time to return home, to re-unite with his wife and see his new son.

Aged 4

With his parents in Goole

Aged about 12

Roomfield School Todmorden
Derek is third from the left in the back row - one of the few wearing a tie.

Army Football Team

Saturday 19th August 1950

England v South Africa, the Oval August 1951 (Central Press Photos Ltd)

MCC Tour to India and Pakistan 1951- 1952

1951 India

Derek & Kathy 1950
(Southern Newspapers Ltd)

With parents & Son Julian

Family Portrait in the mid 50s

Vic Cannings & Shack 1952

Chapter Six

Shack and Vic

Julian was about two months old when his dad saw him for the first time. The tour did not end until 3rd March and then the long journey home by boat meant just a short stay in Todmorden before the new family travelled down to Southampton just before the start of the 1952 season.

They didn't return to their flat in Portswood but, through a friend of Kathy's, they were able to rent the upstairs part of a Victorian house in Cavendish Grove, Southampton which was just a few hundred yards from the county ground. Although it wasn't ideal they would stay there for the best part of two years. At that time it was simply not possible for them to buy a property. Early life together had not been easy, indeed 'together' is not the appropriate word as Derek had spent two winters away and, during the summers, he was frequently in other parts of the country. However, there would now be a little more stability because, although he didn't realise it at the time there would, surprisingly, be no further overseas tours.

Pre-season training had already started (Derek had been allowed a few days grace) but, in his case, this seemed largely irrelevant as he had been bowling almost without a break for two years. Probably a rest was more beneficial. His Hampshire colleagues were, by now, well aware that he was not a great nets man and were happy to accept that, by doing so much bowling, he kept himself extremely fit.

Hampshire had made no new signings and the nucleus of the side would be very similar to that of the previous season. McCorkell had now retired and, with Knott only available for five games, this left Hill as the sole regular survivor from pre-war days not including Harrison who had made only a couple of appearances in 1939.

Although wicketless in the first match against Warwickshire (he bowled only 5 overs in a rain ruined game) Shackleton then took 41 wickets in the next five. As in 1951 he simply continued where he had left off in India ; he was a constant relentless machine and he now carried before him a feared reputation. Even the finest batsmen were becoming more cautious and their cause was not helped with having to face Cannings at the other end.

There were two early encouraging wins against Somerset and Sussex and, in the former, Shackleton had a typical Portsmouth haul of 9-86 with Gimblett collecting a 'pair' being dismissed twice by Derek. Sweet revenge for 1948 when Gimblett scored 88 and 52 on Derek's championship debut and for 1949 when the Somerset opener scored two centuries at Taunton. In this latest match Alan Rayment hit his first century followed by 74 in the second innings.

Whilst Shackleton and Cannings were important, indeed vital, components of the bowling attack the form of Rogers as the premier batsman was just as essential and, until Gray became his regular opening partner, he really was Hampshire's batting at that time.

Rogers would enjoy his best season to date and scored over 2,000 runs in championship matches alone, something no Hampshire player had achieved since Arnold and Mead in 1934. Strangely, although he scored so many runs and averaged 42 he hit only two championship hundreds, both in May (he added a third for T N Pearce's X1, also in May). This really confirmed his consistency and reliability; in very few games did he fail. He certainly wasn't helped by having an effective opening partner in the first half of the season. Quite the reverse, in fact. In the first eighteen championship innings only one score of more than 50 was achieved by the other opener and, at the beginning of July, Gray, who was also enjoying his best season was promoted to open with Rogers at Leicester. In the second innings Gray hit 93 and he and Rogers opened the batting for the remainder of the season.

Another anomaly with Rogers was that his highest score on home grounds in 1952 was only 80 - he certainly travelled well as the following figures testify.

	Inn	NO	Runs	Hst	Ave	100s	50s
Home	25	-	755	80	30.20	-	6
Away	26	3	1259	119	54.73	2	9
TOTAL	51	3	2014	119	41.95	2	15

The most extraordinary match of the season took place at Southampton on May 31st and June 2nd. Traditionally Hampshire played Kent over the Whitsun weekend and there had been many exciting and enjoyable encounters over the years, especially those in 1948 and 1950. In the former, Hampshire had been set a second innings target of 124 in sixty five minutes and won in the last over. Jack Martin, the Kent fast bowler, almost pulled off a dramatic victory by taking 6-37 and certainly did not deserve to receive an unprovoked attack from a 'spectator'. In chasing a ball to the boundary he was joined in the pursuit by a lively, high spirited dog who relished this unexpected activity. It didn't appreciate Martin reaching the ball first and gave him a painful bite on the ankle. In 1950 Hampshire were involved in the second tied game in their history.

The game in 1952 started unpromisingly in miserable weather which restricted the first day's play to three hours. Hampshire limped along to 135 in 63 overs against the unchanged opening attack of Dovey and Martin. What occurred on the Monday was nothing short of sensational with 29 wickets falling in less than a full day. The wicket had become almost unplayable after the rain and the ball either rose alarmingly or nipped through sharply off the seam. Tailor-made conditions for Shackleton and Cannings.

Kent were dismissed for just 32 with their opening batsman, Peter Hearn, carrying his bat with 12 not out. At one time Kent were 18 for nine but Martin hit Shackleton for a four and a six to ensure some 'respectability' and thereby avoiding the ignominy of equalling their lowest ever score of 18 'achieved' in 1867.

On seeing the mayhem which had occurred the Hampshire batsmen adopted a more positive approach in the second innings but it was largely due to skilful innings by Harrison (45) and Gray (61 not out) that enabled Eagar to declare at 144 for eight. Why declare when every single run was vital and with well over a day to spare ? However, the general view, and one put forward by Gerry Hill, was to get Kent back in a second time as soon as possible. The wicket was still unpredictable but could calm down by the following morning. Kent, like Hampshire, tried to be more positive, there was simply no point in just defending. As well as skill and courage an abundance of luck was required to stay for any length of time and, in any case, the Kent batsmen were facing two of the very finest seam bowlers in the country. They did fare better but fell well short of their target and only Godfrey Evans with a sparkling, and occasionally, lucky 34 gave any real resistance.

Shackleton and Cannings had bowled unchanged throughout the match, the former taking 12-67 and his partner 8-55. On looking at the details of that match now it is interesting to note the manner of the dismissals. Of the 38 wickets to fall only five batsmen were bowled and there were no lbw decisions in the bowler's favour. Apart from a stumping by Evans no less than thirty two catches were held, most of them close to the wicket. Fagg, fielding in the slips for Kent, caught seven and, for Hampshire, Cannings caught four in the gully, Eagar four at short leg and Gray four in the slips. The wicket must have been a real flier and, with so much movement and lift, the umpires would have been reluctant to give a batsman out lbw. All twelve of Shackleton's wickets were from catches, a very unusual statistic in his case.

By the time the selectors met to choose the England team for the first test against India Shack had taken 35 wickets at an average of 11.65 and had played in the previous 'full' England side - the fifth test of 1951. He was, though, overlooked not only because of the automatic selection of Alec Bedser but because a relatively inexperienced Yorkshireman was picked, one who was to become the outstanding fast bowler of his generation. Whilst the selectors wanted to pick the best side to beat India they were also aware that, the following year, Australia would be making their second post war trip and their magnificent opening attack of Lindwall and Miller would be in their prime. England had unearthed a genuine fast bowler, Fred Trueman who, hopefully, with Bedser would redress the balance which had swung very much Australia's way in the early post war years. Trueman may have been raw at the time but he had real pace and destroyed the Indian batsmen that summer.

The choice of Bedser was logical, that of Trueman was ambitious but also sensible and there could be no argument with picking Laker. What was slightly illogical was the selection of Roley Jenkins, the Worcestershire leg spinner. A series against one of the weaker countries would seem to have been an ideal time to give further opportunities to a younger player such as Shackleton. Jenkins, a fine leg break bowler in county cricket, had achieved only moderate success at test level, mainly on the 1948/1949 tour to South Africa when he took 16 wickets at 30.93. He was, by now, 34 and with the national team, as well as the counties, trying to build towards the future surely a younger, even simply 'promising' bowler should have been given a chance. Jenkins lasted for two tests and was then replaced by Tony Lock. This was another piece of the jig-saw, now almost complete, the final picture of which would become known as the Golden Age of English Bowling. Equally, Derek would not become part of this puzzle, although he did not know it at the time.

Although opportunities for Derek at test level appeared to be receding he was not completely overlooked at representative level because he was picked for a very strong Players' side against the Gentlemen. In the second innings he had a very high quality quartet of victims - Sheppard, May, Insole and Bailey. Just another reminder that he was consistently capable of troubling the very best batsmen on good wickets. It belied the oft mentioned theory that, whilst he was an acknowledged master in county cricket, 'class' batsmen would find him out. He was never given a prolonged chance to disprove this.

Notwithstanding his non selection for the test side he would continually keep his name to the fore by just taking wickets. The economy of his bowling was already legendary - the number of runs conceded per over average was steadily reducing - to 2.13 that season. In later years this would often fall below 2 per over.

Vic Cannings was giving some tremendous support at this time and they were as formidable an opening pair as any in the country. Les Jackson and Cliff Gladwin of Derbyshire, both of whom were quicker than the Hampshire duo and more hostile, were feared in the same way but no other counties could boast such a potent new ball attack. Statham (Lancashire) and Bedser (Surrey) had little seam support but had the benefit of some high quality spinners. Trueman, due to National Service and test calls, played only a few times for Yorkshire who relied heavily on the left arm spin of Wardle.

It was now expected that 'Shack and Vic' would shoulder the bulk of the bowling and Desmond Eagar based his whole strategy on this tremendous asset which he had at his disposal. They would be sure to keep runs down, could bowl sides out quickly and this would often cover up any cracks in the batting. Counties would frequently bat very slowly against Hampshire and the critics would argue that Eagar's tactics were negative but this would be an unfair judgment. Hampshire often had low totals of their own to defend and runs could not be given away. The general feeling and indeed generally the fact was, that if Rogers failed, they would be lucky to reach 200.

Cannings firmly believes that Hampshire were no more than an average side then and that the assets they had had to be used to the fullest advantage. He and Shackleton, therefore, had to bowl for long periods whatever the state of the wicket and "Shack would be allowed one half volley a season and I would be allowed two". Spinners had few opportunities and, if they were hit for four, they were taken off. Cannings remembers that Mervyn Burden, the unlucky off spinner in the years ahead became frightened to bowl on occasions. He would remark : "If I don't pitch them in the right place straight away I'll be taken off".

Shackleton and Cannings had the knack of getting wickets for each other. There could be no relaxation for the batsmen. Cannings himself was very accurate but he never saw a more accurate bowler than his partner. He could understand the spectators' puzzlement of why he was so successful, because with his gentle run up and general lack of aggression he looked quite harmless, certainly from the comfort of the boundary. If you were the batsman, however, the view would have been very different. Yes, the run up was without apparent menace but it would have been smooth, the head absolutely still with eyes focused directly on the batsman , the wrist cocked at right angles to the arm at the point of delivery and it was the wrist movement which gave him the disconcerting nip. The left elbow was neatly pointing towards the intended victim. Everything about the action was neat, tidy, beautiful with no palpable effort. Finally, and crucially, the ball would be delivered with the unerring accuracy of a well directed bullet. It would pitch on the seam on such a length that, although it was generally agreed it was better to play forward nevertheless, in that split second, there would be a moment's hesitation which would often prove fatal. The ball would come through the air, and particularly off the wicket, much quicker than seemed possible from the gentle run up. Even the best batsmen, especially if the wicket was doing something, were simply happy to survive the over. Even playing forward the ball was often "never quite there" recalls Cannings and "always doing a little bit".

There was, therefore, a general reluctance on Eagar's part to change this format and this policy was never more apparent than on green top wickets such as that at the United Services ground in Portsmouth. Hampshire always played a full complement of seamers there and Knott, and in later seasons, Burden and Wassell, were rarely selected. Their skills were needed at Bournemouth.

Home fixtures at that time were evenly spread between the county headquarters in Southampton, Dean Park in Bournemouth and at Portsmouth.

Derek loved bowling at the United Services ground because whilst he admits it did favour seamers it was a good cricketing wicket with something for the batsmen as well. Because of his successes there he was delighted with the description once given him of 'Hon. Lord Mayor of Portsmouth'. He and Cannings enjoyed bowling in the pre lunch session on the first morning when it would not be too unusual for 5 wickets to fall. In the afternoon the wicket would become more placid when batsmen found life less difficult and a more defensive field would be in place. The two seamers would have frequent discussions and often remark that green patches, which had disappeared during the afternoon, would return at about 5.30 and the ball would be moving around again. As Derek puts it "the tide was coming back in". Hove was a similar wicket - conditions so typical of seaside towns.

Described as a 'sporting pitch' the United Services ground enjoys the benefit of arguably the largest and heaviest roller in the country. Built during the winter of 1921/1922 'Hercules' was, originally, horse drawn with the horses being provided with leather shoes to avoid damage to the wicket. The roller, weighing five and a half tons is still in use and had a complete overhaul in 1995. Doug Welsh, the groundsman when Derek was playing, remarked once : "County players don't refer to Portsmouth by name, just as 'the ground with the big roller!'"

A typical example of Derek's view of the Portsmouth wicket occurred in June with Northamptonshire the opposition. The visitors, batting first, were all out before lunch for 67 with Shackleton and Cannings taking all 10 wickets. Cannings had a spell of 4 wickets in 11 deliveries without conceding a run. Hampshire replied with 154 - Rayment top scoring with 42. It was not the first, nor by any means the last, time that he produced a fine innings in difficult circumstances . With the wicket easing the Northants batsmen fared much better in the second innings totalling 333, built up patiently with Shackleton and Cannings bowling 95 overs between them. Hampshire, with the exception of the ever reliable Rogers, batted poorly in their second innings and lost by 45 runs.

With the 1952 season coming to an end there had been no let up in the work load the county put upon him but Derek never raised any objections. He just loved bowling, something he had been doing almost without a break for two and a half years. He actually missed three games through injury which was very unusual, the most he would miss in one season for this reason. By now there were batsmen who were becoming paranoid about him and although the test selectors were overlooking him the majority of county batsmen were doubting this logic. Many of them would have welcomed him being in the England side if only to take him out of the county circuit for a while !

Although it was disappointing for the county to slip to twelfth in the championship it had been a year which brought further encouragement. At the start of the 1951 season they had won three games by the narrowest of margins which, temporarily, took them to the top of the table. Fortune usually evens itself out and, a little over twelve months later, Hampshire suffered four very close defeats. They were beaten by Northamptonshire by 45 runs, Middlesex by 3 wickets, Lancashire by 25 runs and finally, and without Shackleton, by Yorkshire who beat them by just 17 runs. If two of these results had been reversed they would have finished fifth. Again this emphasises the fine line which can exist between success and failure, in this case a difference of seven places.

Apart from the seam attack and the batting form of Rogers there were other pleasing aspects. Gray had certainly enjoyed his best season to date and, during the latter half, provided excellent opening support for Rogers. They would remain in harness for the next two seasons. As well as his batting form Gray showed his all round qualities by taking 48 wickets. The middle order batting was a little more stable with Harrison, Rayment and Eagar each scoring 1,000 runs in all games.

The standard of the fielding was particularly encouraging and compared favourably with any Hampshire side of the past. The enthusiastic Eagar continued to lead by example. Although the nucleus of the team had been basically unchanged the average age showed a slight fall due to McCorkell's retirement and the infrequent availability of Knott.

The future looked bright when the county made a major signing in September, someone who would not only strengthen the batting in a very positive way but one who would also transform the attitudes of the other batsmen. The West Indian, Roy Marshall, would become the dominant player Hampshire so desperately needed although, due to qualification restrictions, would not be available until 1955.

Finally, waiting in the wings or more specifically in the Forces doing their National Service, were the young quartet of Burden, Heath, Barnard and Sainsbury.

For once, Derek was relieved when the 1952 season ended as he had been playing without a break for two and a half years. Few bowlers would have successfully undertaken such a continuous and arduous spell of work especially as this period included two tours to India, in itself tiring because of the wearisome travelling. He had bowled a total of 4,353 overs between April 1950 and September 1952, taking 476 wickets at an average of 20.87 - highly commendable in view of the pitches and conditions he encountered overseas.

Although he would take a break from cricket he needed to work to supplement his income from Hampshire which was hardly substantial but, not being a wealthy county, they probably couldn't afford to pay him more. When Derek received his county cap in 1949 his wages rose to £7.13.10 and there had been only a small increase since then. He had been able to save a little from his tours to India and from the occasional representative match but, nevertheless, money was tight especially now they had a young baby. Price's bakery at Eastleigh had strong connections with Hampshire and, for some winters, he worked for them. The work was fairly basic but he enjoyed it and provided the essential extra income.

Like 1947 and 1948 the summer of 1953 was one of great expectancy and optimism and not just for cricket lovers. The austerity of the immediate post war years was beginning to wane ; people had a little more money to spend on luxury items with televisions and cars being the main beneficiaries. The Coronation would be the biggest celebration since before the war and this alone had a massive effect on television sales. For many it would be the first time they had seen 'the box' and, on that wet day in June, living rooms across the country were packed with eager faces around a small black and white flickering picture.

It was a year of great sporting achievements starting with the 'Stanley Matthews cup final' when the maestro, at the age of 38, tormented and tortured an injury hit Bolton Wanderers in the last twenty minutes to help Blackpool to a 4-3 victory after being 1-3 down. A national fervour (apart from in Bolton) seemed to will Matthews towards a coveted winner's medal. He was the most famous footballer in the world at the time and had already suffered the disappointment of two loser's medals. In truth he hadn't actually played that well until that last period of the game and it must not be overlooked that Mortensen scored three goals and became the first player to hit a hat-trick in a cup final.

If Matthews was the magical individual in football then Gordon Richards had a similar reputation in horse racing and he rode the famous 'Pinza' to victory in the Derby. Mike Hawthorne became the first Englishman to win a World Championship Grand Prix race since before the war but the crowning glory came when the announcement was made, on Coronation day itself, that Everest had been conquered. With these events setting the mood of the nation there was an Ashes series to savour.

Hampshire started the new season with a very similar playing staff to that which finished the previous one. There was, though, one important signing (apart from Marshall) which, whilst not having any immediate, significant impact, was one which would prove so vital in the years ahead.

Henry Horton was one of the most likeable men to have played for Hampshire. He had very little experience of first class cricket having played just a few games for Worcestershire in 1946 and 1947. His main sporting prowess had been on the football field starting as an amateur with Worcester City, turning professional in November 1946. He was then spotted by Blackburn Rovers and signed for the first division side in January 1947. In those days of packed football grounds he remembers playing in front of a "sea of 30,000 caps" on a murky winter's afternoon. Murky, because the factories of the industrial North were having to work overtime in helping to put Britain on to a sound financial footing - this is where the real wealth of the Nation stems, not the Square Mile in the City of London. Unfortunately, this did not help the air quality at the time and the sun struggled to get through, especially in the winter.

Horton had signed for Blackburn as a wing half but was soon converted to centre half, although he was not the tallest of men. His confidence in that position improved after he watched Neil Franklin of Stoke City and England. Like Horton, Franklin was not that tall but one "who wouldn't be pushed around". Horton was then transferred to Southampton in 1951/1952 and it was when he was playing for the 'Saints' that Arthur Holt, the Hampshire coach and also a former 'Saint', asked him to play cricket for the Hampshire Club and Ground side. He was soon asked if he would like to have another stab at county cricket. Initially he wasn't too keen believing he still had a few years left in league football but the persuasive Arthur finally had his way.

Horton's first experience of watching Derek Shackleton was as a spectator at Southampton and, like so many others, he could not understand how this man could take so many wickets, although did notice the "zip" into the keeper's gloves. He would get a closer insight when he made his county debut in May.

Hampshire started the season modestly with a win, a draw and a defeat from their first three matches. The win by Middlesex at Lord's included a superb century by Robertson, the batsman Shackleton still admired more than any other at the time.

Two matches against Leicestershire deserve special mention. At Loughborough Hampshire achieved a very fine victory in adversity. During the course of the Leicestershire first innings Hampshire lost the services of both Knott and Harrison due to injury. The loss of Knott was particularly galling as the wicket was taking spin and he had taken the first 5 Leicestershire wickets. They totalled 179 and, in reply, Hampshire were skittled out for 68, Rogers carrying his bat with 32 not out. The 'Shack and Vic' partnership demolished Leicestershire in the second innings and Hampshire were left to score 196 to win. Although the wicket was still difficult they won comfortably by 9 wickets after an opening partnership of 160 by Rogers and Gray.

Immediately following this the two sides met in the return fixture at Portsmouth. Leicestershire were bowled out for 91 with Derek taking 6-48 and, in reply, Hampshire declared at 370 for seven after being 25 for three and, later 128 for six. Rogers (as usual) and Horton, on his debut, retrieved the first collapse and Walker, Prouton and Dare later contributed 231 between them. Leicestershire needing 279 to make Hampshire bat again collapsed to 81 for seven and early taxis were ordered to take their players to the station. Their skipper, Charles Palmer, refused to give up hope and found a very worthy partner in Terry Spencer who stayed for just over an hour. The taxis had been sent away and then there was a delay for rain. Upon the resumption their last man Goodwin joined Palmer (Walsh had been injured and couldn't bat) and such was his reputation as a true tail-ender that taxis were ordered again.

Jeffrey Goodwin was a lively left arm opening bowler and took 5 of the 7 Hampshire wickets to fall but his ability as a batsman was, to put it kindly, 'modest in the extreme'. He was probably pleased with his first innings score of 3 which was higher than his previous season's average of 2.84. He would end his career with an average of just over 5. How then did he survive for over two hours on a seamer's wicket against two of the best exponents of this type of wicket in the world ? He not only stayed with Palmer to help save the game, he enabled his skipper to reach a thoroughly deserved century and, in the process, made his own highest ever score - 23 not out. The taxi drivers of Portsmouth cannot have been too happy as they had again been asked to return to base.

Palmer would have shielded his partner as much as possible but, during this two hour period, Goodwin would have faced a considerable number of deliveries from Shackleton and Cannings who were bowlers who could be relied upon to whittle out tail end batsmen without any problems. Derek, when looking back over his twenty year career, cannot recall any other occasion when a genuine tail ender lasted so long. He took 5-67 in 50 overs (11-115 in the match) but, for once, could not make the final breakthrough.

After defeating Kent at Southampton Hampshire briefly led the championship table but soon lost this lofty position not because they started losing games but due to the fact that three of their next four matches were of non championship status.

The England test selectors met during the weekend of 6th June to pick the side for the first test against Australia. There was a great expectancy for the series notwithstanding the 4-1 defeat when the teams last met in 1950/1951. Close scrutiny will show that, although Australia won two tests very comprehensively, they won luckily at Brisbane and by only 28 runs at Melbourne. Bradman had retired and England had their strongest side since before the war.

When the selectors deliberated, Shackleton had already taken 50 wickets in all matches at an average of 16.12 and Hampshire had, at one time, led the championship table which could only help his cause. There were also doubts about the selection of Trueman who had promised so much the previous year. He was still in the Services and did not play for Yorkshire until a period of leave at the end of May. It was not a happy time for, potentially, England's most exciting fast bowler and the selectors appeared reluctant to take a risk. However, they did not turn to Shackleton but chose to take a great gamble by playing only four regular bowlers of which only Bedser and Bailey were seamers. Brian Statham, perhaps not quite so quick as Trueman, was, like Shackleton, extremely accurate, was having a good season and could count himself unlucky to find himself omitted from the original twelve. Bedser was an automatic choice and there could be little argument with the selection of Bailey as the all-rounder. As a bowler, however, Bailey was not the potent force that Trueman, Statham and Shackleton were.

During the same weekend that the England selectors were meeting at Lord's Hampshire played the Australians in a memorable match at

Southampton. The early performances by the tourists bore very favourable comparison with their predecessors of 1948 and their six victories up to this point were all by an innings margin. The wicket at Southampton that season was poor with too much lime being used and, right from the start of the game, there were problems. Before a packed crowd Shackleton bowled the first ball to Graeme Hole. What happened then was quite astonishing. As Alan Rayment described : "A small mushroom shaped 'cloud' rose slowly from the pitch - rather like a miniature atom bomb". This caused great consternation, not only for the batsmen but also to the Hampshire committee who had been 'rubbing their hands with glee' at the size of the crowd which, it is believed, swelled to over 15,000 by the afternoon with many people still outside after the gates closed. The Australians were pulling in large crowds everywhere and there was every prospect of a large gate on the second and third days. But would the match last that long ? Eagar concluded that the wicket would break up on the first day and that the game would end within two days and he was proved entirely correct .

There was much to savour and enjoy in this game although Reg Dare would probably have had reservations. Very early in the Australian first innings he was fielding at short leg when Derek bowled to Hole who, aiming to drive through the covers, took an inside edge and the ball hit Dare full in the face, which swelled dramatically and alarmingly. Ken Gibson, the club doctor, had the idea of treating the swelling with leeches and the remedy proved so successful that no stitches were necessary. Fortunately the Southampton General hospital had some of these blood sucking worms available!

Those lucky enough to be at Southampton on the first day witnessed one of the truly great innings. Neil Harvey treated the crowd to a century of such quality that Derek rates it as good as any he ever saw. The wicket, putting it mildly, was difficult but Harvey gave a perfect lesson in using his feet to the fullest advantage. He pulled and drove to all parts and did not give a single chance.

Hampshire were never seriously in the game but, although they were without Rogers who had injured his thumb in the previous game at Bristol they were able to give a debut to Roy Marshall who was allowed to play in non championship matches. He scored a spectacular 71 in the second innings hitting 5 sixes and 5 fours in a brief, but hugely entertaining, partnership of 96 with Rayment who himself lofted Benaud for six into an adjacent orchard.

As a footnote to this match there was one very significant dismissal in the Australian first innings when Cannings caught and bowled the Australian number X1, Bill Johnston, for 8. There was no reason to give any particular thought to it at the time but it turned out to be the only occasion Johnston was dismissed that season. In 17 innings he was not out 16 times and, in scoring a total of 102, finished top of the Australian batting averages. There were strong rumours later in the tour, when his colleagues realised what was happening, that there were numerous (unsuccessful) attempts to run him out. A thoroughly good humoured cricketer he would greatly enjoy this statistical anomaly. Only Boycott (twice) and Gooch have achieved century averages in post war cricket in England.

Throughout Derek's entire career there was never an extended period when he did not take wickets. He would never lose his impeccable line and length and he would ruthlessly exploit a wicket which gave him assistance. In 1953 this was particularly so in a game against Glamorgan at Newport.

Most wickets that summer had some moisture in them and the Welsh county were mercilessly destroyed. Shackleton, bowling virtually unchanged, nagged away pitching the ball on a very small patch which gradually became worn and this resulted in the ball rising and moving off the seam alarmingly. No other mark was visible apart from this worn circle of approximately six inches in diameter. He had an uncanny ability to pitch the ball exactly where he wanted it EVERY time. On this type of wicket the batsman had to use all his powers of concentration simply to survive and runs, often from involuntary edges, were a hard earned bonus. Shackleton took 9 wickets in an innings for the first time with Dare unfortunately robbing him of the tenth when he caught and bowled the Glamorgan number X1 Don Shepherd. Glamorgan would suffer a similar fate on a wicket at Neath five years later.

There were theories put forth, notably later by Ted Dexter and Bob Barber, that the best method of tackling the Hampshire craftsman was to hit him 'over the top'. This did not really work with either of them but one who did adopt this tactic with more success, albeit briefly, was the Rt. Rev David Sheppard, the former Bishop of Liverpool, and, at that time, captain of Sussex. There were examples of late order batsmen slogging him with varying degrees of success but few legitimate ones were willing to attack him - to take the game to him. Survival was still the main priority.

Sussex were having a good season and their final position of second equalled their previous highest in the championship. They defeated Hampshire at Bournemouth to go top of the table for the first time since 1932 and this win was largely due to an innings of 88 by Sheppard out of a total of 221. Henry Horton remembered this knock because it was so rare for a specialist batsman to loft Derek back over his head.

The retired Bishop himself has distinct memories of the innings :

> "Shack had bowled a great many overs for very few runs. The whole of the match was one in which the ball moved about quite a lot and low scoring was the order of the day.
>
> My memory is that I battled it out, accumulating runs fairly slowly. When I had been in some time, I did indeed decide that I would hit him back over his head if he pitched the ball up to me. I duly did so, not quite middling the ball, so that it went just over the top of mid on. Having got away with that, I must have felt a bit more confident. The next ball he bowled me I hit right in the middle of the bat and it went for 6 over the beer tent. He then bowled a slower off spinner and I hit that for 6 in the same corner of the ground. He then bowled a fast ball which I also hit for 6 in the same direction. It was quite extraordinary that, in the middle of an innings in which I really had to battle for runs, there was this one over in which I hit 22"

As the former Bishop says, this was really an isolated over and not a sustained belligerent attack. Excluding that particular sequence of six deliveries Shackleton took 4-66 in 31 overs.

David Sheppard probably played Derek as well as anyone but had a very high regard for him. He marvelled at the "wonderful economic action, the lightness on the feet and the movement and the accuracy". Like so many others he was often surprised at the pace off the wicket.

The 1953 season ended disappointingly for Hampshire with four draws and seven defeats in their last eleven matches and meant a further fall in the championship, this time to fourteenth. It was not the fault of Shackleton who, in all matches, took 150 wickets for the first time. With so much bowling his batting suffered but, on his 29th birthday, he scored 65 against Glamorgan, his only 50 of the summer. He frequently produced something special on his birthday.

England regained the Ashes with a famous victory at the Oval. With Trueman making his only test appearance that summer the bowling was strong and the start of a period when England had a superb, perfectly balanced attack. Although Bedser's test career would soon be over England would have real, and quality pace, a medium pacer who was a genuine all rounder and two of the finest spinners this country has ever produced.

Derek's chances for England were further receding and he would remain in the test wilderness for some time, but not for ever.

Chapter Seven

A Day on the Beach at Weston

The two following seasons could not have been more different, not simply in the fortunes of Hampshire CCC, but in the contrasts of the weather.

The summer of 1954 turned out to be the wettest and coldest in living memory, certainly the most miserable since 1903. It made even 1946 reasonably tolerable in comparison. A huge number of games were directly affected by rain and those that escaped the drenchings were played on soft, slow wickets. There were only a few consecutive days without rain and even fewer when spectators could leave their macs and umbrellas at home. The sales of these products soared in 1954.

For Derek Shackleton it was to be a relatively modest season although most bowlers would have been more than happy with his final figures. During the twenty consecutive seasons in which he took 100 wickets there were only two when he did not achieve this feat in championship matches alone - in 1949, his first full season, and in 1954. He bowled fewer overs than he was used to - 'only' 1069.5 - due undoubtedly to the appalling weather. Shackleton and Cannings, together with the Derbyshire pair of Jackson and Gladwin, were still a feared opening attack conceding only two runs per over. Batsmen throughout the country were struggling for runs with counties being regularly dismissed for very modest totals, not only because of the inevitable shortened playing time and wet wickets but also the slow outfields.

Derek's work load, therefore, was not so onerous but, for a man who loves the warm sunshine, it was a year when he, perhaps, didn't enjoy his cricketing life as much as usual. There were a few times during his career when it took him a few games to warm up at the beginning of the season. In 1954 his barren period came towards the end - only 27 wickets in the final twelve matches.

The season had started optimistically enough with the knowledge that several very promising Hampshire born players would now be available after completing their National Service. Sainsbury, Burden, Heath and Barnard were to be given several opportunities but, due to 'Anno Domini', there were final appearances for Knott and Hill. They had contributed so much for the county and were the last remaining stalwarts from the pre-war side .

Hampshire won two of their first four matches but only two more throughout the remainder of the season. Half of their games were undecided with thirteen draws and one 'no decision'. The weather wrought havoc with the championship - Lancashire suffering most with seven 'no decisions', a quarter of their fixtures totally ruined. Only the woefully weak Somerset escaped this particular outcome but, quite often, opposition counties needed only two days or less to wrap up victory ; delays brought about by the rain did not have so much effect on their results.

Hampshire lost their opening game at Lord's mainly due to a superb all round performance by Denis Compton. He not only scored 117 and 64 but also had match bowling figures of 8-77. This, allegedly, after turning up late on the first morning following a party the previous night! His century was not a swashbuckling innings of 1947 vintage - the knee had seen to that - but it held the Middlesex first innings together. He was, though, made to work hard for his runs with Shackleton and Cannings conceding only 92 runs in 40 overs.

The Hampshire batsmen were disappointing but the twenty year old Colin Ingleby-Mackenzie made a fine 54 in the second innings and Rayment who, as an amateur, had once played for Middlesex 2nd X1 top scored in both innings with 40 and 65 which gave him great satisfaction.

Ingleby-Mackenzie had made his championship debut in 1951 just a few days short of his 18th birthday and played a handful of games the following year. Fresh out of Eton he was somewhat in awe of players of the stature of Edrich and Compton but, in 1952 in another match against Middlesex, he had hit an aggressive 61 in an hour and a half before being bowled by Compton. They were to form a life long friendship and their attitude to cricket, and to life, was that it had to be enjoyed to the full.

Charlie Knott had the great satisfaction of dismissing Compton in the first of his final three matches for Hampshire although, by then, he had scored 117 and Knott had been dealt some heavy handed treatment. A few weeks later in his last appearance for the county he took 5-87 against Kent. Born and bred in Southampton he was Hampshire through and through and a road near the county ground is named after him. Unfortunately for Hampshire he was heavily tied in to the family's fishmongers' business and he remained an amateur.

This, together with other business commitments in the city, severely restricted his appearances.

Knott recalls his first appearance for Hampshire in 1938. Serving in the shop one August morning he received a telephone call asking if he would be available to play for the county at Canterbury. He readily accepted and, bowling seamers, took 1-92 and then 0-80 in the next game at Worcester. The county were on a brief away tour and the final match of the three was against Gloucestershire at Cheltenham when, turning to spinners, he "took a few wickets".

It was at Canterbury that he was approached by a young man and his friend asking if they could get a lift to Worcester in Knott's car. He turned out to be a Southampton policeman who was taking his annual holiday watching Hampshire on this tour. Leo Harrison already knew him as being a cricket fanatic and one who was always at home games watching both the play and those practising in the nets. When Harrison came out of the RAF and listened to the radio after the war he immediately recognised the distinctive voice of John Arlott.

For all of Arlott's many achievements one which gave him most joy and satisfaction was when he appeared as Hampshire's twelfth man at Worcester in 1938. For some reason the county had only eleven players with them and there was a short period, due to an injury, when he was asked (or did he volunteer ?) if he would step into the breach. No matter, there was absolutely no hesitation. He had to borrow some kit including a large size pair of boots from the Worcestershire opening bowler, Reg Perks. Arlott was in heaven and this must have inspired him to write his first published poem which begins :

"Dozing in deck-chair's gentle curve
Through half closed eyes I watched the cricket
Knowing the sporting press would say
'Perks bowled well on a perfect wicket'"

The introduction of Mike Barnard to the side added further strength to the Shackleton armoury. He had made solitary appearances in 1952 and 1953 but, having now completed his National Service, he was more available but not completely so. He was also a talented inside forward with Portsmouth, then in the old first division and there would, inevitably, be a conflict of interests. Derek has always paid tribute to the fine close fieldsmen and he considers Barnard to be the best slip catcher he has ever seen. Hampshire now had expert close catchers on the leg side in the form of Eagar, Rogers and Horton and, shortly, Sainsbury would become the best of them all. This contingent gobbled up those batsmen ensnared by the in swing and, with the rapid development of the outswinger, Barnard and Gray provided a hugely successful trap in the slips.

The tourists that year were from Pakistan who were making their first visit to England and what they would have made of the weather is anybody's guess. They were, perhaps, fortunate in drawing the test series because the weather saved them from certain defeat at Old Trafford, although even there they suffered from much the worst of the conditions. However, they won the fourth and final test at the Oval on merit and became the only side to win a test match on a first visit to England.

Derek played no part in the test series and was probably further away from selection than he was the previous year. Hutton, with a winter series against Australia on the horizon, was very much in favour of pace as Bedser would realise shortly after the start of that tour. During the summer of 1954 England used Bedser, Statham, Loader and Tyson augmented by Bailey, Appleyard and Wardle. Surprisingly, or perhaps not so, Trueman who was having a good season with Yorkshire wasn't selected, almost certainly as a result of his controversial tour to the West Indies the previous winter. The conservatively minded selectors were not prepared, it seems, to forgive his apparent misdemeanors which, in any case, were wildly exaggerated. What was even more astonishing was his omission from the touring party to Australia which was announced at the end of July. The next day, after hearing the news, he vented his indignation on the unfortunate Derbyshire batsmen with a truly hostile spell. Really wound up he took the first 3 wickets in seven deliveries without conceding a run.

With Derek now thirty and with younger, faster bowlers around, it appeared likely that his brief test career was over.

Another significant newcomer for Hampshire, Peter Sainsbury, made his debut against Nottinghamshire at Southampton scoring a confident 63 not out in the second innings batting at number nine. It was particularly pleasing for the county that there was now so much home grown talent coming through. Sainsbury, born in Southampton, would play for the county for over twenty years and is the only Hampshire player to have been in both their championship sides. Another quite exceptional fielder, this time on the leg side, he would hover, lethally, at short leg and dismissals 'caught Sainsbury bowled Shackleton' would become commonplace over the next fourteen seasons.

Hampshire now had a superb group of close catchers and, if indeed Shackleton and Cannings needed any encouragement, they would certainly have been inspired by the safe, and utterly reliable, pairs of hands around the batsman. Often the catching was quite breathtaking and, when assessing Shackleton's career, it is essential that full credit is given to the fielders.

By bowling so straight and beating the bat so frequently there were, in every game, a considerable number of appeals for lbw. Shackleton was, though, a fair if vociferous appealer. Being so accurate meant that if any appeals did not go in his favour it was due to the late movement or lift which would have put doubt in the umpire's mind. Leo Harrison recalls an umpire at Derby " who got so carried away that he appealed for lbw before Derek did, it was so plumb".

He wasn't so successful with another umpire on the circuit at that time, someone who seemed to uphold all Vic Cannings' appeals but who would turn down the majority of his own. On seeing this umpire arriving for a match against Sussex and noting the position he was taking up on the field Derek said to his partner "I suppose you want that bloody end". "Not half" was the reply. During the game Derek did not win one appeal from that particular umpire but Cannings won a dubious one against David Sheppard.

The miserable season spluttered to a welcome close. The two seamers had both taken 100 wickets at reasonable cost but the last major success they had in a game together that year was against Leicestershire at Portsmouth in mid July. Hampshire won by an innings with Shackleton having match figures of 8-52 and Cannings taking 10-83. They worked well together professionally and were also good friends. Although Shack would always take the first over there were no arguments as to which end each would bowl from. The decision would be based on any breeze or slope which would help Derek's natural in swing and Cannings' away swinger.

Hampshire had, by now, another seam option in the making. Malcolm Heath was a very tall (6 foot 5 inches) fast bowler who, Neville Rogers was pleased to observe, "made opposing batsmen duck and weave about for a change". Outstanding though they were neither Shackleton nor Cannings could be described as hostile and an alternative pace option was welcomed. Heath was considered to be a 'made' bowler rather than a natural one and Arthur Holt spent hours and hours with him to improve his run up and his general action and to try to get full benefit from his height. It was indeed the height which made him an awkward proposition and if he had been more aggressive he would have been even more impressive. A genuinely nice man who did not like seeing a batsman hurt. Like the heavyweight boxer a fast bowler needs a killer instinct to be truly successful, something perhaps, Heath lacked. Even so there were occasions when he produced spells of true hostility especially in 1958, his most lucrative season. Those who faced him at Neath and at Burton that year will testify to that.

Heath topped the Hampshire bowling averages in 1954 with 17 wickets at 15.41. Two of those were the highly prized ones of Len

Hutton who he dismissed twice at Bournemouth, a game Derek missed because he was slightly injured after falling off a ladder.

Few people lamented the passing of the 1954 season, including the players and administrators of Hampshire. Every April since the war there had been 'optimism for the season ahead' but, in reality, their performances rarely matched this quest. Between 1946 and 1954 they had finished no higher than ninth and simply did not have the strength in depth to improve upon this position. But the younger players were becoming more experienced and, with Marshall available in 1955, the promise of better things would turn into fact. Also, the weather could only improve.

Before the 1954 season had ended Kathy went back to Todmorden to be with her mother as she and Derek were expecting their second child. Caroline was born on 2nd September. Although Hampshire's season had ended two days beforehand Derek had been picked for a couple of representative matches at Hastings and Torquay. These games earned him a little extra cash but he was keen to travel north himself which he did immediately after the game in Devon.

The following year , 1955 , turned out to be the most satisfying season to date in the County's history. They finished third in the championship, their highest ever position at that point in their history and it was achieved through a wonderful, cohesive, team effort from basically just twelve players. Apart from the twelve Heath played in only seven matches, although taking 32 valuable wickets, and Ingleby-Mackenzie stepped in as an emergency wicket keeper when Harrison was selected for the Players v. Gentlemen.

For Derek it was a summer of unrelenting success taking 159 wickets at an average of 13.72 and a year which contained the most extraordinary bowling performance of his career.

Hampshire were celebrating their Diamond Jubilee year but, initially, this did not seem to inspire the players and they won just the first of six matches, five of which were rain affected. Surely the season couldn't be as wet as the previous year ? The sole victory in this opening spell was against Glamorgan but this was followed with defeats by Nottinghamshire and then by Middlesex in a remarkably low scoring game at Lord's. The highest total by either side was 102 and Hampshire were dismissed twice for less than 100. For Shackleton and Cannings it was personal triumphs again taking 18 of the 20 wickets to fall. After two drawn matches against Worcestershire and Lancashire there was to be a similar low scoring game against Kent. The highest total this time was 127 in Hampshire's second innings and Kent, set 167 to win, were in dire straits at 54 for eight . An unlikely unbroken stand of 63 between Ted Witherden and Doug Wright saved the Kent side from defeat which had appeared certain at one stage.

The turning point in the County's fortunes coincided with a change in the weather which resulted in almost unbroken sunshine for the remainder of the summer.

Hampshire beat Northamptonshire at Peterborough, the start of a spell when they won five and drew one of six matches. They soundly defeated the Midlands county due to a fine all round batting performance backed up by excellent bowling from Shackleton and Sainsbury in particular. Derek actually remembers this game because of his batting.

When asked who he considered was the fastest bowler he ever faced, Derek, without a moment's hesitation, said "The Typhoon". Frank Tyson fresh from his triumphs in Australia was bowling at Peterborough on a slightly more helpful wicket than the flat one he usually experienced at Northampton. On observing the quite ferocious pace being generated by Tyson, Derek, at the non-striker's end, called to the batsman waiting (apprehensively) for the next delivery: "Two's, four's or nowt, lad". Peterborough is not one of the largest of grounds and Tyson's run appeared to start from the steps of the pavilion with the wicket keeper, Keith Andrew, and the slip cordon close to the opposite boundary. Derek had never seen slip fielders so deep and wondered if they were positioned to stop edged sixes ! He remembers receiving one extremely painful delivery on the inside of his thigh leaving the actual imprint of the ball. However, he did score 47 brave, and occasionally, fortuitous runs which would prove to be his highest championship score of the summer.

Most of Derek's colleagues agree that, on his day, Tyson was the quickest bowler they encountered. One of those in agreement is Alan Rayment who recalls another example of Tyson's awesome pace. It happened a year later at Portsmouth when Ray Flood, a gutsy little player from Lyndhurst in the New Forest, came to the crease towards the end of a day's play with instructions from his skipper to 'just stay there'. A tall order for a 20 year old playing in only his second championship game and facing the fastest bowler in the world on a lively wicket. He had the distinctly uncomfortable sight of Tyson as a speck in the far distance and, looking behind him, could see the keeper and slips so far away as to make conversation superfluous. Umpire Laurie Gray at square leg, perhaps sympathising with the batsman, asked "How are you, Floody ?" "Bloody lonely" was the reply. Flood survived the onslaught but was dismissed early the next morning stumped off the left arm spin bowling of George Tribe.

That same morning Rayment remembers his skipper, Desmond Eagar, receiving a delivery from Tyson which spun his Harlequin cap through 180 degrees and, after being caught at the wicket, returned ashen faced to the pavilion where he slowly regained his composure.

In a fearsome spell by Tyson Eagar was one of three victims in one over - the others being Derek and Vic Cannings, both having their stumps uprooted and, if the truth be known, perfectly happy to be back in the sanctuary of the pavilion.

Both Tyson and Shackleton opened the bowling for their respective counties but they could hardly be more contrasting. They were utilised in totally different ways. Tyson would not be expected to bowl for long spells but, in short bursts, could be devastating and he would be a real test of a batsman's character and mental and physical courage. One person who played him better than most was Roy Marshall and, in the aforementioned match at Portsmouth, hit a rapid 48 mostly off Tyson who was visibly riled. About ten days beforehand Marshall had hit a century off Northamptonshire on a slow wicket at Rushden but facing Tyson at the United Services ground was an entirely different proposition. Marshall had a theory at that time of 'simply throwing the bat' against fast bowling on a lively wicket. This is what he did at Portsmouth knowing that if he got an edge it would fly through the slip cordon at such a height and speed that it was unlikely he would be caught. The ball seemed to go everywhere and Tyson was getting angrier and angrier and, although the Hampshire players were enjoying the spectacle , they must also have felt a little apprehensive as to what they might expect to receive when it was their turn to bat. Marshall was being over modest when he said he just threw the bat - he was too good a player - and he had a very impressive record over the years against the very best pace bowlers.

Shackleton was also an opening bowler but that is where the comparison ends. In his entire career he never tried to bowl too fast, it would have been a quite unnecessary waste of important energy. His tried and tested method was proving ever more successful so why change ?

Whilst Derek was still the main front line bowler (he was, by now, beginning to bowl considerably more overs than Cannings) Hampshire had their best balanced attack since before the war. This was largely due to the considerable advance made by Peter Sainsbury who, as a slow left arm bowler, took 96 championship wickets (102 in all matches) in his first full season and was picked for the MCC tour to Pakistan the following winter. In addition Burden took 59 wickets with his off breaks and there was important back up from Gray with his deceptive in swingers. Finally Heath who, although only playing in seven matches, took 32 wickets at an average of under 20.

Even on the better wickets of 1955 matches involving Hampshire tended to be low scoring affairs. It was the strength of the bowling which was the main reason they won so many games; they were now able to defend quite modest totals of their own.

There were a few occasions that season when rain and a subsequent drying wicket had a bearing on certain games and Sainsbury took full advantage of the conditions in two matches in June. Against Essex he had superb second innings figures of 7-25 but he gave an even more impressive performance in the next game at Bradford, a match he would always remember.

Hampshire, batting first, scored what appeared to be a relatively modest 224 against a very strong Yorkshire side. However, the northern county were caught on a drying wicket on the Monday and were twice dismissed in a day for 62 and 119. Sainsbury had match figures of 9-62 from 42 overs and took the wicket of Hutton in both innings. What a way to celebrate his 21st birthday and the England captain presented him with the ball.

In the same match Marshall also took 9 wickets for just 50 runs. Although signed as a batsman the county had expected him to bowl reasonably regularly. As the years progressed he bowled less and less but in 1955 topped the bowling, as well as the batting, averages with 25 wickets at 11.92. Most of these wickets were taken in the two games against Yorkshire. After his performance at Bradford he took another 7 wickets against them at Bournemouth in June bringing his tally in the two encounters to 16.

Although Yorkshire won the game at Bournemouth and Hampshire then failed to win the next two their spirits weren't dampened and they embarked on a sequence of ten wins, two draws and a single defeat from their last thirteen matches. Derek took a staggering 85 wickets during this period with a further 6 in the game against the South African tourists.

After a narrow defeat against Leicestershire , Hampshire won five consecutive matches including yet another enthralling encounter with Kent at Canterbury with Hampshire winning off the very last ball, Wright being trapped lbw by Cannings.

The Portsmouth cricket week in August saw a comfortable win over Sussex and a closer one against Lancashire. As usual seam bowlers dominated in both games with Derek picking up 15 wickets and, in the second match, Heath, showing real hostility, caused the Lancashire batsmen all sorts of problems.

After a tight game with Nottinghamshire the side travelled to Weston-Super-Mare, the scene of Derek's most remarkable bowling analysis.

Bare facts show that in 11.1 overs he took 8 Somerset wickets for 4 runs with just four singles (at least two of which were edges) scored off him. Taking a further 6 wickets in the second innings he had match figures of 14-29 and, not surprisingly, Hampshire won comfortably. This was a typical example of Shack exploiting what was obviously a difficult wicket, albeit this time his figures were spectacular in the extreme. Two days when virtually everything went his way. On another occasion he would have bowled equally as well with a slightly more modest outcome. The match itself deserves further comment and also a comparison to another match at Weston in 1927.

In the 1955 game Hampshire batted first and at 78 for one appeared to be cruising towards a useful total. There was no indication of the devastation to follow. After Gray and Horton had each been dismissed for 43 a collapse ensued and Hampshire were all out for 154. James Hilton, bowling off breaks, took 6-49 including a hat trick - the victims being Harrison, Shackleton and Burden. A drying wicket was beginning to create serious problems for batsmen and, after Hilton's success, it was widely expected that Sainsbury and Burden would do most of the damage for Hampshire. However, right from the first over Shackleton became virtually unplayable, it was simply a question of survival for the Somerset batsmen and, with one exception, they had no answer. They finally reached a total of 37 with Harold Stephenson, their wicket keeper, remaining undefeated on 18.

Most bowlers would have been in ecstasy with figures of 8-4 and, deep down, Derek was highly delighted. What upset him was that the final analysis could so easily have been 9-4 which, at the season's end, would have brought him a considerable financial prize. John McMahon, a true tail-ender, was a player who Derek would not normally have had any problem in dismissing especially on that particular wicket. McMahon edged one delivery to the left of Peter Sainsbury and set off for a single. This was Sainsbury's first full season and his reputation as a fieldsman of extraordinary ability was not, then, so well known. Quick as a flash Sainsbury swooped, picked up and threw in one motion leaving McMahon stranded. This denied Derek a crucial wicket and deprived him of the annual Brylcreem award for the best bowling performance of the season. " 'Sains', you've just robbed me of 100 guineas" with tongue (slightly) in cheek. Still on a modest income and with his first benefit a few years away the extra cash would have been very welcome. Sainsbury also took the other wicket to fall to a bowler but they still remain good friends !

In a later season Derek would have a very justifiable complaint at missing out on a cash prize. The reward in 1955 went to Jack Flavell of Worcestershire who took 9-30 against Kent but there was another extraordinary statistical performance that year from Charles Palmer of Leicestershire. Against Surrey he took 8-7 in the first innings and, in the second, conceded only one run in 13 overs giving him a match analysis of : 27-24-8-8.

After the debacle of the Somerset innings Hampshire, batting a second time, soon lost two wickets but Horton scored a typically determined 59 and Rayment an extravagant 104. Rayment was an enigma. A batsman of considerable natural talent he had the knack of producing his finest innings on difficult wickets but, annoyingly, did not score as heavily as his talent suggested he would when he first joined Hampshire. To him cricket was a game to be enjoyed to the full and averages were of no great consequence. His Hampshire average of just over 20 is modest but the majority of his 6,000 plus runs and his time at the crease would have brought great joy to those watching. He was never boring. It is no surprise that his idol was Denis Compton and that he would later have the greatest admiration for Colin Ingleby-Mackenzie and his attitudes when captaining Hampshire. At Weston Rayment realised that, if he simply tried to defend, he wouldn't last long and so, in his own words, "went bananas". He attacked virtually every ball, dancing down the wicket 'a la Compton' to totally unsettle the two spinners, Hilton and McMahon. His task was made easier as Somerset did not possess a seam bowler remotely in Shackleton's class but, nevertheless, it was a magnificent knock in the circumstances and could not have been bettered by Compton himself. It was to be his finest hour and it was sad that this very talented, but slightly unfulfilled, player should leave the game a few years later to concentrate on other, and very varied, business interests.

Somerset, needing 363 to win, soon lost five wickets and, despite a courageous 52 from Stephenson, were all out for 98.

Yawar Saeed was a young Somerset batsman who probably rather reluctantly remembers this game. He was out in both innings 'caught Barnard bowled Shackleton 0', not necessarily that unusual except that both times he was caught off his thumb. He had a brief spell with Somerset and, on another occasion, had the distinction of hitting Frank Tyson for six . He apparently said later "I didn't see the ball. It came off my right thumb and went over the wicket keeper's head". Perhaps it was a good thing he didn't have a long cricket career, he may not have had many fingers and thumbs left. Although he had a career away from cricket he later managed the highly successful Pakistan tour of England in 1996.

What was additionally surprising about the Weston-Super-Mare game was that Shackleton took 14 wickets and Cannings none. During their period together in the 1950s their ratio of wickets would have been about 5 or 6 to 4 in Derek's favour so why, in this game, should it be 14-0 ? Admittedly Cannings was given only four overs in the first innings but Shack already had several wickets by the end of his fourth over. It was one of those times when everything falls into place for one player and nothing clicks for another. Why did Laker take 19 wickets in a test match and his great spin partner, Lock, only 1 ? In the same season for Surrey Laker took all 10 wickets in the Australian first innings and Lock none in 33 overs but, in the second innings, Lock took 7 wickets and Laker only 2. Such anomalies are thrown up from time to time for which there are no apparent good reasons.

It is also worth recalling a not dissimilar game 28 years beforehand, again at Weston. As in 1955 Hampshire played Somerset in the festival week. Jack Newman, virtually on his own, destroyed the Somerset batting taking 8 wickets in each innings and ending with match figures of 16-88. He, like Shackleton, was unplayable and again a similar question can be asked. Why did Newman take 16 wickets and his famous partner Alec Kennedy only 3 ? In this instance each bowler delivered exactly the same number of overs. On another day Kennedy would have been the arch destroyer.

With the sun continuing to shine Hampshire ended a happy season with wins over Surrey and Worcestershire at Bournemouth. The victory against Surrey was especially pleasing as they were the side to beat - the existing champions and also champions elect. Whilst never seriously challenging Surrey and Yorkshire for the championship Hampshire did have the satisfaction of beating both counties and deservedly so.

Derek always liked playing at Bournemouth although, for a while, didn't enjoy quite the success which came to him so automatically at Portsmouth and, on away grounds, at Lord's and Hove. With the large influx of visitors to the town in the holiday months there was generally a good crowd and atmosphere, especially in August, and his father would often be a spectator when he and Derek's mother took their annual holiday.

England and South Africa had fought out an exciting test series with the host nation winning 3-2. Although they managed two totals of 500 or more the South Africans were let down by their batting, with the notable exception of Jackie McGlew. England were almost totally reliant on May and Compton for their runs but, overall, their batting was stronger than that of their opponents who failed to reach 200 in seven of their ten innings.

With the series ended, and with the weather set fair, the tourists came to Southampton and, in an entertaining match, defeated Hampshire by the comfortable margin of 275 runs. Derek had a good game taking 6 wickets and also top scoring in the first innings with a rapid 50. He drove 'Toey' Tayfield, still the finest off spinner South Africa has produced, for 3 sixes in one over which delighted his father who was in the crowd.

To finish third in the championship crowned the Diamond Jubilee year and everyone played a major part. Above all there was a wonderful team spirit. It was a genuinely happy side and as Desmond Eagar mentioned in 'Hampshire County Cricket, The Official History'

"No captain can ever have led a more pleasant, equable or friendly side". Great credit for this must go to the skipper himself. No county had a more enthusiastic leader and no one individual could have been more hard working in promoting his county. After the last match that year at Bournemouth an emotional 'EDR' presented each player with a pair of silver cuff links to commemorate this special year and which were paid for out of his own pocket.

Derek had enjoyed another fine season bowling yet more overs than ever before and reaping a record haul, at that time, of 159 wickets. His average fell to 13.72 and, ignoring D.F. Cox of Surrey who took only 14 wickets, he was second only to Bob Appleyard in the national averages. The difference to Hampshire in 1955 was that Shackleton and Cannings were not alone, there was considerable support from the other bowlers.

Marshall had a good first season with the bat although he would become even more dominant in later years. He averaged just under 35 (strangely only he and Horton had averages in excess of 25 in what was a very successful season for the county) but scored quickly and gave the other batsmen the confidence to attack rather than let the opposition take the initiative.

At last the pre-season optimism was well founded and the final outcome gave Hampshire the confidence and self belief that they could achieve even greater heights.

The classical action photographed by Patrick Eagar

Chapter Eight

Kennedy and Shackleton

During the immediate post war years when Hampshire were actively seeking younger players and, importantly, a new seam attack those who had supported the county between the wars harked back to a golden era when Kennedy and Newman were so prolific. However, by the end of 1955 the Shackleton/Cannings partnership was receiving similar plaudits and Shack was certainly being looked upon as the new Kennedy. Comparisons such as this do little justice to either player. There was only one Kennedy as there was only one Shackleton and it has been proved so often how difficult and inconclusive it is to compare or contrast the merits of two individuals from quite separate eras. Suffice to say both have made huge contributions to the success of Hampshire CCC. There were, though, certain similarities which justify comment and analysis.

Alec Kennedy, like Derek, came from northern 'climes', indeed from Edinburgh, but moved south at a much younger age, in fact his parents came to live in Southampton when he was only five. It was whilst he was still at school that he used to spend hours in the nets at the County ground and he joined the groundstaff when he was 14 and made his debut in 1907 when he was only 16 and a half. His career, therefore, started much earlier than Derek's but was disrupted by the first world war.

There is a description of Kennedy in 'Hampshire County Cricket, The Official History" which is worth quoting verbatim because, for the most part, it could apply equally to Shackleton. A Hampshire supporter, whose knowledge may be limited to post second world war cricket, on reading this, and without a hint of the subject matter, would immediately assume it was about Derek Shackleton.

"He is an essentially serious cricketer. Hour after hour he would bowl ; five measured walking paces and then eight unhurried running strides, planting his feet so precisely in the same place each time that, on a damp ground, I have seen the tracks of his run up and walk back cut to the exact shape of his boots by his machine-like regularity. He walked back erect as a guardsman, turned and plomped smoothly in, to bowl with his right arm as high and straight as a hop-pole : in fact his bowling arm brushed his right ear as it came over.
"His pace was about medium, sometimes, with the new ball, a little above medium. He bowled mainly in-swingers while the seam was sharp, but his most consistently effective ball was the leg cutter, which he bowled with remarkable accuracy and varied with a true off- spinner of little less pace. With just a little sympathy from the atmosphere, his leg cutter would dip in to the leg stump and turn away off the pitch. On good wickets, where his cutter would not turn, his weapon was length, length, length, with slight variations of pace and infinite patience".

A description of Derek would have only very slight variations.

A man in a somewhat unique position to make valid points about both bowlers is Neil McCorkell who kept wicket to Kennedy between 1932 and 1936 and to Shackleton between 1948 and 1951.

McCorkell, writing from his home in South Africa, recalls that Kennedy was a very serious minded cricketer, indeed a hard man and, to the young McCorkell in 1932, it was always 'Mister' Kennedy. He was a man who was treated with the utmost respect by other county sides and McCorkell confirms his mastery of length and movement off the pitch. He remembers Kennedy calling him aside one day and, in his deep voice, the conversation went as follows :

A.K. "'Nipper' (he always called McCorkell 'Nipper'), can you see when I bowl my leg cutter ?"
N.M. "No, Mr. Kennedy"
A.K. "Can you see my in-swinger ?"
N.M. "No, Mr. Kennedy"
A.K. "Can you see my away swinger ?"
N.M. "No, Mr. Kennedy"
A.K. "Can you see my off spinner ?"
N.M. "No, Mr. Kennedy"

McCorkell said that if he had said 'yes' to any of these questions he would have received a reply along the lines : 'Some kid, thinks he knows everything in a very short time'. His reason for answering 'No' was in the hope that Kennedy would say 'Come in the nets, Nipper, and I will demonstrate to you'. But the response was not so kindly. His reply was "Then you had better find out, you're no bloody good to me otherwise".

Shackleton was a serious cricketer and, due to his quiet nature, would not necessarily go out of his way to give advice but, if asked, would readily give it. Kennedy's attitude seems self defeating because a good understanding between bowler and wicket-keeper is so essential. Whilst McCorkell did not see Kennedy at his peak he was still ' a very good bowler ' in those latter years.

McCorkell's description of Shackleton is more kindly. He remembers him in those early years "dropping the ball on a good length, moving the ball into or away from the batsman and could bowl and bowl and bowl. He had remarkable patience and was a good team man with no pomp".

It is quite clear from McCorkell's comments that he preferred Derek as a person but said that both were truly great bowlers. Statistically there are some interesting comparisons.

In all matches Kennedy took 2874 wickets at an average of 21.23 and Shackleton 2857 at 18.65. These two Hampshire bowlers occupy seventh and eighth positions for the total number of first class wickets taken and, with the reduction in the number of first class matches played in this country and elsewhere, these records will, almost certainly, remain in perpetuity.

In matches for Hampshire Shackleton has the slight edge. His total of 2669 wickets at 18.23 is marginally better than Kennedy's 2549 at 21.16. Shackleton's best performance was 9-30 and Kennedy's was 9-33 and, for Hampshire, Derek took 5 wickets in an innings on 190 occasions and his predecessor achieved this 205 times.

Neither player was treated generously by the England selectors - Kennedy was picked just five times and Shackleton seven.

There is little point in trying to ascertain who, of the two, was the 'best' bowler. There can only be a few people alive today who saw Kennedy in his prime and it would be almost impossible to come to a reasoned decision. Many of Derek's colleagues, without hesitation, would choose him as first choice bowler if selecting a best ever Hampshire X1. There is a theory, and quite a legitimate one, that the game became far more professional after the second world war and that the standard of the game in this country in the 1950s was better than it had ever been. There were, of course, many outstanding players between the wars, indeed some of the greatest the game has seen - such as Hobbs, Sutcliffe, Hammond, Mead, Woolley, Tate,

Larwood, Verity and Freeman amongst others and Compton and Hutton started their careers in the 1930s. However, against this there were a large number of players who were not first class material in the cricketing sense particularly many amateurs who, because of their financial means could pick and choose games when they really weren't worth a place on merit. This began to die out after the war and, by the 1950s , those amateurs who remained were players of some considerable stature - May, Cowdrey, Sheppard, Dexter and Bailey were unquestionably test quality.

How do you, sensibly, go about selecting a best ever side from a history of 100 years ? It would be good fun and interesting and it would broach a lot of argument but it would be inconclusive. In Hampshire's case and with specific reference to the opening bowling attack there would be little argument up to the end of the 1950s. John Arlott wrote in 1957 :

> "When, one day on the Elysian Fields, a Hampshire
> eleven picked from all time goes into the field
> Derek Shackleton and Alec Kennedy, by
> inalienable right, will open its bowling"

Since then, though, Hampshire have been lucky enough to have benefited from two of the greatest West Indian test bowlers - Andy Roberts and Malcolm Marshall - and two other English born pacemen, Butch White and Bob Cottam, all of whom could have a valid claim made for inclusion. All sorts of bowling combinations could be permutated but for sheer unbroken consistency over such a long period, and with the weight of the number of wickets taken, Shackleton and Kennedy must be automatic choices. Probably one of them would have to be first change as most of the 'selectors' would almost certainly, and quite rightly, pick Marshall to open.

Before the start of the 1956 season Neville Rogers announced his retirement for business reasons. In 1955 he had, unselfishly, moved down the order to allow Roy Marshall to open with Gray and, whilst it wasn't one of his best seasons, he still produced several important innings especially against Essex and Kent when his batting was the prime reason for these two victories.

Rogers scored over 15,000 runs for Hampshire, a figure which would have been substantially higher if the war had not halted his career before it had even started. An average of 32 does not do him full justice. It must always be borne in mind the huge responsibility he carried because, if he failed, so invariably did Hampshire. He frequently 'carried his bat' and was, without doubt, one of the very finest batsmen never to have represented his country. Certainly less talented have done so. If he had been batting in the 1980s and 1990s on covered, flat wickets his career average would have been appreciably higher.

Rogers had skippered the Hampshire Seconds in 1948 in the match against Wiltshire when Derek bowled seamers for the first time for Hampshire and immediately knew that he was, perhaps, going to be something special. "Right from the start he was so accurate, it was uncanny. If he had been asked to bowl in the dark he would have pitched it on a length".

Fortunately, Rogers still keeps close ties with the county, his love for the game undiminished, and to listen to him and to his great pal, Leo Harrison, is a true joy. Raconteurs par excellence, their double act, as Ingleby-Mackenzie says, is something akin to Morecambe and Wise.

Rogers and Harrison, like so many others, agree that it was Derek's equable and unflappable temperament that helped make him such a fine bowler. Everything about him was neat, tidy, economical and thrifty allied to an immaculate appearance. He was a very smart man in the way he dressed and groomed himself. He would never look untidy either on the cricket field or when in 'civvies'. Harrison, mischievously, tried to rattle Derek when they travelled by train. Pretending to be asleep he would casually stretch his feet across the compartment in an effort to scuff Derek's very shiny shoes and "he used to get a bit upset about that!"

Harrison kept wicket to Shackleton more than any other keeper and, after the early years, would normally stand up to the stumps which Derek preferred. This would deter the batsman from taking a guard outside the crease and restrict the footwork ; by now almost everyone was playing him off the front foot. Also there was the chance of a stumping and Derek had ten dismissals in this fashion between 1953 and 1955. Harrison did stand back if, on a particular day, the away swinger was more prevalent. Just one of so many, Harrison has never seen a more accurate and economic bowler. He was "someone who didn't like giving anything away" adding impishly "least of all his cigarettes !" " But he was, and is, a very likeable man".

In 1956 Derek was quickly into his usual rhythm with two impressive performances at Lord's before Hampshire's championship season got under way on May 12th.

He had been chosen to represent the MCC in a fixture against the county champions, Surrey. Match figures of 6-96 off 50 overs helped MCC to victory and, at Lord's again, in the following match, but now playing for Hampshire against the MCC, he took another 5 wickets. Eleven wickets in two matches at Headquarters again proved he could dismiss quality batsmen on good wickets. By now no proof was necessary - he would continually, and always, trouble the very best batsmen.

The wickets he took in these opening matches included those of Micky Stewart, Bernard Constable, Peter May, Jack Robertson, Tom Graveney and Arthur Milton. In addition, just as a reminder that he could still bat a bit, he scored a fine 64 in the MCC second innings mainly with powerful drives off the front foot. Bear in mind a Surrey attack of Bedser, Loader, Laker and Lock.

Hampshire started the season in the same vein as they had finished the previous one. Three wins and three draws (two of which were definitely in their favour) was the ideal start and, with the confidence of a successful season behind them, there was a genuine belief that they could break the Surrey stranglehold on the championship. One of these draws was against Worcestershire in Hampshire's first fixture on the Isle of Wight since before the war. This game produced a moment so out of character for Derek that all his colleagues playing that day remember the incident clearly.

Hampshire, batting first, declared at 370 for seven after an outstanding attacking century by Ingleby-Mackenzie who, later, made several good scores at Cowes. The balmy relaxing Isle of Wight air obviously suited him as did the conviviality of the Royal Yacht Club ! Worcestershire, in reply, could only manage 196 and were asked to follow on.

The 'incident' involved Laddie Outschoorn, the Worcestershire opening batsman. Outschoorn was one of the first Ceylonese players to succeed in English cricket after coming to this country after the war for rehabilitation after suffering severely at the hands of the Japanese. A stylish batsman, but one who could be very dogged in a crisis, he produced a stubborn innings of 154 not out to deny Hampshire victory. Technically, he was 'dismissed' in a somewhat unusual manner, especially bearing in mind the nature of the man responsible.

Worcestershire had lost two early second innings wickets including that of Kenyon, who was to Worcestershire what Rogers had been to Hampshire. There was no hope of a Worcestershire win and Outschoorn dug in scoring the majority of his runs either attacking Heath and Marshall or by continually nudging Shackleton through the slips or down to long leg. The Hampshire seamer would concede only 58 runs from 39 overs on a very warm day but he just could not shift Outschoorn. The frustration finally got to him and, when bowling to Martin Horton, he noticed Outschoorn backing up and well out of his crease. Without any warning he whipped off the bails in his delivery stride and appealed for a run out which the umpire was obliged to uphold. Desmond Eagar had not immediately noticed this from his short leg position and wondered why Outschoorn was walking back to the pavilion. "What's going on, Shack ?" "I've run him out" was the reply. "Then you can jolly well call him back, we don't play cricket like that in Hampshire". Outschoorn returned to the crease and a somewhat sheepish Shackleton continued bowling.

This story may seem, forty years on, just a little trivial but is worth relating as it was so out of character and stories against Derek Shackleton are virtually non existent.

Over a twenty year career there appears to have been only one other occasion when he showed a little annoyance.

Bryan Timms, Hampshire's keeper in the 1960s remembers a match against Leicestershire in 1963. Shack, over the years, had experienced a few duels with Maurice Hallam, their opening batsman. During this game Derek heard that he had been selected for England again, for the fourth test against the West Indies. For some reason he got cross with Hallam and, after dismissing him in the second innings, caught by Horton at short leg, he 'ushered' him to the pavilion. Not in an aggressive manner but a gentle 'on your way' gesture. Whether or not the confirmation of his test place had any bearing on his action is unclear but would be difficult to believe as he was one of the least big headed players imaginable but perhaps he was on a high with the adrenaline flowing.

Derek was never overtly aggressive. Competitive, yes - he had given and would continue to give everything for his adoptive county but always within strict codes. He knew that it was his quite extraordinary equable temperament which helped make him such a fine bowler. These two instances of emotion would not necessarily be important to mention but for the mere fact they are the only examples of their kind.

Whilst Surrey were undoubtedly the strongest county side during the 1950s Hampshire had defeated them at the end of 1955 and did so again at Portsmouth the following June. Admittedly in 1956 Surrey were without May, Laker and Lock who were on test duty but the two spinners were hardly missed with Bedser and Loader bowling unchanged in Hampshire's second innings which totalled only 71. However, May's absence was probably crucial with Hampshire winning by just 28 runs.

Hampshire were then comprehensively beaten by Glamorgan being dismissed twice for less than 100 - their third two figure total in a row, but returned to form again by beating Middlesex at Lord's.

How times had changed for the Metropolitan county since their glories of 1947. There has always been an impression that 1947 was a year of totally unbroken sunshine and runs being scored off every ball. Neither, of course, was true. Middlesex were exceptional but matches between less talented counties did not produce such fast scoring run feasts and, indeed looking at Middlesex themselves, two of their bowlers that year conceded only two runs per over.

In 1956 Middlesex, including Robertson and Edrich but not Compton, were skittled out for 59 in a fraction under 50 overs. The Lord's wicket was grassy, but not unplayable, and the Middlesex batsmen seemed to freeze. In contrast Marshall scored a superb 112 ; his 16 fours comprised mainly drives, pulls and magnificent hooks. Derek dismissed his old adversary Robertson in both innings and, like he did with Kenyon, began to get the upperhand of someone who previously had given him so many problems.

A breakdown of Robertson's performances against a Shackleton led Hampshire attack is as interesting and illuminating as that about Kenyon.

	Inn	NO	Runs	Hst	Ave	100s	Dismissed by Shackleton
1948-53	16	-	879	141	54.93	3	4
1954-58	18	-	315	71	17.50	-	9

These figures are not, of course, conclusive evidence that Shackleton was completely responsible for the change in Robertson's fortunes against Hampshire. It would be detrimental to the other bowlers to suggest this but, in the latter period, he dismissed him 50% of the time whereas in the first period it was only 25% and then generally only after Robertson had scored heavily. This change in fortune is very similar to that experienced by Kenyon.

Robertson and Kenyon were two examples of very fine batsmen who were unlucky that they did not represent their country on more occasions

Cowdrey and Graveney, however, did play for England regularly and their records against Derek make interesting reading but in a different way. They were both genuine test class, a niche slightly higher than Robertson and Kenyon. In contrast, their form against Hampshire improved as the years progressed, in Cowdrey's case quite dramatically. Perhaps they had that extra bit of class necessary to successfully combat him.

Cowdrey, like Graveney, had difficulties in his early days with both Shackleton and Cannings. Modestly he says :

> "Derek was a great bowler, impossible to master
> from my point of view. I found it difficult
> to pick the outswinger from the inswinger.
> There was also a very slight, subtle change

of pace which was very difficult to spot"

On his first encounter with the Hampshire duo in 1951, at the age of 18, his confidence was damaged so much he asked to be stood down from the Kent side. His scores were 0 and 4, Shackleton dismissing him in the first innings and Cannings in the second. Sensibly his skipper insisted that he persevered and this helped him to restore his confidence. Derek considers Cowdrey and May to be the classiest English batsmen he ever encountered. "They simply had so much class, so much time to play their shots".

Cowdrey's and Graveney's performances against Hampshire can be split into two very distinct periods.

Cowdrey

	Inn	NO	Runs	Hst	Ave	100s	Dismissed by Shackleton
1951-58	23	1	654	90	29.72	-	5
1959-68	30	3	1497	156	55.44	6	7

Graveney

	Inn	NO	Runs	Hst	Ave	100s	Dismissed by Shackleton
1949-60	33	1	728	71	22.75	-	8
1962-67	12	1	424	106	38.54	2	5

The split in the figures for Graveney coincides with his move from Gloucestershire to Worcestershire.

Again these statistics do not necessarily prove a lot and Derek continued to take their wickets quite regularly but, in both instances Cowdrey, especially, and Graveney were scoring more heavily in the second halves of their careers.

Peter May did not play so many times against Hampshire but produced innings of the very highest quality and all the Hampshire bowlers of that period confirmed him to be the one truly great English batsman to have emerged since the war. Derek did get him out on a few occasions especially with, he remembers, an unplayable delivery two years later, but generally he scored heavily and, in county championship matches against Hampshire, he averaged over 59. Even Derek was occasionally nonplussed and when Butch White turned to him for advice and solace after being on driven for three successive fours he replied : "Just bowl straight, Sunshine, there's nowt else".

Hampshire's 1956 season, like the weather, was more changeable than the previous year with a real mix of wins, draws and defeats. Shackleton, though, continued to have a relentless stream of victims. Bowling standards, undoubtedly helped by uncovered wickets, were then as high as they had ever been and scoring rates were beginning to plummet. It would soon afflict the England side. In December 1958 on the third day of the first test against Australia just 122 runs were scored to equal the previous, dubious record only for this new 'achievement' to be broken the following day with 106. E.W. Swanton, reporting in the 'Daily Telegraph' wrote : "Sterile cricket, not worth winning. Cricket like this poses the question 'How long will people watch ?'" And this about an England side that included May, Cowdrey and Graveney !

With the dual problems of uncovered wickets and high bowling standards the average county batsman was not prepared to take risks against opening bowlers of the calibre of Shackleton, Cannings, Gladwin, Jackson, Trueman, Statham, Bedser, Loader and many more. No batsman that year had an average of 50 or above but thirty bowlers averaged less than 20. How, in the 90s, the balance has shifted.

Hampshire fell from third to sixth but were reasonably pleased. Only twice before, in 1914 and 1955, had they finished higher. Shack's best performances that year were 7-62, 7-48 and 7-38 against Surrey, Sussex and Warwickshire respectively, all on away grounds. However, in the penultimate match of the season, he produced another remarkable performance against Somerset, this time at Bournemouth.

The West Country side who had been so humiliated at Weston-Super-Mare the year before were bowled out for 37 equalling their debacle of 1955, although this time lasting 36.4 overs, 14 more than before. A run rate of 1 per over - Middlesex, at Lord's, earlier in the season, just managed to beat this with 1.2 runs an over. This time Derek took 5-5 in 15.4 overs and Sainsbury 5-15.

In the four matches against Somerset in 1955 and 1956 his astonishing figures were as follows :

Overs	Maidens	Runs	Wickets	Average
149	63	206	36	5.72

Somerset, by now, would have liked to have seen the back of him but, a year later, he took another 14 wickets !

As a final anecdote to the game at Bournemouth Malcolm Heath, who was frequently twelfth man that year, remembers the Somerset

number X1 coming to the wicket and receiving an almost unheard of half volley from Shackleton. Ken Biddulph, a true tail-ender with no batting pretensions whatsoever, and who ended the season with an average of 2.72, actually hit it back quite powerfully only to see the ball inadvertently trapped by the bowler's boot. Harrison, behind the stumps, remarked casually to the disappointed batsman "that's the only half volley he's bowled all season" (it was now the end of August). Biddulph felt very aggrieved !

Mention should be made of the Australian tour not because Shackleton had any participation in the test series but, quite the contrary. He had very little chance of selection that year. The strength of the English attack had reached its zenith and he was realistic enough to appreciate that, with Trueman, Statham, Tyson, Bailey, Laker and Lock at their peaks, his own abilities and proven experience would not be sufficient to force his way into the test side. In any event, that summer, the wickets were tailor made for the spin of Laker and Lock.

It seemed in 1955 that, with the advances being made by Hampshire's younger players, the heavy work load being borne by Shackleton and Cannings would reduce. In fact Derek bowled just as many (uncomplaining) overs in 1956 and, in 1957, the gap between himself and the other bowlers simply widened. Hampshire were very reliant on their senior bowler and, in the batting, on Marshall, Gray and Horton. As 'Wisden' pointed out :

> "If evidence were needed of the side's
> dependence on certain individuals none better
> could be given than the remarkable record
> of Shackleton. Far from having his style of
> in-swing attack cramped by the restriction
> placed on leg-side fieldsmen he bowled more
> overs than anyone in the Championship"

'Wisden' was referring to the 1957 season. The statement is not quite correct as two leg break bowlers, Eric Hollies and Bruce Dooland, slightly exceeded his output but Derek certainly bowled more overs than any other seamer.

The leg side restriction referred to a change in the law whereby 'not more than two may be behind the popping crease at the instant of the bowler's delivery'. With his out swinger now a potent weapon Shackleton did not worry unduly about this change.

The 1957 season started with a defeat by Essex, a draw with Northamptonshire and wins over Leicestershire and Middlesex. Against Leicestershire Hampshire led by only 28 on first innings but

Shackleton produced one of his deadly spells in the second innings taking 7-20 in 30 overs, 19 of which were maidens.

In the next game at Portsmouth against Middlesex he had match figures of 11-72 on a difficult, but not vicious, wicket. Marshall and Horton batted well for the home side and Compton and Edrich with half centuries, and Robertson with 49, partially revived memories of days past. Even for batsmen of their ability they had to fight hard for these runs with Derek conceding only 41 runs in 32 overs in the second innings .

He had taken 31 wickets in his first four matches and there would be little change to this ratio throughout the remainder of the season. Whilst he would continue in his own unerring way the side itself was inconsistent and victories few and far between.

With Shackleton's performances it would be so easy to get carried away with a mass of statistics in which case almost every game would have something of interest. It was another 'typical' season for him (was any season 'untypical' ?) but three games are worth mentioning.

Hampshire's third win of the summer was against Somerset at Bath. Compared with the devastation of the two previous years Derek had a modest first innings return of 6-42 and just two wickets in the second ! The game was a triumph for Malcolm Heath who grasped the opportunity offered by Cannings' injury with match figures of 11-106. There was a curious incident in this game. Following a run out, Horton returned to the pavilion but, after the umpires had discussed matters, it was decided that Gray should have been the batsman given out. Horton returned to the crease only to be run out 'again', and conclusively, shortly afterwards.

Whilst Hampshire had beaten Surrey in 1955 and 1956 they felt the full might of the eventual champions (yet again) in 1957 with two defeats by an innings. Vic Cannings believes that the Surrey batting performance at Portsmouth in the second of the two games was the only occasion when both he and Derek were totally dominated. It was certainly rare but Cannings obviously forgot some distinctly unflattering figures they each had in a match against Worcestershire in 1950. But it was certainly unusual. There were times when one or the other may have bowled a lot of overs without taking wickets but very rarely together and rarely expensively. The Surrey batsmen, that day, treated the large crowd to a superb display of batsmanship with Peter May quite outstanding. He scored an immaculate 97 in just over two hours against an attack containing two of the meanest bowlers around and on a wicket which usually gave them assistance. Their highly uncharacteristic figures were :

	Overs	Maidens	Runs	Wickets
Shackleton	30	4	97	0
Cannings	20	1	77	0

Peter Sainsbury was another player who remembers May's innings and has no hesitation in naming him the most difficult batsman he bowled to. "Although he didn't appear to be scoring quickly you found he had reached 50 in very little time".

Hampshire had been outplayed in spite of two superb innings by Roy Marshall. He scored 56 out of 120 in the first innings and a brilliant 111 in under two hours in the second. This against an attack of Bedser, Loader, Laker and Lock. Over the years he developed a great liking for the Surrey bowling and became particularly severe on Lock. A top quality bowling attack was the sort of challenge he relished.

The West Indian tourists were, frankly, annihilated by England although this did not seem likely at the end of the first day of the first test. England were bowled out for 186 with Ramadhin weaving his magic again in taking 7-49 in 31 overs. However, once May (285 not out) and Cowdrey (154) mastered him in the second innings the series went dramatically England's way. Ramadhin took only seven further wickets and they were to cost him 498 runs. With Ramadhin and Valentine reduced to impotency and Worrell, Weekes and Walcott past their best there has never been a more one sided series between the two countries when the results have been in England's favour.

Unfortunately, rain called a halt to Hampshire's match with the tourists but not before Shackleton had a second innings return of 7-103. Ten wickets in all, nine of which required no help from the fielders. Heath recalls one of the umpires said that one delivery was "dead unfair, it was so unplayable". In this game Derek was once again a victim of a hat-trick, Tom Dewdney claiming Derek as the first of his three scalps.

Hampshire fell to thirteenth in the championship and another era came to an end with the retirement of Desmond Eagar both as player and skipper. He had given so much for the benefit of Hampshire cricket but, fortunately, he remained as secretary and was, therefore, able to keep a very close involvement with the club. An exciting new chapter was to begin with the appointment of Colin Ingleby-Mackenzie as captain.

Just One of 2857 !

Chapter Nine

A Lesson for Malcolm

The year began sadly for Hampshire with the news that Philip Mead, their greatest batsman, had died on 26th March but, thereafter, 1958 was one of the happiest in the county's history and which ended with their highest ever position to date - second . The only disappointment came in mid August when, after leading the championship table, they experienced their worst run of the season enabling Surrey to overhaul them to win their seventh consecutive championship.

Great credit must be given to Colin Ingleby-Mackenzie, their new young captain, who was only 24 when the season started. The plan to make him skipper was the idea of Harry Altham, the Club President at the time, and Desmond Eagar. What an inspired choice it would turn out to be. He had a totally different approach to that of his predecessor but his cavalier attitude should not deflect from his keenness for Hampshire to succeed. If there was the slimmest chance of a victory then it had to be grasped even though, on frequent occasions, there could be a real danger of defeat. If Hampshire had had a more orthodox captain during the Ingleby-Mackenzie period there may have been fewer defeats but there would definitely have been far fewer victories. More importantly the public's imagination would not have been captured as it was in 1958 and, even more so, in 1961.

It is also to his credit that Ingleby-Mackenzie was, immediately, able to get the players to respond to his somewhat unorthodox style. Here was an Old Etonian, still at a relatively tender age captaining a team of professionals many of whom had been playing for the county for at least ten years. But it worked. When Derek was asked how he got on with his new skipper he replied "I would have bowled to the end of the Earth for him". And he frequently did. It is difficult to believe that Ingleby-Mackenzie would have had the same positive responses if, say, he had been asked to captain the Yorkshire team at the time.

Hampshire were already a happy unit of good professionals but the new captain gave them an important added dimension.

Hampshire's first three matches were on the 'Northern tour' and they met with no success whatsoever. Both Ingleby-Mackenzie and Shackleton had cause to remember the first match against Yorkshire at Bradford. No play was possible on the first two days - it was to be another wretched summer - and the game became, effectively, a one day affair with the side leading on first innings taking eight points.

Hampshire won the toss which was rare that season. They, occasionally, had certain luck with the weather but lost the toss in twenty two of their twenty eight championship matches. Ingleby-Mackenzie decided to bat first, which he soon realised was a mistake, and then declared leaving Yorkshire to score 106 in fifty five minutes. This they achieved with comparative ease mainly because Trueman, promoted in the order to number four, scored 58 not out in under half an hour. He belligerently hit 3 sixes and 6 fours mainly off a bemused Shackleton who was simply not used to this treatment. It was not the first, nor the last, time that Trueman attacked the Hampshire seamer with no little success. He was a better batsman than the usual lower order slogger but was certainly not recognised as a true batsman. Perhaps Derek's immaculate line and length suited Fred's approach - one foot down the wicket and 'bang'. Shack was so used to pitching the ball on exactly the same spot it was not in his general nature to make great changes to combat such an onslaught. All his success had been based on a quite exceptional line and length with movement off the seam and why change this method when someone occasionally tried to hit him out of the attack ? He knew that the batsman would not last too long but the problem with someone like Trueman was that considerable damage could be done in five or six overs. Derek was, though, an intelligent bowler and there would be subtle changes of pace and of length but Trueman was certainly more successful than most in dealing with him.

Although technically the game with Yorkshire was drawn Hampshire were beaten, comprehensively, at Trent Bridge and at Old Trafford. No hint yet of the successes to come.

The first wins came against Worcestershire and Kent at Portsmouth and Southampton. Hampshire had, in fact, been largely outplayed by Kent but magnificent centuries by a very much in form Marshall and by Ingleby-Mackenzie helped pull off an enterprising victory.

For Derek it had been only a moderate start and, after five matches, he had taken just 14 wickets at an average of 31 - uncharacteristic but perhaps not surprising in view of the damp cold start to the season. He, like Denis Compton, thrived with the sun on his back.

Everything went well from the next match at Leicester. He took all six Leicestershire second innings wickets to fall in an honourable draw, with Willie Watson using all his fighting qualities saving his side with 62 not out from a total of 97 for six. Eleven wickets followed at Lord's, although Hampshire lost, and then nine in the return fixture against Leicestershire at Cowes.

He haunted Somerset yet again with second innings figures of 5-17 off 26 overs. He had a lean return of just one wicket from the second of back to back matches against Somerset, a game Hampshire were desperately unlucky not to win, so outplayed were the West Country side. Fine batting by Marshall, Gray, Horton and Ingleby-Mackenzie, who scored the fastest century of the season in 61 minutes, put Hampshire in complete control but a determined rearguard action by Somerset against superb spin bowling by Burden resulted in a draw.

Derek then took 13 wickets in a victory over Gloucestershire at Bristol to be followed by a remarkable performance against Glamorgan at Neath, remembered in particular by Leo Harrison and Jimmy Gray.

The first day's play had been lost due to rain and, on a drying wicket, Shackleton and Heath, bowling unchanged, were virtually unplayable. The Welsh side were all out for 72 with Allan Watkins scoring 42. No one else reached double figures. Gray considers Shackleton's performance as quite extraordinary.

Neath is a small ground and the wicket was flat although a little grassy. It was also wet on top and Shackleton ruthlessly exploited this as probably only he could have done. After the first over there was no other mark on the ball apart from on the seam itself. Harrison had seen this before but not only was the 'round' of the ball unmarked the only evidence of a ball pitching on the wicket was a very small patch of just a few inches circumference where every delivery had pitched. Gray recalls that:

"At the end of the innings the team studied the pitch and noted with some astonishment and awe that there was one very small area with no mark outside it. This was after 25 overs - 150 deliveries".

"We were worried, though, that Glamorgan's Don Shepherd might use this to his advantage but, for him, it was too short. He went on the other end to make his own mark"

After Hampshire had declared on 120 for six - wisely as the weather would deteriorate again - Glamorgan were routed in their second innings for 46. Shack came on at the same end and, with the wicket now much drier, destroyed the Glamorgan batsmen. Hitting the same spot with the seam batting became a nightmare. This destruction was quite ruthlessly thought out and executed and no other bowler could have done this in such a spectacular way. He and Heath once again bowled throughout, apart from one over of spin by Burden. This odd over would not have been to allow the two seamers to change ends - it would have been impossible to prise Shackleton away from his end and from the patch he had so carefully nurtured. He had match figures of 9-46 from 47 overs but Heath's performance must not be overlooked. Whilst not hitting the seam quite so relentlessly he had also bowled extremely well and the Glamorgan batsmen found the bounce generated from his height disconcerting to say the least.

Derek had received some help from the natural elements. There was another time when he allegedly had some 'artificial' assistance. During a Hampshire match at Bournemouth the players were enjoying some considerable hospitality after the end of a day's play in one of the many marquees. Unfortunately the only toilets were situated in the pavilion at the opposite end of the ground and some of the players found the journey far too long. 'Relief' took place on the wicket, indeed on a spot which Derek, with his usual great accuracy , again ruthlessly exploited. He was not one of the culprits but those apparently involved remain mysteriously nameless!

After the win at Neath Hampshire had moved to the top of the championship table and, apart from a very brief period, remained there until August 22nd.

They had the better of a draw against a full strength Surrey at Guildford. Shackleton was, by now, rampant taking wickets galore and his only 'failure' during the remainder of the season was at Bournemouth in late August when he took only one Yorkshire wicket. At Guildford he took 7-34 in 25.4 overs and, among his victims, were Stewart, Constable, May and Barrington. Ingleby-Mackenzie described the ball which bowled May as one of the finest he had ever seen. It swung into him, pitched on the seam on a perfect length and nipped away to take off stump. May was probably the finest batsman in the world at the time and, in a thoroughly depressing season for batsmen, he was the only one to average over 50 - and at 63.74 by some distance. Only three others averaged in excess of 40 and, in contrast, forty three bowlers had averages below 20. The balance had shifted still further.

Hampshire were on a roll, in the middle of a sequence of fifteen matches of which nine were won and six drawn.

It is important to mention the significant part played by Malcolm Heath who was enjoying his best season and, with the declining effectiveness of Cannings, providing Shackleton with very valuable help. Everything came right for him that year. He was an automatic selection which greatly helped his confidence; his run up and action, after hours of coaching by 'dear old Arthur (Holt)', were in harmony and he was making full use of his considerable height which made him an uncomfortable proposition on an awkward wicket.

Heath achieved his finest analysis that year in the match against Sussex at Portsmouth in July. It was another game which Hampshire won inside two days. Much was made of Hampshire's good fortune with the weather in 1958 but, more relevantly, they had the capabilities of achieving a positive result within two days to beat the weather. Marshall and Ingleby-Mackenzie could be devastating when quick runs were needed and Shackleton and Heath were frequently capable of destroying any side. In addition, Ingleby-Mackenzie would constantly consider declarations to try and beat any inclement conditions.

Against Sussex Shackleton and Heath shared the honours in the first innings but, in the second, Heath took 8-43 and his eighth wicket was that of Robin Marlar who was caught by Derek at mid-on. He threw the ball in the air with genuine boyish enthusiasm so delighted was he for Heath's success. The meanness of his bowling did not extend to his general attitude.

Because of his quiet nature Derek did not proffer advice readily but would always be willing to help if approached. It was, therefore, unexpected when, one day, he pulled the young Heath aside in the nets. "I'm going to show you something". He then proceeded to run up to bowl and knocked down the off stump. The next ball he took out the middle stump and with the third delivery knocked over the leg. "I've seen everything now, Shack" remarked an astonished Heath. "No you haven't" was the reply. The stumps were put back up and he simply did the feat in reverse. Leg, then middle, then off. This made quite an impression on Heath and he believes that, whilst some bowlers might do this occasionally, in Shack's case it was quite spontaneous and probably could have been done at will.

Heath remembers, very early in his career, sharing the new ball with his senior partner. At the end of the second over, and Heath's first, Derek came up to him and said : "Hey, son, what the bloody hell have you been doing with this then ?" noticing marks all over the ball. "Polish it up". Heath soon learned not to give the ball back to him unless it was well polished. Shackleton and Cannings had always kept the ball in pristine condition.

After ten years with Hampshire Derek was awarded a well deserved benefit and he chose the fixture against, what he thought at the time was his home county, Lancashire. When, later, he found out he was a Yorkshireman his second benefit in 1967 was taken in the match against them. Obviously he was hoping for a good financial return. The opposition were attractive, Hampshire were leading the championship table and there would be a good influx of visitors to Bournemouth at that time of the year.

Derek was not, and would never be, a wealthy man by any stretch of the imagination. He had come from a humble background where money was scarce and was hard earned. This made him a very cautious spender and, although his income wasn't large, getting into debt would have been abhorrent to him. There was a real justification and logic that he would always be careful in financial matters. Basically his income was derived from his wages with Hampshire plus win bonuses and from any representative honours which were, by now largely non-existent. He received a small income from winter employment with, first, Price's bakery in Eastleigh and then a short spell with Dimplex in Southampton before, later, he would take over the running of the indoor school at the County Ground. There were no cricketers' pensions schemes at the time and, for most players, a good benefit match was crucial. However, in those days, benefits were not so well organised as they are today and agents and sponsors were unheard of and few cricketers and footballers had cars. Alan Rayment remembers the astonishment on the faces of the large crowd queueing for the match against the Australians in 1953. Rayment arrived at the ground on a bicycle to play against some of the finest cricketers in the world and even this he says with some chagrin "wasn't sponsored!" In 1946 Denis Compton, who was one of the two or three most famous players was only earning £300 a year plus a match fee of £8. For a test appearance he received £36. Even allowing for the vastly different value of money now these were not substantial sums bearing in mind the stature of the player. He would receive far more remuneration from the Brylcreem advertisement and, later, writing for the Sunday Express.

From Derek's point of view there were good, and distinctly frustrating, aspects of his benefit match.

Hampshire won, which consolidated their position at the head of the table and, although he only took 5 wickets in all (mere mortals would have been perfectly happy with this), they were all crucial ones. Wharton and Pullar in the first innings and Barber, Marner and Washbrook in the second. He also took his 100th wicket of the season.

He was disappointed, though, that the match was completed within two days thus reducing the collection monies. Also, the collection did not go too well on the second day and Ingleby-Mackenzie, with his passion for the horses, suggested to Derek that he placed the lot on a horse. Risking money like this was certainly not in his nature - he would have had an in-built and natural warning system - and he promptly declined. The horse romped home at odds of 100-8 and would have netted over £1,000. Shack was, in Ingleby-Mackenzie's words, "dismayed and furious". He still flinches slightly when he is reminded !

Derek received about £5,000 from this benefit, a reasonably tidy sum in those days and would enable Kathy and him to purchase their first house. They had been living in an old property in Lodge Road just off the Avenue in Southampton and had not been particularly happy there and the timing of the benefit monies could not have been more opportune. They would live in Water Lane in Totton, a few miles to the west of Southampton and, in this relatively small town, Kathy would run a lingerie and childrens' clothes shop. They paid £2,325 for the house but Kathy remembers there was a last minute panic as they found they were £25 short.

At the same time Derek purchased his first car although he had not yet passed his driving test. He has never really enjoyed driving partly because of his eye problem. He took his test three or four times before passing and someone mentioned to him that if the examiner realised he was a famous cricketer he might receive preferential treatment. So, on one of his tests, he loaded his cricket gear on the back seat in the hope this would be noticed and he also had to hope that the examiner was a cricket lover. It was all to no avail, Derek failed !

Hampshire followed up the Lancashire victory with an innings win over Nottinghamshire. Although the seamers played their usual part, centuries by Marshall and Gray dominated the match. Gray also took 4-90 in Nottinghamshire's second innings. Kent were then beaten by four wickets at Canterbury with Derek taking 7-71 in the Kent first innings but, after this, things started to go horribly wrong.

There was to be only one further victory during the final eight matches and the championship was retained by Surrey. Many reasons have been put forward for their demise but, realistically, the main cause was the loss of form of most of the batsmen during the run in and it was too much for the bowlers to retrieve. For Marshall, Gray and Horton, the pillars of the Hampshire batting, it was a nightmare period and, during the eight matches, their combined average was only just over 16.

There was an extraordinary match in mid August against Derbyshire at Burton-On-Trent which was completed in little over a day. Play was limited to twenty minutes on the first day before rain intervened with the Derbyshire score standing at 8 for one. The next day 39 wickets fell on a drying pitch. Shackleton and Heath bowled unchanged throughout the entire game, only the second time this had occurred since 1935. Derek was involved the other time - with Cannings in 1952. At Neath earlier in the season only one solitary over by Burden put stop to another unchanged Shackleton/Heath partnership.

When Derbyshire were all out for 74 before lunch on the second day Hampshire were quite happy little realising what was to follow. They, in turn, were dismissed for 23 in 16 hostile overs from Jackson and Rhodes with Barnard and Horton top scoring with 5 apiece! It was the lowest total in England since 1939 but they are now spared this ignominy following Surrey's 14 against Essex in 1983, and that on a covered wicket.

Derbyshire, batting for a second time, had reached 40 for four when their skipper Donald Carr joined Derek Morgan and a partnership began to develop. During one over from Shackleton, Morgan received two or three deliveries which came through reasonably comfortably. He called to Carr "Skip, I think it's eased up now". The next ball hit him straight between the eyes ! However, he and Carr bravely put together 54. Hampshire were set a target of 159 and they never had the confidence that they would achieve an unlikely victory. The last wicket fell at 55 with Barnard again top scorer with 16.

Derek had just bowled and bowled all season and his stamina was now legendary. Ingleby-Mackenzie, like his predecessor, would throw him the ball and could forget one end. Later, on a private tour to the West Indies, which Ingleby-Mackenzie skippered, he gave the ball to Alan Moss, the Middlesex fast bowler, on a very hot day. After a long spell of bowling, Moss, feeling he was being forgotten, shouted to his captain "Hey, Colin, my name's not Derek Shackleton, you know !"

Many players had their own theories about Derek's fitness but basically he was a totally uncomplicated man in all aspects of his life and this simplicity had a bearing on his avoidance of injuries. He remained a slim man throughout his playing career, the only noticeable difference in his appearance being the greying of his always neat hair. Unfortunately, he did not benefit financially from TruGel as Compton did from Brylcreem ! He had a constant weight of about eleven stone and basically he kept fit simply by bowling. He did very little pre-season training and was, frankly, casual with net practice. He was also extremely light on his feet and, as Neville Rogers observed, "he didn't leave any foot marks....as though he had bowled in slippers". There was, therefore, no great strain on his back, legs or feet and his beautiful high action ensured he did not develop shoulder or upper arm muscular problems. Whilst he was a sound fielder with a safe pair of hands he would not have considered diving full length on the boundary to convert a certain four into a three . That would have meant risk of injury and neither he, nor the county, would have welcomed him being out of action for any length of time.

In over twenty years with Hampshire Derek missed only thirteen matches through injury, an absence rate of one game every one and a half seasons - years when there were a minimum of twenty eight championship matches and sometimes as many as thirty two . Test calls and other representative matches accounted for a further thirteen , but he was an almost ever present for two decades. Only Mead, Kennedy and Sainsbury, the latter two only marginally, exceeded Derek's record of 583 matches for the county. Once he established himself from the third game of 1949 he was an automatic choice and injuries seldom came into the reckoning.

Alan Rayment, whose last season this was, has a theory that there were less muscular problems in that era because children had more opportunities of developing their muscles at a young age. With less danger from traffic they played a lot of street cricket and football and would have walked to and from school, sometimes for several miles. Social, as well as traffic problems, and a considerable change of leisure habits and interests have meant a slower build up of muscle strength. A theory, perhaps, but a very plausible one.

Derek may have been quite exceptional in keeping clear of injuries but the great fast bowlers of that period, those who put far more effort and exertion into their action, rarely suffered injuries. Trueman, Statham, Lindwall, Miller, Hall and Griffith were very fit men.

An example of Derek's serene temperament was remembered by Malcolm Heath. Most players have a look at the wicket before the start of play and, when the Hampshire team arrived at a particular ground, Rayment, having seen what looked to be a 'green top', rushed back to the pavilion and, seeing Derek in the corner of the dressing room quietly enjoying a cigarette, said "Shack, have you seen the wicket ?" "No, it's still twenty two yards isn't it ?" Whatever the state of the pitch it would have been unlikely to have affected the way he bowled. On another occasion at Lord's he declined a similar offer to look at the wicket by saying "It's too far to walk".

There was one match, though, when the wicket was not the regulatory twenty two yards and which Derek spotted almost immediately after starting to bowl. After delivering two or three half volleys he asked the umpires to measure the wicket. It was found to be only twenty one yards and the game had to restart a little later. He could not believe he would bowl three half volleys, as he was only allowed one per season ! He instinctively knew that the length of the pitch was the problem. There was to be a very similar occurrence ten years later.

There were other bowlers who would bowl automatically 'on the right spot'. One such bowler was Cliff Gladwin of Derbyshire and one who Neville Rogers faced many times between 1946 and 1955. Facing him at Derby Rogers could not believe his luck when he received three long hops, all of which were despatched for four . Gladwin said to the umpire: "the pitch is too long". This time it was discovered to be twenty four yards. Gladwin, like Shackleton, just knew he wasn't pitching the ball where he wanted it. In fact he was, it was the length of the wicket which was the problem.

Notwithstanding the disappointing results in August it had been a highly successful season for Hampshire finishing second behind

Surrey. For Shackleton, another best ever year with 165 wickets at an average of 15.44. He had bowled more overs and taken more wickets than ever and at an economy rate of 1.93 runs conceded per over. Equally impressive was a strike rate of a wicket every 48 deliveries. He was achieving a lot of his success with total proof of his accuracy; 111 of his 165 victims were bowled, lbw or caught behind and, once again judging from the scorecards for 1958, most of the remainder were catches by the close fieldsmen.

He was now 34 but only at the half way stage of his cricketing career.

Chapter Ten

Late Afternoon in Portsmouth

After Hampshire had enjoyed such a good season in 1958 the main thought in the minds of their supporters was 'could they go one better in 1959 ?' Two immediate wins served to fuel these ideas but, ultimately, they would finish eighth. Perhaps disappointing but they actually finished only eighteen points behind Gloucestershire in second place. One further win and a draw and Hampshire would have retained second position themselves. Yorkshire won the championship to break the impressive Surrey sequence of seven successive wins.

The summer of 1959 was hot and sunny, a total contrast to the previous year. The summers during the 1950s appeared to be one extreme or another but perhaps memories are now playing tricks some forty years on. There were no doubts about 1959 with the hot weather starting as early as May which isn't always the case in a good summer.

One of Hampshire's recurring problems since the end of the war was the lack of consistency in their middle order batting. Players such as Barnard, Rayment, Flood and Pitman all promised much and, on occasions, contributed many useful and attractive innings, but their form, by and large, was inconsistent. Marshall, Gray and Horton were now, in their contrasting ways, regularly providing the county with a good solid base - August 1958 an unhappy exception - and all three would score over 2,000 runs in 1959.

Rayment had now left to concentrate on many diverse business ventures. To replace him Dennis Baldry, like Rayment ten years beforehand, was signed from Middlesex. He had a dream debut scoring 151 against Glamorgan and, within a month, had scored three centuries and nearly 750 runs in nine matches averaging just under 50. Unfortunately, this glut of runs flattered to deceive and he did not score another century during the remainder of his four year spell with Hampshire. The county still had a problem in that department.

The hard, fast wickets that season demanded accurate seam

bowling and even more onus was placed on Shackleton because Heath's form fell away and Cannings, in his final year, was nowhere near as effective as he had been in the past. However, another bowler would soon make a considerable impact and would become Derek's regular opening partner the following year. David 'Butch' White had made his debut in 1957 and played a handful of games in 1959.

When he started his career Derek's opening partners were either George Heath, Lofty Herman or Vic Ransom. Then came the very productive partnership with Vic Cannings followed, relatively briefly, with Malcolm Heath. Now it seemed someone else was on the horizon. He took it all in his stride and just got on with the job of bowling, accepting the changes at the other end in his usual phlegmatic way.

With the Shack and Vic pairing coming to its end it is appropriate to analyse their special relationship which lasted for nearly ten years.

Hampshire's main strength during that period was the total reliability of the seam attack. Until 1955 the batting had to rely so heavily on Rogers and, after that, it was some years before Marshall, Gray and Horton batted with such consistency together.

It has been argued that Hampshire adopted too negative an approach at the time but Eagar had very little option but to contain the opposition as much as possible in view of the frailty of the batting. He had two of the most accurate bowlers in the country but this does not necessarily mean they were automatically negative. Shackleton's strike rate throughout his career was a wicket every 55 deliveries and, during some seasons, was down to the mid 40s. Batting, generally, had become extremely defensive and, added to this, many counties with less skilful bowlers were adopting a very blatant leg side theory which, undoubtedly, had a direct bearing on the subsequent change in the laws restricting the number of fieldsmen on the leg side.

Nevertheless, batting against Hampshire was never going to be easy due to the accuracy of the bowling and the quality of the close fielders.

The negative attitudes prevalent in English cricket surprised Roy Marshall when he first played for Hampshire. A player with all the strokes in the book it took even him a little while to adjust. In a match against the Army in 1954 Marshall watched, incredulously, as Cannings set his field - a slip, gully and extra cover with six men on the leg side. This for a bowler who was a natural away swinger to the right hander. He bowled outside the line of the leg stump and his 'out' swing would actually take the ball IN to the batsman on his leg stump and scoring became almost impossible.

A similar instance was recalled by Gerry Hill, again from the early 1950s. Cyril Washbrook complained bitterly that Cannings was bowling deliberately at the leg stump with a strong leg side field and scoring had almost come to a halt. Whilst acknowledging this criticism with a certain amount of sympathy Hampshire also had to play to their strengths. Eagar had painstakingly worked to build up the team towards his most successful year in charge - 1955 - and which was beginning to form the basis of the even more rewarding seasons of 1958 and 1961. He had a happy team, the fielding had improved beyond all recognition and, although the batting was not strong, he could rely totally on his seam attack of Shackleton and Cannings. It was all very well having a happy side but to capture the public's imagination, to get them coming through the turnstiles and to increase membership, which was so vital to their finances, they also had to win matches. If this meant a slightly negative approach, so be it.

Cannings, himself, remarked that when he signed for Hampshire he did not expect to be on the winning side too often and he also believes that it was partly due to an inferiority complex that they slipped up so badly in the run in to the climax of the 1958 season, when the championship was snatched away from their grasp.

At that time Hampshire simply could not compete with the strengths of some of the other counties. The all round power of Yorkshire and Surrey, the Middlesex batting and the Lancashire bowling. All these sides could afford to be more positive, they had the necessary fire power. Hampshire had to play to their own strengths.

Leo Harrison, who was in a prime position to evaluate the merits of the two bowlers, holds them both in very high regard. He believes that Cannings never, knowingly, bowled an in swinger but continually used his brain. An intelligent man who could think a batsman out. He and Shackleton certainly took wickets for each other. Very often a batsman, so completely bogged down by one of the two, would take an unnecessary and calamitous risk against the other.

It took batsmen of the highest quality to score reasonably freely off both of them and the best example of this was the entertaining partnership between May and Barrington in 1957, but this was a rare incident. Many eminent test batsmen did not relish facing Shackleton and Cannings. They seemed to accept it if someone like Trueman, Statham, Tyson, Laker and Lock took their wicket but, for a while at first, it appeared an affront to their dignity if a 'somewhat innocuous' medium pacer dismissed them. As time passed, however, they would learn to treat Shackleton and Cannings with the utmost respect.

The famous partnership was nearing its end and Cannings would go forth to the playing fields of Eton. No more the regular, springy if slightly flat footed approach to the stumps of eleven paces by someone who, like his colleague, could surprise batsmen with his pace. A slightly more volatile man than his partner he was never quite his equal as a bowler but, for a few years, there was very little to choose between them as a measure of their value to Hampshire. He also had a good sense of humour and was not averse to the occasional leg-pull. One year he turned this talent on the Sussex players.

Arthur Price was an enthusiastic Hampshire supporter and ran Price's Bakeries, a firm based in Eastleigh and where Derek worked for a while. From time to time when the county embarked on one of their away tours, often for three matches, he would come with the team with his Rolls Royce. It was well known that he was not a good driver and, one season, Cannings was nominated to drive the prestigious vehicle to Eastbourne. On arriving at the ground the Sussex players swarmed round the car with surprised and envious looks and asked him how he came to be driving such a beautiful motor vehicle. It was still relatively rare for a cricketer to be driving any sort of car. However, quick as a flash, Cannings replied that he had had a large win on the pools and one of the many items he had bought was this handsome Rolls Royce. Envy and disbelief were quite evident amongst the players and the word spread through the counties that Cannings had won the pools. It was some time before the truth was known.

With cars being used more and more for travelling Derek, being a naturally cautious and careful individual, liked to choose who he would ride with, there being certain drivers with whom he felt distinctly uncomfortable. One was Arthur Price and there was a sense of great relief when one of the players was asked to drive the Rolls. Derek recalls with some horror a journey to the Midlands in Alan Rayment's Jaguar. A lovely car but, in those days, Rayment drove a "bit hastily" and Derek also discovered, on the journey, that there were four bald tyres. No MOTs then . The Sunday was a free day and Rayment suggested a drive over the moors. Derek quickly declined imagining being stranded miles from anywhere, and indeed one of the tyres got a puncture and the journey back to the hotel was severely delayed. Rayment has since disputed the claim that, in his younger days, he was a dangerous driver. "You should have been with Ingleby if you really wanted excitement!"

Although Derek would later use his own car he frequently allowed some of his colleagues to drive because of his aversion to getting behind the wheel. He was even more careful with his choice of driver!

Cannings was now 39 and, being of heavier build than Derek, probably would not have had his partner's stamina to continue for much longer. He had been coaching in Trinidad during the preceding winter and received two air mail letters in one week, one from Eton and one from Tonbridge. Colin Cowdrey wanted him for his old school but Cannings decided on Eton who were able to pay a bit more. He coached there for twenty five years, retiring in 1984, but then had three seasons with the Threepenny Boys - the first years. During his time at Eton he coached several boys who went on to first class cricket - notably John Barclay and Mark Faber of Sussex and Matthew Fleming of Kent.

Cannings had a fine reputation at Eton and, on one occasion, Neville Rogers asked Colin Ingleby-Mackenzie how Vic was getting on. "How do you mean ?" said Colin. "Coaching". "I don't know about the coaching, but he's given them a few winners !" Ingleby-Mackenzie wasn't slow in placing a few bets himself when he was at Eton.

The two early victories of 1959 were against Glamorgan and Gloucestershire and, for the second consecutive year at Bristol, Derek took nine wickets in an innings. He achieved this feat four times in his career, twice at Bristol. Hampshire then lost three matches and, although they finally won eleven games, these victories were regularly interspersed with defeats and draws and they were never able to put together a good lengthy sequence of wins as they had done the previous year. The required momentum to seriously challenge Yorkshire did not materialise.

Although Derek took slightly fewer wickets in 1959 compared to 1958, and at an increased average, this was to be expected in a hot dry summer. He bowled 270 more overs than anyone else in the country and, for Hampshire in championship matches, took 126 wickets with only Heath (with 68) of the other bowlers taking more than 50. Whereas in 1958 he had been assisted by rain affected pitches this was rarely the case in 1959 - only at Ebbw Vale did he get substantial help from the wicket in taking 5-32 in 30 overs.

He turned in very fine performances against Yorkshire, Middlesex, Surrey and Lancashire, all strong sides, on pitches giving him little help and, in all of these games, a high proportion of his wickets were top of the order batsmen, many of whom were test players. This season, like that of 1955, belied the theory that he would only do well on wet wickets. In 1959 they were generally dry, the outfields fast and the huge work load he had to undertake for Hampshire did not seem to tire him.

Apart from in championship matches Derek created more problems for certain test players when Hampshire played the MCC at Lord's. He had match figures of 11-88 including the wickets of Peter Richardson (twice), Cowdrey, Parfitt and Titmus.

How would his Hampshire colleagues have fared against him ? This was often a talking point amongst the players over a number of years because it appeared no one had ever faced Derek competitively, not even in meaningful net practice. In fact, Roy Marshall did so on the West Indian tour of England in 1950 and, in his book 'Test Outcast', he mentions that, during his fine innings, "Derek Shackleton worried me and kept me in check. In the end I played a disgusting shot against Shack. I tried to hit him over square leg which was a silly thing to do and lost my middle stump". Watching Derek over so many years Marshall had no doubts that, if he had ever faced him again, he would have played him off the front foot. This method was the generally agreed consensus amongst the Hampshire batsmen, to play back would have been fatal. They were absolutely delighted that such a fine bowler would be in their side but, secretly, would have loved an opportunity to pit their wits against him.

The following year was disappointing. As Ingleby-Mackenzie simply put it "1960 was not a good season". For the first time for more than a decade some blame was put on the fielding - several matches were lost as a direct result of dropped catches. Apart from that it was difficult to pinpoint the reasons for the fall to twelfth in the championship table. The batting was sound with Marshall, Gray and Horton maintaining their form of 1959 and Sainsbury also scored over 1,000 runs. Danny Livingstone, an attractive left handed batsman from Antigua was another to show 'considerable promise' in the fated middle order position but his best years were ahead. Shackleton remained as consistent as ever and with Butch White making the breakthrough and Heath and Sainsbury providing solid support the bowling was strong. Perhaps, therefore, it was simply the fielding lapses which cost so dearly - another twenty points and they would have finished fifth , a rise of three places instead of a drop of four.

One of the early matches of 1960 resulted in a quite extraordinary win against Warwickshire at Portsmouth. All the drama occurred during the last forty minutes on the third day due to an extravagant piece of Ingleby-Mackenzie inspiration and to a spell of bowling by Shackleton which was both devastating and remarkable even by his standards. It was, importantly, to earn him a financial reward.

After somewhat pedestrian batting by both sides in their respective first innings an attacking knock of 81 from Marshall relieved the tedium and enabled Hampshire to declare in their second innings leaving Warwickshire 289 to win.

Two early wickets fell, both to Shackleton, and Warwickshire 'shut up shop' making no effort to go for victory. At about 4.15 they were still about 100 runs short of the target with a maximum of forty five minutes left. The game was scheduled to finish at 4.30 with the option of an extra half an hour if a result seemed likely. Ingleby-Mackenzie had given Derek a rest shortly after 4 o'clock after bowling fifteen consecutive overs but, just a few minutes later and with, crucially, the Warwickshire score at 196 for four (crucial, because in those days the new ball could be taken at 200), he recalled Shackleton for one final effort. The bowler was somewhat miffed and could not really understand the decision and was even more peeved when his skipper told him to give the batsman four runs in order that the new ball could be taken. Although he could see the logic, and would certainly comply with his captain's instructions, it hurt to give away four precious runs. Fred Gardner had opened the innings and was 75 not out at the time. If he had realised the ploy - and surely he must have been surprised to receive an inviting full toss from the tightest bowler in the country - he, probably, would not have stroked the first ball of this new spell to the boundary .

Derek still didn't seriously consider a win was likely and, talking to Syd Buller, the umpire, said that within a quarter of an hour they would be enjoying a cigarette in the pavilion. However, after that first delivery to Gardner, the Warwickshire opener was out the very next ball caught behind the wicket and, in just twenty six deliveries, Shackleton took 6 wickets without conceding a run, finishing with his best ever analysis of 9-30.

He later recalled that the new ball had "moved all over the place" and was so typical of a late afternoon at the United Services ground. Harrison took five catches in the innings, four in that last spell. With the fall of each wicket Shackleton's confidence was sky high and the middle and late order Warwickshire batsmen were arriving at the crease in trepidation, if not panic.

He often relished little contests within the main battle and he remembers Alan Townsend, the Warwickshire number six, saying to Roly Thompson who came in at number ten "I'll take Shack, you just drop anchor at the other end". Next delivery Townsend's off stump was uprooted after the ball pitched on middle and leg. "That'll teach him for trying to take me on". If he did hear of a batsman prepared to state his intentions, it produced just a little bit of added edge.

Great credit must go to Ingleby-Mackenzie for this win. Even he must have had considerable doubts that a victory could be achieved but he was prepared to take a gamble which paid off handsomely. He also had the best bowler in the country to exploit the conditions which prevailed and probably his most difficult task was persuading Derek to give away four runs!

Not only would this performance provide him with his best ever analysis - although his 8-4 at Weston-Super-Mare seems more imprinted in most minds - but earned Derek the annual Brylcreem award for the best bowling performance of the season. This was the not inconsiderable sum in those days of 100 guineas. He was, therefore, delighted with his captain's decision not to give up an apparent lost cause.

A typical example of dropped catches losing games that season was an early fixture at Lord's against Middlesex. It was a low scoring affair and, in the final innings, Middlesex were left with a seemingly easy target of 81. Shackleton and Heath, bowling unchanged, reduced the home side to 35 for six and then 63 for eight and, with two very genuine tail enders, Warr and Moss, at numbers ten and eleven , it appeared that Hampshire would pull off a remarkable win. John Murray was, though, a more than useful number eight and was the dangerman from Hampshire's point of view. Warr was out with the score at 73 and, immediately afterwards, Moss was dropped at slip. That was Hampshire's final opportunity of winning because Murray bravely hit Shackleton for six to clinch a close victory. Whilst this missed chance proved so costly there had been several other dropped catches earlier in the game and, for the first and possibly only season during the 1950s and early 1960s, the results were being seriously and adversely affected by careless fielding.

Three successive wins at the end of May and beginning of June only flattered to deceive because they won only three more throughout the remainder of the season. In fact there were very few matches in 1960 which linger in the memory but two can be singled out for special mention. One proved that, in cricket, nothing can be taken for granted ; the other giving Hampshire one of their most one sided victories ever.

At Coalville in May Leicestershire, not for the first time against Hampshire, saved a game when all seemed lost. At one stage in their second innings Leicestershire had been reduced to 52 for eight still needing 30 to avoid an innings defeat. Robin Gardner, the Leicestershire number four, was then joined by his skipper, Willie Watson, who came in at number ten due to a cracked rib sustained earlier in the match. The two batsmen then put together a valiant partnership worth 125 and although Shackleton took 4-33 in 38 overs he failed to make the breakthrough. Watson made 76 and Gardner 78 but no other batsman reached doubled figures. It was the third occasion in just a very few years that Leicestershire had thwarted Hampshire against all odds

In the second fixture that season against Middlesex Hampshire gained ample revenge for the earlier defeat winning by an innings and 26 runs. In itself the margin may not seem that dramatic but a look at the scorecard will show that Hampshire lost only two wickets in the match. Marshall (168) and Gray (88) put on 249 before being separated, a county first wicket record at that time.

Butch White did considerable damage in the Middlesex game ending with match figures of 10-97. He was a powerfully built man and had genuine pace and hostility, certainly the fastest bowler Hampshire had until Andy Roberts and Malcolm Marshall came along. Who was the fastest of the three can only be the subject of conjecture.

White had made his debut in 1957 but now, due to Cannings'

retirement and the slight decline in Heath's effectiveness, he had become a regular in the side. His rapid improvement was undoubtedly the bright spot in a somewhat disappointing season. Shackleton, therefore, had a new opening partner and, together, they were a distinctly uncomfortable proposition for batsmen. Much, quite rightly, has been made of Derek's reserves of stamina but White had immense strength because he, too, was asked to put in long spells of bowling. He would charge in like a battering ram off a lengthy run up but rarely lost his accuracy. In 1960 he took 114 championship wickets at an average of 18.78 and at a very laudable strike rate of a wicket every 40 deliveries.

Like many others, White remembers Shackleton inspiring by example rather than in any other more direct form. He felt it a privilege to be bowling with "this lovely guy" and there was never any resentment that White, although by far the quicker of the two, always conceded the first over to his senior partner. Choice of ends would be resolved amicably and without fuss but Shack would always send down the first delivery. Batsmen were often quite anxious to get away from White, certainly on a lively wicket, but they were then lured into the web of the cunning veteran. Both agree that they took wickets for each other, probably more so than the Shackleton/Cannings partnership.

White was born in Sutton Coldfield and, as a youngster, played for Aston Unity in the Birmingham league. His opening bowling partner was the former Lancashire fast medium bowler Dick Pollard who played four times for England in the late 1940s. White went on to play a handful of games for Warwickshire Second X1 and, a compatriot of his, Dennis Amiss recalls that he was a big in swing bowler off a shortish run and who, at that time, also opened the batting. Amiss firmly believes that Shackleton was ideal for White's development and that they were perfect foils for each other.

It seemed fortuitous for White that he made such an impact in 1960 because his performances should have been noticed by the England selectors. During the 1950s England had been blessed with three of the finest fast bowlers in their history - Trueman, Statham and Tyson. Tyson announced his retirement at the end of the 1960 season and, although the other two were still very formidable, the selectors would, or certainly should, have been looking to the future for adequate replacements. White was probably now the fastest bowler in the country and his form in 1960 would have done him no harm but for one apparent 'blemish'. Inexplicably, and unfairly, he was called for throwing by umpire Paul Gibb in a game against Sussex at Hove and this isolated incident probably cost him a place on the winter tour to New Zealand.

Throwing was a major issue during that period and the level of concern reached a peak in 1960 when the South African, Geoff Griffin, was 'called' on numerous occasions, his individual nightmare coming to a head in the second test at Lord's. This seemed to spark a spate of such incidents but White, it is generally agreed by colleagues and opponents alike, was genuinely unlucky as his action was considered to be very sound. From Hampshire's viewpoint there was no problem and the new partnership of Shackleton and White was one of the county's saving graces that year.

Chapter Eleven

Champions

The ultimate ambition of every cricketer is to represent his country. For a few it becomes almost immediately apparent at a young age that the necessary class and, importantly, temperament are there to enable them to play at the highest level. For others the progress is slower, those perhaps who have to work harder when the complexities of the game have not come to them so naturally. Finally there are the majority who, whilst they may still harbour dreams of a telephone call from Lord's, know that any honours that come their way, certainly in England, will be with their county. There are now, of course, four separate domestic competitions but in 1961 there was still only the county championship to play for. Many very fine players of that era missed out on honours altogether, a prime example for Hampshire being Neville Rogers.

It would turn out to be the most exciting season the county had ever experienced and, as win followed win in August with the tense nail biting climax at Bournemouth on September 1st, Hampshire supporters were given the present which had eluded the county since its admission to the county championship in 1895. At last Hampshire had come to full maturity, and this was proved in the way they handled the pressure in those last few matches, something they certainly didn't do in 1958 when they had such a miserable August.

Derek had enjoyed a fairly relaxing winter continuing to be in charge of the indoor school in Southampton. The lingerie business, run largely by Kathy on her own, was doing reasonably well and life was comfortable but they certainly couldn't afford an exorbitant lifestyle. Because of Derek's evening work and with two young children, both of whom were now at school, there was not a great deal of time for social and other leisure activities. Whenever possible they would go out and Bella Knights, who ran the bar at the county ground and who was wife of the groundsman, would occasionally baby-sit. Often it would be a visit to the cinema or to a cricket related function.

The players were frequently asked to attend dinners and parties and when Eagar was skipper it was normally only the players who were invited, with the wives largely ignored. "Cricket ruled", according to Kathy and it reached the stage when Derek told Eagar that there would be no more dinner acceptances unless Kathy came as well. He relied to a very large extent, throughout his career, on her support and they both felt, very strongly, that it was important the wives should not be ignored. Life is not too easy for a cricketer's wife and Kathy believed that they fully deserved some of the perks which were going. She, herself, mixes easily with people and has admitted that she greatly enjoyed meeting the 'rich and famous'. Dukes, ambassadors, politicians, actors and bandleaders.

Derek is quieter but has never had a problem on a one to one basis whoever he may have met.

"I'm shy in front of an audience" he once said. This did not appear to ring true when he was a guest of the Hampshire Cricket Society at their annual supper in December 1997. He replied to a large number of interesting questions from an enthusiastic and enthralled audience in a concise, clear, and above all hugely entertaining manner. It was an extremely confident performance. The nerves certainly did not show then.

Before the season started Ingleby-Mackenzie had a premonition that this could be Hampshire's year. He was confident and on ' a high' following several wins at the races and indeed wrote to his friend, E.W. Swanton, suggesting he put some money on a Hampshire championship. Probably the advice was not taken and who could blame him ? After achieving second place in 1958 the county had slipped to eighth and twelfth in the following two years and the playing staff remained virtually unchanged. There was no real reason to suggest they would mount a serious challenge to the powerful Yorkshire side notwithstanding the likelihood of test calls being made upon them.

After a drawn, rain ruined, game against Worcestershire at Bournemouth Hampshire defeated Somerset at Frome, narrowly, by just 18 runs. The wicket took spin right from the start and Burden, with his off spinners, had match figures of 12-108. In the Somerset second innings Ingleby-Mackenzie, not the most nimble fielder, ran out two with throws from mid on. Stephenson, the Somerset skipper, was the second victim and considered himself especially unlucky. Having witnessed the first run out he could not believe it could happen again ! Perhaps this was another omen for the new season.

Field placing was easy when Derek was bowling and Jimmy Gray and Peter Sainsbury remember all the players going automatically to their respective positions, certainly when the wicket was 'decent'.

He rarely had more than two slips and a gully unless the wicket was poor when “it was all round the bat”. Horton would then come in to forward short leg with whoever was at fine leg often coming up into the slip cordon. The close fieldsmen were all experts in their particular field and they, in turn, had confidence knowing there would be few, if any, loose or unpredictable deliveries. Equally Shackleton had a firm trust in his fielders. A very mutual admiration society but fully justified.

A typical field in 1961 would have looked something like this :

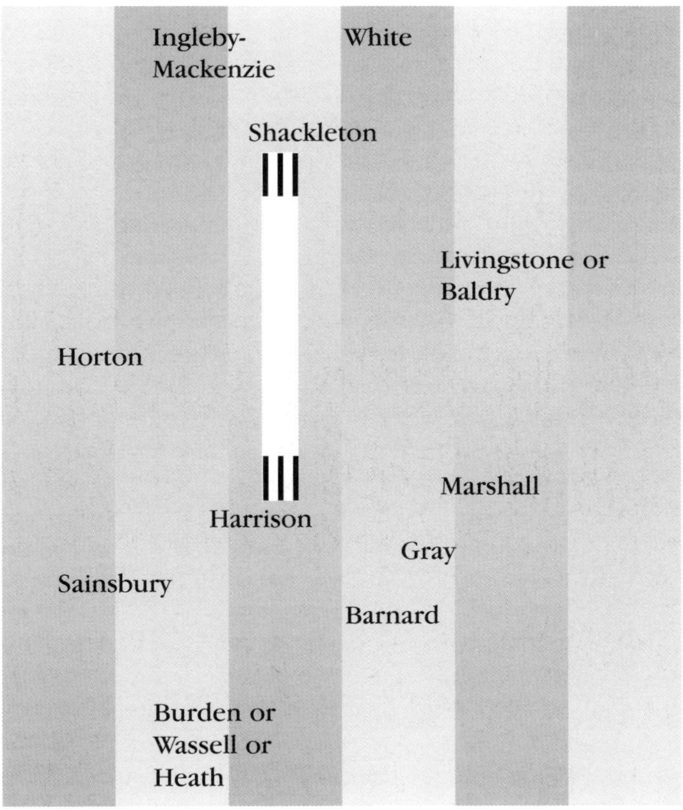

Hampshire had many close victories that summer, many due to enterprising declarations, but if they had a truly lucky one it was surely the early win against Surrey at the Oval.

Surrey, with attacking centuries from Barrington (who did not always enjoy complete freedom against Shackleton) and John Edrich, declared their first innings at 356 for four and Hampshire were thankful that May was dismissed for a modest 23 - lbw to Shackleton. In reply, Hampshire struggled to 190 and were grateful for a stubborn innings of 85 not out by the ever reliable Horton. Under a change in the rules Surrey were unable to enforce the follow on and, batting a second time, declared at 141 for two . With a first innings lead of 166, and together with hindsight, Surrey should have scored more quickly in their second innings - their 141 taking up 57 overs. May, generously, left Hampshire five and a half hours to score 308 which was risky with the ominous threat of Marshall. Indeed he batted majestically scoring 153 out of 280 in under two and a half hours. His partnership with Horton, who also scored quickly, produced 180 runs and ensured victory with ample time to spare. Galling for Surrey who lost only six wickets in the game.

Much credence has rightly been given to the importance of Ingleby-Mackenzie's declarations. These decisions were often based on Marshall's ability to score at a very fast pace and on Shackleton and White making early inroads into the opposition batting. Derek, of course, also had the vital asset of putting a brake on the run rate. Gray, though, has a very valid additional theory that it was the unlikely Horton who won many games for Hampshire when they had to chase runs. Horton is widely remembered for his crouching, somewhat ugly stance at the crease, and for being such a stubborn reliable number three for many years during an important era in the county's history. Gray believes Horton could pace his innings better than Marshall and was capable, especially when set and when circumstances demanded it, of scoring very quickly. His 84 in the second innings at the Oval coming in under one and a half hours which contrasted with his four hour stay in the first innings when scoring 85. Each innings was perfect for the situation which prevailed at the time. Bowlers always thought they had a chance of dismissing Marshall, much less so with Horton.

Derek had made a modest start to the season, just 8 wickets from the first four matches at an average of 30 - it had been cold once again - but 7 wickets in the next game at Portsmouth against Lancashire got the momentum going .

Hampshire beat Lancashire, closely, but E.W. Swanton, reporting on the game, mentioned to Ingleby-Mackenzie during the match that because Hampshire were employing as many as five seam bowlers they wouldn't win and laid odds of 3-1 against a Hampshire victory. Admittedly Burden and Wassell did not play, as they rarely did at Portsmouth, and Hampshire did include their full complement of seamers - Shackleton, White, Heath and Gray. However, Jim Swanton wasn't quite correct because the left arm spinner, Sainsbury, was the fifth bowler. It was logical to play the seamers at Portsmouth but a more spin orientated attack at, say, Bournemouth. That year the bowling line up was extremely flexible and fluid enough to meet whatever conditions they faced.

Fortunately, in a low scoring game, Lancashire were without Statham, so often a thorn in Hampshire's side, someone who could so easily have swung the game in their favour. In the return fixture at Old Trafford ten days later a fully fit Statham had match figures of 8-47 ensuring a comfortable Lancashire victory by 8 wickets. By the end of May Hampshire had won three of their eight matches with the margin of victory being extremely close on two occasions and the third win somewhat fortuitous. Nothing at this stage to seriously suggest they would soon be challenging for the championship. Suddenly, though, there was a sequence of six straight wins which ensured a rapid rise up the table. The first of these, against Somerset at Bournemouth, included a 10 wicket match haul for the desperately unlucky Burden. Unlucky because, at this stage, he had taken 39 wickets in seven matches but would only be selected on five further occasions that season and he took only 6 more wickets. The emphasis on seam was ever more evident and to add to Burden's insecurity was the rapid advancement of Wassell.

Burden finished second only to Shackleton in the bowling averages that season but after Wassell took 5 wickets against Glamorgan at the beginning of June he was generally selected ahead of Burden. In that same match at Swansea Derek had his first 5 wickets in an innings haul of 1961, a feat he would repeat a further eleven times in all matches before the season ended.

The next game at Portsmouth against Gloucestershire produced an astonishing victory following, what appeared to be, a bizarre declaration by Ingleby-Mackenzie. Due to outstanding bowling by Shackleton and White with respective analyses of 5-45 and 4-69 Gloucestershire were all out for 176. However, the second day was completely washed out and it seemed that the only points at stake would be those for first innings lead. Marshall and Gray, opening the innings as usual, took the score to 96 without trouble and Marshall, on 71, appeared to be well set for the fastest century of the season. They were not happy, therefore, when they perceived their skipper ushering them back to the pavilion as he had taken the decision to declare. In a later era such declarations are not unusual but were fairly innovative at the time. Marshall was furious and there were often times when he queried his skipper's judgment. He was, though, one of the first to concede, especially in 1961, that, more often than not, Ingleby-Mackenzie was right. If he had backed horses that year - and there would be little doubt he did, and frequently - he should have made a fortune!

Gloucestershire accepted the challenge, although had difficulty in forcing the pace against some extremely accurate bowling from Shackleton who took 4-27 in 19 overs. They declared at 118 for eight leaving the home side to score 199 at 88 per hour. Marshall hit a brisk 38 and with Horton, again proving he could score quickly when necessary, and Ingleby-Mackenzie both scoring half centuries, the game swung Hampshire's way. Such is the beauty and uncertainty of cricket that the whole scenario changed very quickly. Five wickets fell for 29 runs and with twenty minutes remaining 37 runs were still needed. Butch White, hitting with great power, scored 33 in eighteen minutes to clinch a quite remarkable and important victory. Derek had stayed with him in this vital unbroken stand of 37.

Hampshire then had three very comprehensive wins over Northamptonshire, Worcestershire and Leicestershire (not even Willie Watson could save them this time) and this sequence took them, for the first time in 1961, to the top of the table.

Most of the team now shared their captain's optimism that this indeed would be their year. They now actually expected to win most matches, they had dispelled the inferiority complex which had afflicted them in the past. Their first six victories had been close, results which could so easily have gone the other way and it was important, therefore, to prove to any doubters that they could also dominate. These three latest wins were very convincing - by margins of 172 runs, 185 runs and 10 wickets. There were excellent performances by all concerned and showed the rest of the counties that Hampshire were a genuine force to be reckoned with. They were oozing confidence and were now used to winning. Provided they could keep clear of injuries it would be difficult to break the winning habit.

Derek just continued to take his usual crop of wickets but not spectacularly so - almost half would come in the final crucial third of the season, an important factor in the strong finish. Hampshire, in 1961, probably had their most complete bowling attack in its history. White was a belligerent force, a player who could do real physical damage and batsmen were quite happy to get away from him only to be drawn into a chess like contest with the canny, cunning veteran. Total and absolute concentration and patience was then required and those who became completely becalmed took their chances at the other end. In addition to White there was still Heath, if the wicket was green, or the spinners - Sainsbury, Burden or Wassell if it was a turner. Finally, there was the added bonus of Gray's little in-swingers. Various permutations could be used depending on conditions but there has never been a better balanced Hampshire bowling attack, not even in the days of Kennedy and Newman.

Between the end of June and the early part of August Hampshire won only five out of a possible twelve matches and whilst this may have been a satisfactory ratio in previous seasons it did cause a little concern in 1961. For the first, and only, time that summer there was a slight flutter of nerves. Would they capitulate to the big guns of Yorkshire and Middlesex? That year, though, there was a tremendous belief in their own abilities. It would not mean they would underestimate the competition but they did not feel inferior either.

After being well beaten by Middlesex at Lord's Hampshire's travels took them to the Isle of Wight for their annual 'overseas' fixture, sadly no longer the case. They were to pull off an improbable victory over Essex largely based on a brilliant innings by Ingleby-Mackenzie, more penetrative and containing bowling by Shackleton, a generous declaration by Trevor Bailey and a little bit of cunning.

Essex declared their first innings on 321 for nine but Marshall, when fielding, slipped and strained a hamstring. He could hardly walk and the leg was heavily bandaged but he was able to bat, albeit at number seven, and, in some considerable discomfort, scored 10. Essex had a first innings lead of 90 and, on the last day, declared again leaving Hampshire to score 241 in 215 minutes. Unbeknown to Bailey, Marshall had discovered on the ferry between Southampton and Cowes that his leg was moving much more freely and, although it was agreed he wouldn't open, he would certainly bat if required. Bailey later recalled that he considered the declaration to be right at the time but that if it had been later in the season, when Hampshire were in serious contention for the title, he may not have been so generous. He had based his decision on Marshall being unable to bat.

With Hampshire reduced to 35 for four there seemed little doubt Essex would win, and comfortably. Ingleby-Mackenzie then proceeded to hit the highest of his ten career centuries in a brilliant, inventive and, occasionally, outrageous innings. He received invaluable support from, first Livingstone, and then, crucially from Marshall who, coming in at number eight with a runner, hit 36 in forty four minutes showing he could be almost as effective on one leg. Even some of his colleagues were not convinced he would bat and Shackleton was actually walking down the pavilion steps when Marshall overtook him!

Bailey was yet another test player full of regard for Derek's abilities as a seam bowler. He faced him as much as anyone during those two decades and honours were just about even . He probably saw more of Derek than he did of anyone else in the Hampshire team "because every time I went to the wicket he seemed to be bowling". With Bailey's well known occupancy of the crease it is just possible Derek bowled more deliveries to him than to any other player. It would have been a real battle of very patient wits. When he was asked who he considered the most difficult batsman to try and dismiss, Derek, without a moment's hesitation, said 'Trevor Bailey'; at the same time giving an example of that famous forward defensive stroke!

Hampshire were keeping in touch with the leaders with regular, if not consecutive, victories but, at the end of July, Derek started on, statistically at least, his most rewarding form of the season. This was to be so important to the clinching of the championship title. During the first twenty one matches he had taken 84 championship wickets at 21.72 but, in the last eleven, he took 69 at 15.97 when the pressure was really on.

This personal sequence started at Bristol, a ground where he always seemed to do well. Throughout his career only at Canterbury , Leicester and Lord's did he take more wickets on away grounds. He captured 6 wickets in the win over Gloucestershire and 9 in the drawn match with Middlesex. Marshall, captaining the side in the temporary absence of the injured Ingleby-Mackenzie, was not prepared to give a generous declaration to opponents who were now one of Hampshire's closest rivals for the championship. The next game resulted in a vital win for Hampshire and a great individual performance from a fired up White.

At Portsmouth, Hampshire led Sussex by 38 runs on first innings and, towards the end of the second day, Sussex had reached 179 for four in their second innings; a reasonable situation for them in a low scoring game.

Marshall gave the ball to White for one final effort. It was well past 6.30 and, although not actually raining, it was a stormy evening with a strong wind sweeping in from the Solent. White, roaring in with the gale behind him, was a truly awesome sight although the first delivery was only brisk medium but caused Jim Parks to play on to his wicket. The next batsman was Ian Thomson, sent in as night watchman. He was caught behind first ball and White's tail was really up. He was now firing on all cylinders and, next ball, took out Don Smith's off stump to complete his hat-trick. Smith, not expecting to bat that evening, had already changed and was on his way to the Lord Mayor's tent for drinks when the over had started. He had had to make a hurried return to the pavilion and then made an equally quick return after his brief 'innings'. Jimmy Gray then just failed to hold on to a difficult slip chance given by the next batsman, Graham Cooper, but, trying to hook the next ball, Cooper gave a catch to Henry Horton. White's 4 wickets in five deliveries transformed the match and Ted Dexter, standing at the non-striker's end, could only behold the mayhem with some incredulity. The final 2 Sussex wickets went down early the next morning and they had slumped from 179 for four to 180 all out. Hampshire won easily with a brilliant cameo from Marshall who scored a rapid 51 including a deliberate upper cut for six over third man off Dexter.

Dexter had a renowned theory of how to combat Shackleton and other bowlers of his type. A simple philosophy of hitting him 'on the up', straight back over his head. One year, after seeing his Sussex colleagues struggle against Shackleton, he said he would show them his method. He was dismissed for 0 and 4 and returned, somewhat sheepishly, to the pavilion much to the amusement of the other Sussex players. In the 1961 match he tried this again in the first innings only to sky the ball to Baldry at mid on. Dexter was far more cautious the second time around.

A draw against Kent and defeat by Essex caused a few hearts to flutter and the pessimists were saying that Hampshire would blow it as they had done in 1958. However, this time they were not going to capitulate and won their next five matches. In this sequence Derek took 39 wickets.

The first and last games in this important five match run were against Derbyshire who, in the past, had proved to be something of a bogey side. At Derby Hampshire declared on 350 for eight and, snatching an early wicket, were very pleased with their day's work. There had been yet another vital innings of 141 by the reliable Horton.

The following day was a so called rest day. In fact, there was little rest in those pre-Sunday league times as the players were often asked to play in charity or benefit games. Colin Ingleby-Mackenzie had arranged for himself, Roy Marshall, Leo Harrison and Derek to play in a charity fixture at Newmarket and the four drove down from Derby on the Saturday evening when the festivities started. These carried on throughout Sunday when, "a little cricket was played in a most convivial atmosphere", and continued well into the evening. It was the sort of situation which inspired the much quoted statement that the skipper was happy provided his team were in bed by breakfast. There was very little sleep that weekend and the four arrived back at the ground not long before play was due to restart and with varying degrees of hangovers. They also had the prospect of a long day in the field.

Remarkably, Shackleton bowled 36 overs and took 6-90 and simply bowled himself out of any hangover he may have been nursing. Generally, after a day's play, he would have a cigarette in the corner of the dressing room perhaps reflecting on the events of the day. He would also often have a glass of milk and then, after neatly packing his gear, he may have had a pint or two in the bar before going to bed at a reasonable hour. This would be just part of his careful and routine pattern. He was not, and never would be, a heavy drinker. He knew he had to look after himself and also, as is the way with drinking sessions, it would be a severe drain on his wallet, although he had to be wary of the many followers on who are more than willing to buy drinks. Those, who next day, will boast they bought a drink for 'such and such a player'.

Derek certainly drank more than his usual quota during the Newmarket weekend but he could drink 'slowly' to keep reasonable control. He unwound in these situations and would be very enjoyable company with a quiet uncomplicated sense of humour. Although a natural introvert he stood out in company due to his tall handsome appearance, a disarming smile and always immaculate grooming. Ingleby-Mackenzie was a totally different character with life to be enjoyed to the full and no moment to be wasted; someone who had great charm and charisma. Their cricket epitomised their contrasting personalities; the beauty was they had great respect and liking for each other.

Hampshire completed the victory over Derbyshire even though Derek had twisted an ankle and had to bowl off three paces in the second innings. Fortunately, the injury was not serious and he was able to play in the next match against Warwickshire which began the following day.

It is appropriate to reflect on a decision taken during the weekend of the Derbyshire match, one, which at first, did not appear to directly affect Hampshire but, with hindsight, was one which could have had an adverse bearing on their championship aspirations.

Due to an historic spell of leg spin bowling by Richie Benaud in the fourth test at Old Trafford Australia had retained the 'Ashes' taking a 2-1 lead in the series with just the fifth test at the Oval to come. The England selectors met during the weekend of 12th and 13th August and decided to take the controversial decision to drop Trueman. He had not been at his best at Old Trafford but, at Headingley in the third test, had bowled magnificently taking 11-88. With twenty wickets in his four tests he was still England's most successful bowler that summer. However, having made that decision, the selectors would surely have considered either Shackleton or White as a replacement. Admittedly Derek was now 37 but, as a temporary measure, in an effort to level the series, he might have been a good choice. Perhaps, more logically, the selectors should have turned to White. Now considered to be the quickest bowler in the country he had proven strength to bowl for long spells and, because of his efforts for Hampshire, deserved the opportunity. The county were now serious challengers for the championship and receiving more than their usual quota of national press coverage. This doesn't do any harm when test sides are being considered.

In fact neither Hampshire player was picked but this raises an interesting and unanswerable question. How would Hampshire have fared if one, or the other, had been selected? It would have meant that, for two vital championship matches, they would have been without a key bowler. The two games were against Warwickshire and Leicestershire at Southampton and Portsmouth respectively. Of the 39 wickets to fall Shackleton and White took 34!. It would be too much to the detriment of the other players, in particular Malcolm Heath who could have filled the breach perfectly, to suggest they would have failed to win either match - there were relatively comfortable margins of 8 wickets and 152 runs - but the combined efforts of the two bowlers was so colossal it does point to an interesting discussion. With the final outcome of the championship so close it could have cost them dearly.

Another player to make a very important and timely contribution that August was Mike Barnard. A largely unsung hero he had not held a regular place that year because of indifferent early season form but in that sequence of five successive wins he scored 380 runs at an average of 63 including a superb not out century against Warwickshire. A quite brilliant slip fielder and outstanding athlete he was one of the last cricketer/footballers. The problem was obvious. The seasons would overlap and this, undoubtedly, was a hindrance to both his sporting careers. Fielding at slip he, like Gray, had the greatest admiration for Shackleton and quite simply marvelled at the exceptional accuracy and temperament. By the time Barnard had started with Hampshire Derek had developed his outswinger and, therefore, became very reliant on the slip fielders - Barnard was considered to be one of the best in the country. He likened the seamer's temperament and general demeanour to the Pompey and England international, Jimmy Dickinson. Both modest men, without histrionics, who went about their business loyally, professionally and without fuss. Gentlemen both; men who attracted great respect and no enemies.

An excellent all round performance against Nottinghamshire secured maximum points and then came a break from the exciting, but nerve wracking, championship race with a match against the Australians. So important were Shackleton and White to Hampshire they were rested for this game although the county did come in for some criticism. In those days matches against touring sides were prestigious affairs and counties generally fielded their strongest teams. Earlier in the season Hampshire would, undoubtedly, have done so but, with their first championship within their grasp, it was a very justifiable decision to take.

And so to Bournemouth, and to the success which came to a southern county for the first time - excluding those bordering London. Sussex, Somerset and Gloucestershire still await their first championship.

Hampshire went into the game against Derbyshire with the knowledge that victory would ensure them of the championship. The weather was fine, the pitch flat with the possibility of taking spin later and there was an exhilarating and expectant atmosphere. Bournemouth, in August, ensured a good crowd.

They were soon off to a good start with an opening stand of 120 by Marshall and Gray but the innings then faltered at 182 for five . Were nerves having an effect? However, the last 5 wickets produced another 124 runs; Derek contributing a valuable 27 not out. Derbyshire soon lost an early wicket - another unerring throw by the skipper from mid off accounting for Lee - but enterprising batting from Laurie Johnson, who hit a fine 112, put the visitors in a strong position at 212 for two. The game appeared to be drifting away from Hampshire and, at this stage, Shackleton was wicketless. In four previous matches at Dean Park that year he had taken only 7 rather expensive wickets. The turning point of the game came during the late afternoon and evening on the second day when Shackleton and Wassell bowled in harness and from 212 for two Derbyshire could only reach 318, a lead of just twelve. Shackleton took 3-70 from 39 overs and Wassell 5-132 from 42.

Hampshire started their second innings badly losing Gray and Horton for 16 and, with Livingstone gone with the score at 40, things looked bleak. However, another brilliant innings from Marshall, together with vital half centuries from Sainsbury and Barnard, enabled Ingleby-Mackenzie to declare setting Derbyshire a target of 252 in 192 minutes. The burning question was 'could Hampshire dismiss their opponents in just over three hours ?' A draw would be of little consequence . Anything less than outright victory would mean they would have to go into the last match against Yorkshire, their nearest rivals, with everything to play for.

Derek, when recalling that late afternoon in early September, had no specific plan other than to 'bowl straight'. He was only too well aware of the significance of the situation but only on very rare occasions would nerves unsettle him and this was not one of them. He does remember, though, that he considered it imperative that Johnson was dismissed quickly. In addition to his first innings century the hard hitting Barbadian had top scored in both innings at Derby earlier in the month.

He then produced arguably the most important spell of bowling of his life. Immediately after lunch on that third day he took the first 4 wickets for 8 runs (including that of Johnson) and, at 24 for four , the back of the Derbyshire innings was broken - irretrievably as it would turn out. With two batsmen bowled, one lbw and one edge to the keeper he had done the damage largely on his own. Wassell took the next two wickets and then Shack claimed two more - both bowled - to have Derbyshire reeling at 52 for eight and the match was theirs. Or was it ? With the crowd now quite literally on the edges of their seats there was an annoying stand of 52 between Bob Taylor and Harold Rhodes which doubled the Derbyshire total before Sainsbury dismissed them both and the championship was won.

Derek's performances throughout the season had, yet again, been of the highest quality culminating in the climax at Bournemouth. He had bowled more overs than anyone else in the country and, of his total of 158 wickets, more than half were taken without the aid of fielders. In particular, it was when the pressure was really on in those final weeks that his skill and experience proved so invaluable. His analyses in that five match winning sequence were as follows:

	Overs	Maidens	Runs	Wickets	Ave
Derbyshire	36.1	13	90	6	
	25	4	58	1	
Warwickshire	27	6	88	5	
	23.5	12	36	6	
Leicestershire	19	7	36	5	
	18	6	22	1	
Nottinghamshire	33.1	5	111	4	
	8	2	15	2	
Derbyshire	39	15	70	3	
	24	10	39	6	
Total	253.1	80	565	39	14.48

Of the nine wickets in the second Derbyshire game, five were bowled, one lbw, two caught at the wicket and one in the slips. This on an unresponsive pitch! Small wonder, therefore, that he led the side off the field on that September afternoon although it was difficult to pass through the cordon of spectators who had thronged in front of the pavilion. Photographs show that, notwithstanding he had bowled 24 overs, his short sleeve sweater was immaculately in place, his shirt sleeves neatly rolled to the elbows and his hair still beautifully groomed, although a little greyer than in his younger days. An absolutely impeccable appearance even after the champagne flowed!.

Walter Shackleton, watching his son that day, could not have been more proud, and, at the same time, pleased to have advised Derek, all those years ago, to take up the offer of a contract with Hampshire.

It should not be overlooked, of course, that Hampshire's success was very much a great team effort - an unfashionable side led by a charismatic captain prepared to gamble. It was also a popular victory amongst neutrals if only because the dominance of years of Surrey and Yorkshire championships had been broken. The (few) critics would argue that they were lucky with the absence of test calls, the fact that many of their wins were by slender margins and that declarations by the opposition were over generous. These would be churlish criticisms for which there are good valid arguments by way of response.

Yorkshire missed Trueman for a few games due to his selection for England and Illingworth was absent with his two test appearances. To offset this the Northern county had a much stronger and larger squad of players and were able to absorb these occasional absences better than one of the smaller counties. It was often their boast that they could have fielded a second X1 which would have more than held its own in the championship. Middlesex were only without their wicket keeper, John Murray, because of test duties and Surrey, although frequently without May, Barrington and Lock, finished fifteenth that summer, too far behind Hampshire for those absences to have made such a significant difference.

Some of Hampshire's early wins were, indeed, close but, as the season progressed, they began to dominate and to dictate terms and the margins of victories became quite substantial.

The experimental law that year which did not allow the follow-on (provided play was possible on the first day) called for intelligent declarations and Ingleby-Mackenzie had a magic touch. It is far too easy and glib to say he was simply a lucky gambler. He was much too astute and not to be underestimated. The timings of many of his declarations were often perfect, just enough to tease the opposition into self destruction. With regard to those occasions when the opposition declared and Hampshire had to score runs in the fourth innings to win they had mixed success - three wins, two defeats, and one draw. In hindsight two of these declarations (both of which resulted in a Hampshire victory) could be construed as generous. However, in both matches they were asked to score more than they had done in their respective first innings and, against Surrey at the Oval, relied heavily on a brilliant innings of 153 by Marshall and, at Cowes against Essex, on an astonishing knock by the skipper after his side were in deep trouble.

Hampshire were, in fact, very worthy champions and, to be fair, one of the first to offer his congratulations was Vic Wilson, the Yorkshire captain. They gained some consolation by beating Hampshire in the final game with, once again, Trueman launching a successful assault on Shackleton (and White).

If 1961 was a triumph for the players it was a truly emotional time for many others who had worked so hard towards this achievement.

Particularly the President, Harry Altham, the secretary and former captain, Desmond Eagar, whose enthusiasm was unbounded, and Arthur Holt, who was responsible for the development of so many of the younger players.

Although three of the senior players were now 35 or over and a further three in their 30s the side would look forward optimistically to 1962. It would prove to be false optimism as they slumped alarmingly to tenth position but no blame could be attributed to the so dependable man from Todmorden.

Hampshire County Champions 1961 (Sport and General)

Celebration September 1st 1961
(Southern Newspapers Ltd)

Derek showing his father how the damage was done September 1st 1961

Cricket can be fun (Southern Newspapers Ltd)

And tiring

Leo Harrison, Derek and Colin Ingleby-Mackenzie

South Africa 1966

Cape Town with daughter
Caroline

Kathy watching Derek bowl.
This was the view from their flat
(Southern Newspapers Ltd)

Reunions in the 1990s (The above photos by kind permission of Susanne Marlow).

With Caroline and Kathy

and Julian

Lord's June 1963 (Sport and General)

Chapter Twelve

Back , Centre Stage

In 1962 Derek experienced his poorest ever start to a season and his figures after three matches in the chilly early days of May were:

Overs	Maidens	Runs	Wickets
104	32	242	2

And yet, perversely, he would finish the season with a total of 172 wickets which would prove to be his best ever tally. It was to be the first of four consecutive years when he was the leading wicket taker in the country.

Henry Horton, who was often Derek's room-mate, remembers those few occasions when not everything clicked for him. They were very rare and, almost always, right at the beginning of the season and Horton believes it was because he took net practice far too casually. He would bowl off two or three paces which would make the delivery 'all arm action' and, when he started bowling in earnest, some of the natural rhythm wasn't there. Without exception, all would come right very quickly, and he never had a lengthy period throughout his entire career when his wicket taking completely dried up. All his colleagues understood his general reluctance in the nets; they knew he would quickly bowl himself into form. If proof of this theory was needed two of his best ever starts to an English season were in 1951 and 1952 when he had been bowling throughout the preceding winters. In 1962, approaching the age of 38, he bowled 1717 overs, almost 300 more than anyone else.

Horton would often field at mid wicket or forward short leg and, when fielding close, did not feel at all uncomfortable when Derek was bowling. He felt quite safe because he knew there would be no long hops. Horton was involved in many bat/pad dismissals.

At this time Alan Wassell was frequently fielding in the gully, another uncomfortable position if the bowler is wayward or pitching short. He was a little nervous when Derek would say to him "in a bit. in a bit", but he soon had great faith in the ability he had of pitching on exactly the same spot. Derek, over the years, had become used to a fairly close in gully position stretching back to when Vic Cannings joined Hampshire. Cannings had fielded in the gully during his time with Warwickshire and, when he was first asked to field there by Tom Dollery, he was told that he must stand several yards closer to the wicket than the normal gully. Cannings got used to being in this potentially dangerous position but knew he would be relatively safe fielding to Shack as there would be no short deliveries.

Unfortunately for Hampshire in 1962 Derek did not get the seam support that he had done during the championship season. Both White and Heath took far fewer wickets and at a higher cost. White wasn't at the peak of fitness and, great trier that he was, the opposition were now less likely to be blasted out. The three spinners, Sainsbury, Burden and Wassell, all took over 50 wickets but, like the two pacemen, were more expensive.

The gap between Shackleton's performances and those of his colleagues widened alarmingly. He bowled 1595 overs in championship matches - the next best was White with 723 - and took 161 wickets with, again, White the closest with 71. The many narrow wins of 1961 were now turning into draws. During 1962 Hampshire actually lost two fewer matches than in the year before but the number of wins went down from nineteen to seven with draws increasing from six to nineteen.

Although it took him a few games to settle into his usual bowling rhythm Derek gave early reminders that he could still bat with two very contrasting innings. He helped retrieve a desperate situation at Edgbaston in a stubborn ninth wicket partnership with Wassell in the face of some difficult bowling by Bannister and Cartwright. Cartwright, like Derek, had started his career as a batsman but had developed into a seam bowler of the highest class and, as the years progressed, was likened very much to his southern rival. Against Lancashire at Southampton Derek hit a quick and crucial 44 not out winning the game with a massive six with just two balls remaining.

There were many outstanding performances by Shackleton that year. When was this not the case? Again , without going into all the impressive statistics there was one feat that warrants special mention. Against Glamorgan at Cardiff the Welsh county were cruising along nicely at 91 for one when he was brought back for a second spell. Derek then took all eight remaining wickets (Wheatley was absent hurt) and Glamorgan slumped to 114 all out. His final analysis was 8-36 from 28 overs.

Lack of overall penetration in the bowling, lapses in the field and the inspired declarations of 1961 not quite coming off meant that 1962 was something of an anticlimax. It was a pity because the batting was consistently good with six players scoring over 1000 runs in championship games and it was this strength which helped the side remain unbeaten until the fifteenth match when they were defeated by Yorkshire by just 5 runs - notwithstanding Derek having match figures of 12-145. Any remote hopes of retaining the championship were dashed when they failed to win any of their final twelve games.

For Derek, though, it had been another thoroughly successful season and he had, yet again, fully earned his modest income - he simply was Hampshire's bowling that season. Fortunately, although he was now 38 he had no immediate thoughts of retirement; he loved what he did and, importantly, a second benefit would become due within a few years. He was still remarkably fit and the dedication to his job and his unrelenting skills were to be rewarded in unexpected fashion the following season.

Again a slow start to the 1963 campaign with just 5 wickets from the first three games at an average of 41 but then he hit a rich vein of form.

There were two significant changes in the Hampshire side that season. Bryan Timms, a highly rated young wicket keeper from the village of Ropley in that central part of the county so familiar to John Arlott, took over from Leo Harrison, the last of the players from pre war days. Timms had made a few appearances before but this would be his first full season. The second change was the signing of Bob Cottam, a tall fast medium bowler, who replaced Malcolm Heath whose contract had not been renewed.

Harrison's keeping and general cricketing expertise had been so important to Hampshire and to Shackleton. He never failed to be amazed at the sheer consistency and extraordinary skills of the veteran seamer, because out of the ordinary they certainly were. Harrison, also, was one of the very few who seemed to be able to pick the outswinger. When asked about this in later years Harrison couldn't clearly define the reason for this, merely saying "there was a slight change in the first four steps of Shack's run up; nothing I could clearly pinpoint, but you just had this feeling". Marshall and Gray, who regularly fielded in the slips and, like Harrison, were very intelligent readers of the game also made this same observation.

Timms, like his predecessor, would invariably stand up to the stumps when keeping to Shackleton. He had made the occasional appearance for Hampshire prior to 1963 but, generally, had been keeping wicket for the second X1 and had not come across someone of Derek's stature. The ball pitching consistently on the seam was legendary and Timms would now experience this phenomenon at first hand. He, too, noticed the very slight variation in approach for the away swinger. What he also remembers is, that during the flight of the ball, it actually appeared to be stationary, a somewhat uncanny experience and due to the fact that the ball did not wobble in mid air. The first two fingers of the bowler's hand would have been astride the ball at the point of release and, with it pitching exactly on the seam, there was a strange sensation of a moment frozen in time as the ball was in the air. Timms never saw any other bowler have this effect.

It is quite noticeable in the 1990s that, although England have used a considerable number of fast or medium fast bowlers, not one uses the seam to such an extent. This is not to criticise bowlers of a different generation because there were few, if any, of Shackleton's era who would hit the seam so frequently. With the availability of high technology cameras and the slow motion facility viewers can now clearly see the 'roll' of the ball and, often, it becomes a matter of luck if it should pitch on the seam.

Timms also recalls Derek's equable temperament but remembers one occasion when he did experience a problem with which he had difficulty coping. Strangely it occurred during the first match of 1963, right at the start of Timms' first full season.

The opening game was against Warwickshire at Coventry and, after Hampshire had been dismissed for 122, the home county lost two wickets cheaply, although neither to a bowler. Ibadulla was given out 'obstructing the field' and Barber was run out. However, Horner and MJK Smith retrieved the situation with a fine partnership and had little difficulty in dealing with Shackleton. Smith was particularly severe scoring 115 - 90 in boundaries. For some reason that day Shack did not have his usual control, the ball going all over the place and Timms remembers it so clearly because it was so rare - almost unheard of - and other players could not recall any other similar situation.

Derek left the field that evening a deeply worried man and was in such a state of mind he got very little sleep. This was a new experience and he simply did not know how to handle it. He was a 'natural' bowler and, for the past fifteen years, had not had any problem with co-ordination , smoothness of action or rhythm. It was a major crisis for him but it proved to be a short lived phenomenon. The next morning he was back to his normal self, hitting the seam with his customary accuracy. He took only 1 wicket in the match but, in the second innings, conceded just 22 runs in 16 overs. A happy and contented man again. To put matters further into perspective it had been a seamer's wicket and he would have expected to have been amongst the wickets. In contrast, his Warwickshire counterpart, Cartwright, had match figures of 12-101; Derek had taken 1-87.

What was the reason for this slight hiccup? He was basically like a well oiled machine which would just run and run until switched off. At the beginning of the season the engine had not been running for some months and, in the often cold weeks of April and May, took a while to get all cylinders going again. This was not helped when he rarely bowled legitimately in the nets and it is worth re-emphasising that two of his best starts to an English season were to follow two overseas winter tours.

Cottam made his debut at the beginning of June against Kent at Southampton at the age of eighteen. Born in Lincolnshire he went to school in Berkshire and, after Arthur Holt became aware of his promise, was offered a trial with Hampshire. Honoured, but not overawed, Cottam shared the new ball with someone twenty years his senior. His first victim was Stuart Leary and Cottam remembers Shackleton coming up to him, shaking his hand and saying "Well done, young 'un, just 999 to go" . This stuck in Cottam's mind and he set himself a very determined target of 1000 wickets. He ultimately achieved this although not all of them were for Hampshire.

Cottam made an even bigger impression in the next game against Middlesex at Lord's. He and Shackleton bowled unchanged in the first innings, something rarely achieved by an eighteen year old; probably even more unusually by two men of such a wide age difference. Shack bowled unchanged again in the second innings and only a few overs from Gray interrupted Cottam's spell. Cottam finished with match figures of 9-144, Shackleton with 10-76. The man with fifteen years experience behind him had yet another opening partner.

Throughout the 1960s Hampshire generally fielded a three pronged seam attack but, although White and Cottam were appreciably quicker, it was, as always, the senior bowler who took the first over. Once again there was never any animosity about this and indeed it seemed sensible and logical for the country's most accurate bowler to immediately make the opening batsmen play at every delivery. Truly fast bowlers, even the best, will often bowl an early loose delivery which might give the batsman confidence, perhaps an early boundary or two. With Derek there was no such luxury. Right from the very first ball the batsmen knew they dare not miss because they would be making a very quick return to the pavilion. Not only did they immediately have to acclimatise to the light and to the pace of the wicket they had to cope with both the movement through the air and off the seam without the benefit of an occasional 'free look'. Derek was pitching on the spot straight away; he did not need a few balls to loosen up, no deliveries would sail harmlessly way outside off stump. The batsmen had to concentrate totally and would need all their powers in keeping their minds focused on surviving, certainly at the start of their innings; they could think about scoring later.

Cottam, like Heath and White before him, soon learned to keep the ball in perfect condition. In his first game against Kent Derek had stressed to him the importance of hitting the seam. Cottam was pleased, therefore, that in his next match, even though he bowled two long spells, the marks on the 'round' of the ball had been reduced. He never received any formal coaching from Derek but there were often quiet words of advice and his example alone was invaluable experience.

Up to the middle of June Hampshire had had a mixed bag of results with four wins, three draws and four defeats. By the end of the game at the Oval against Surrey Derek had taken 58 wickets at 15.81 and, once again, was well up in the national averages. Suddenly, and totally unexpectedly, he was pitched into a taut and intriguing test series which captured the public imagination that year.

The West Indies were making their sixth visit to England and, when they arrived in April, there was already tremendous anticipation, mainly due to their reputation following the tour to Australia two years earlier resulting in one of the genuinely great test series which included the famous tied game at Brisbane.

Frank Worrell, born in the same month as Derek, was an even more respected figure than on his two previous visits to England and now had the immense good fortune to lead a beautifully balanced side. The hugely successful team of 1950 had its strengths in the awesome batting of the 'Three Ws' and Rae and Stollmeyer together with the unique and, at the time, surprising spin talent of Ramadhin and Valentine who took 59 wickets between them. No real pacemen then. The 1957 visit was a great disappointment, due to the general failure of the batting, the mastery by the English batsmen over Ramadhin and, again, the absence of a quality pace attack. Gilchrist was quick but erratic and his 10 wickets in the series were expensive. It was also a year when England had a very powerful all round side with few, if any, weaknesses.

The 1963 tourists were strong in every department and, significantly, possessed two fast bowlers of undoubted quality and hostility, the forerunners of a continuous supply of unrelenting pace attacks which were to dominate West Indian cricket over the next three decades.

Apart from a defeat by Yorkshire the West Indians went into the first test with a fine set of results behind them. They outplayed England at Old Trafford to win comfortably by ten wickets with all the England bowlers suffering, none more so than Statham who, uncharacteristically, was wicketless and expensive on his home ground.

When the selectors met during the weekend of 15th June they came to a decision which not only took the public by surprise but greatly astonished the individual concerned. Derek Shackleton, just two months short of his 39th birthday and who had not played in a test match for over eleven years, was picked for the second test at Lord's.

This raises two valid questions which deserve enlarging upon. First of all, why was he now selected at this late juncture, and secondly, if he was considered good enough now, why had he played so few times for England in the past ?

Regarding the first question it must be said straight away that Statham, who had been dropped, must have considered himself to be extremely unlucky as he and Trueman were still the finest pace bowlers in the country. The wicket at Old Trafford had been a batsman's paradise and to leave Statham out for Lord's, where seamers usually thrived, appeared to be a panic measure. It was perfectly logical to bring in another quality seamer but surely to the exclusion of one of the two off spinners, either Titmus or Allen ? There had been, for years, a widely held contention among many test players, notably Colin Cowdrey, that Shackleton, or a similar bowler, should have been regularly picked for tests at Lord's.

The apparent theory behind the selection was that he would keep one end quiet whilst the main assault would come from Trueman who was probably, at that time, bowling better than he had ever done. Ted Dexter, the England captain, must have had significant influence in the selection because, over the years, he had faced Derek frequently and had been 'won over'. Also, earlier in the month, Derek had taken ten wickets at Lord's against Middlesex conceding only 76 runs from 60 overs. It was this economy which was the deciding factor in his selection. There was a general consensus of opinion that the natural stroke play of the West Indian batsmen was more likely to be curbed with Shackleton's relentless accuracy and that risks might be taken against Trueman. However surprised he may have been Derek was delighted that he had been picked and, this time, was more than ever determined to keep his place.

Why had he played in only three tests before ? Many of his Hampshire colleagues and other eminent test players have their own particular theories.

One of the most powerful reasons is that during the 1950s England, arguably, had their most potent bowling force ever. Who can think of a more dangerous or better balanced attack than Trueman, Statham, Bailey, Laker and Lock ? Think of all the others during this period - Tyson, Bedser, Loader, Wardle, Appleyard etc - and the strength of bowling available to the selectors was obvious. The problem for Derek can stem back to the very early post war days when all the test sides were having to rebuild.

In 1946 England were fortunate that their pre war batting line up remained relatively intact and, although Hammond would soon retire, the first four batting places were taken by Hutton, Washbrook, Edrich and Compton. No problems there. The bowling, however, was a different matter. In the final pre war season of 1939 England had used three seamers - Copson, Bowes and Perks - with spin bowling provided by Verity, Goddard and Wright. Tragically, Verity was killed during the war but, of the remainder, only Wright may have felt that he had a few years of test cricket left. After the war ended all three seamers were over 35 and Goddard was 45 and, understandably, the England selectors were desperate to unearth fresh bowling talent.

The gem that fell into their laps in 1946 was a truly lion-hearted bowler who was to give his all for his country over the following eight years. Alec Bedser was a well built man of over six feet who developed into one of the greatest of all fast medium bowlers and who was likened by many to Maurice Tate. Born, with his twin brother Eric, in Reading in 1918 (the Berkshire town can, justifiably, be proud of its contribution to the fine Surrey side of the 1950s as it was also the birthplace of May and Barrington) he was picked for all three tests against India in 1946. Such was his dominance that his 24 wickets in the series exceeded, by one, the total number of wickets taken by the twelve other bowlers used. When Derek was asked why he felt he did not have many more opportunities early in his career he immediately conceded that "Alec was well established in the England side when I started and then England turned to genuine pace". If he had been around in 1946 he would certainly have been a more appropriate choice than any of the other bowlers used, Bedser excepted.

When Hutton became captain it was soon apparent that he wanted a pace attack that could equal that of Australia. He, more than anyone, had borne the brunt of the Lindwall/Miller onslaught and desperately wanted to get his own back. How sweet it must have been for him therefore when, in 1954/1955 the Ashes were retained due, in no small part, to the ferocious pace of Tyson backed up so superbly by Statham who was only slightly less quick.

Possibly just as much an obstacle to Derek and an England place was Trevor Bailey. Bailey was a genuine test class all rounder who could legitimately hold down the number six batting position and was also a fine fast medium bowler who took over 2000 wickets in a long career. Whilst not quite such a destroyer of batsmen as Shackleton he was, importantly, a better batsman and fielder. Bailey would supply the seam option for an England captain after the initial work done by the pacemen. Indeed, on occasions, he opened the bowling for England and did so, with spectacular success, at Sabina Park, Jamaica in 1953/1954 when he took 7-34.

Another pertinent theory is that Derek did not play for a more fashionable county. If, for example, he had played for Middlesex he would constantly have been in the selectors' minds simply by playing at Lord's and because of the extra media coverage given to those counties bordering London. With almost all of Middlesex's home matches played at Lord's, where he loved bowling and on a pitch that favoured seam bowling, his final tally of wickets, assuming he continued playing as long as he did with Hampshire, would probably have been well in excess of 3000, taking him into the top three or four of all wicket takers. It would have been impossible for the selectors to have ignored this.

Basically he was the right man at the wrong time but, even so, there were times when he should have been picked, certainly at Lord's. His former colleagues agree with this and are of the firm belief that he would not have let his country down in any way.

Both Charles Knott and Jimmy Gray, who should know a thing or two about cricket at most levels with their long association with Hampshire, have both stressed the problems some players have of bridging the vast gaps which exist between the various stages of their careers. From school/youth cricket to club cricket; then possibly to a county second X1 and finally to the county first team. Each separate jump is substantial and many promising players don't make it. For a few others there is another climb up the ladder to a test place which is probably the most difficult to achieve, certainly to stay at the top. In addition to the required high standard of skill necessary, temperament and the ability to withstand tremendous pressure come into being. Derek already had a renowned reputation for regularly causing problems to batsmen who were quite used to test cricket. There was absolutely no reason to suggest this success rate would not continue if he had been given an extended run for England, notwithstanding the wickets would generally be better. There is also no doubt he had the necessary temperament.

Belated though it may have been Derek was going to enjoy the test match and it was to turn out to be one of the most memorable ever played in England.

He remembers being slightly nervous on the first morning especially as England would be fielding first and, to add to the tension, there had been a twenty five minute delay because of rain. He wanted to start bowling as soon as possible and prayed that Trueman would choose to bowl from the Pavilion end. Derek always preferred to bowl from the Nursery end. Trueman duly obliged and there was a dramatic start with Conrad Hunte hitting the Yorkshireman for four on each of his first three deliveries. Shackleton wondered what he might be in for but settled into his groove straight away and runs simply dried up. Twelve runs from the first three balls and then only 35 in just over an hour and a half in the pre-lunch period, during which Derek bowled unchanged. He continually troubled Hunte who gave two chances off him, frequently edged him and was totally ill at ease. Dexter later recalled:

> "Derek played a key role in the great drawn test at Lord's in 1963. How he failed to take wickets on the first morning remains a mystery. He beat the bat consistently and the ball was in the air time and time again - but never quite to hand".

Trueman later claimed the scalp of Hunte which, by right, should have been Shackleton's and he had to be content with the last three wickets taken in four deliveries. Footage of him in action is very rare although there is a short sequence taken on video from the Lord's test. He was then bowling off a run up of just eight steps and was little more than medium pace but the beautifully controlled action is so clear. The right arm in the delivery stride was still as high as it had ever been with the wrist cocked at right angles and the head so still. Each of the four balls shown pitched on, or a fraction outside, off stump only to cut back sharply into the right handed batsmen. His first victim was Solomon who was plumb lbw, then he had Griffith brilliantly caught by Cowdrey. The next ball, which would have brought him his first hat trick, completely beat Gibbs, again pitching on off and being taken by Parks down the leg side. However, with the next delivery Gibbs was well caught by Stewart at short leg.

A little hitch of the flannels, the sweater placed casually but neatly over his shoulder he walked off the ground a happy man - and not a hair out of place! He had taken 3-93 off 50.2 overs but had deserved so much more. In the second innings his analysis was 34-14-72-4 and his wickets included those of Hunte (justice done), Kanhai and Butcher.

And so to the climax of this remarkable match. England were set a target of 234 to win and were in real trouble on the fourth day when they lost the wickets of Stewart, John Edrich and Dexter for 31. Although they progressed to 116 for three before rained intervened for the day England had effectively lost Cowdrey who had had his arm broken by Wes Hall.

Play did not recommence until 2.20 the next afternoon and Barrington was soon out for 60. Brian Close was playing one of his finest innings for England and, after a considerable amount of resolute defending, decided to attack. This worked for a while but he then perished for 70 bringing Derek to the wicket to join David Allen. At this stage 15 runs were required with nineteen minutes left and, after a few nervous singles, 8 were still needed when the final over began - from a rampant Wes Hall. He had been bowling unchanged since the delayed start, well over three hours, and had shown he had a remarkable stamina to go with his proven skill; there have been few finer fast bowlers. He was still bowling very fast and, on a murky evening, would not have been a comfortable proposition for the best of batsmen. For someone like Derek who, at this time of his career, was now a tail-ender rather than a late middle order batsman, who did not have the security of a protective helmet and only one good eye the situation he now found himself in must have been quite terrifying. When, in later years, this was mentioned to his Hampshire colleague, Peter Sainsbury, he said with a little wry smile "It wouldn't have been a lot of fun!" Quite an understatement.

Singles were taken off the second and third balls and all four results were possible. This, in effect, was the last partnership as Cowdrey was not expected to bat. The fourth delivery beat Derek outside off stump going straight through to the wicket keeper, Deryck Murray. Allen called for a somewhat optimistic single, although in truth if Derek had heard the call immediately there probably was one run. However, there was a fraction of a delay in setting off and Murray chose to throw the ball to Worrell fielding at short leg. It then developed into a race between two elderly gentlemen, both of whom were approaching their 39th birthday, as to who would reach the non striker's end first - Worrell had decided to carry the ball rather than risk possible overthrows. Worrell won by a whisker. Famously, Cowdrey came out to bat with his left arm in plaster but did not have to face the bowling and the match was drawn. Shortly after the test Derek met George Duckworth who had been watching from a side on position and felt that he had made the crease before Worrell. However, the video evidence would prove the umpire right although it was close.

The 1963 Lord's test is one of the most memorable and exciting matches ever staged and Shack had played his full part. He had bowled 84 economical overs, had taken 7 wickets and had successfully carried out what he had been required to do - he had given Trueman invaluable support. He, also, did not have his fair share of luck. With this belated recall to the England side he knew that, at his age, it was obvious he would not have a long test career ahead of him. He, therefore, wanted to make the most of 1963 and would have been peeved to say the least if, this time, he did not hold his place. He need not have worried; the selectors meeting during the following weekend picked him for the third test at Edgbaston.

In the meantime Hampshire had only very narrowly failed to beat the tourists at Southampton with Shackleton taking another six wickets. Alan Wassell had a particularly good match with figures of 8-71 and in scoring 40 in Hampshire's first innings.

Derek has always been a quiet, somewhat reserved man and, whilst his chosen career meant spending a lot of time in big cities, he was more comfortable in less crowded, less potentially hostile surroundings. He, Kathy and their two children were still living in Totton, situated a few miles to the west of Southampton and, which at the time, was little more than a large village. The close proximity to Southampton made it almost a suburb but it was, nevertheless, sufficient distance away from the hurly-burly of a large city. When they lived for a few years in Southampton itself it was generally in a pleasant area very close to the county ground - indeed later on they would spend a short period in a flat overlooking the ground - and it was relatively tranquil. He was not a 'man of the world' in the widely accepted sense and would have found the lifestyle of say London, Birmingham or Manchester daunting. He was also much more at ease staying in a local pub or guest house rather than in a large impersonal hotel.

During the Lord's test Kathy had joined Derek at one stage and an incident occurred which obviously concerned him. They were sharing a taxi with Derek's cousin when a woman asked if she, too, could join them as she was going their way. It quickly became apparent that she was, in fact, a prostitute and promptly propositioned Derek. He, totally taken aback, told her "You obviously don't realise who this lady is sitting next to me. It's my wife". Quite unabashed and undeterred the 'lady of the night' as Derek described her turned to the cousin to see if she could be more successful with him. She wasn't.

This type of situation would not be uncommon in a city such as London but Derek was a little bit of the 'innocent abroad' and this would remain firmly fixed in his mind. Handsome sportsmen, among others, are often the target of the opposite sex and cricketers are by no means exempt, especially with being away from home so frequently. Derek had, and has, old fashioned values and all his colleagues agree he would have been the very last person to be led astray. He would have been appalled at all the likely complications which would be brought to his life. This would not have fitted in with his highly orderly life style which transposed itself on to the cricket field. But most importantly he had a very stable and happy marriage which he would not have wanted to jeopardise.

It was during the third test at Edgbaston that Derek learned he was a Yorkshireman! A reporter from the Sunday People said to him on the Saturday evening, "Buy the paper tomorrow, you will find something interesting". The headline read, above an article by Fred Trueman, "Shack, you are one of us". A little research had proved that Todmorden, both geographically and for administration purposes, was definitely in Yorkshire, although the official county boundary had, for so long, run through the middle of the town. The people of Todmorden were probably a little upset that there was a certain ignorance among the country at large as to their true identity but it has never been a big issue with Derek as to whether he is a Lancastrian or a Yorkshireman. He was perfectly happy to be known as being from Todmorden.

An early nickname of 'Top end Tod' was given to him following his two tours to India in the 1950s. Malcolm Heath remembers hearing this from someone who went on one of these tours. It appeared that whenever he was asked which end he would prefer to bowl from the answer was always the 'top end' whatever the conditions.

Derek, throughout his career, never bothered unduly as to which end he would take - the Nursery end preference at Lord's being one of the few exceptions. In any case, as Desmond Eagar once remarked ruefully, "If Shack picked his end, it would invariably prove to be the wrong one for him".

Another little quirk of Derek's stemmed from those two overseas tours. Each time he rejoined his Hampshire team mates he was asked what the weather was like. The reply was always "100 degrees in the shade". Nothing added, nothing embroidered. A simple statement that it was hot, not 90 degrees nor 110, always 100. According to Derek that was sufficient to give a clear picture of the prevailing weather conditions.

England won the third test comfortably with Trueman again the main destroyer but he was given very able support by Shackleton whose three wickets were those of Kanhai, Carew and Sobers. With England levelling the series interest mounted for the final two tests.

Because of his test appearances that summer Derek missed more matches for Hampshire than in any other year. Between the third and fourth tests he would miss yet another when he was picked for the Rest of England in a curious fixture against a team selected from the previous winter's MCC tour to Australia. There seemed to be little logic to the game but it was another representative honour and another welcome fee. He took seven wickets in the match and, in a deadly spell in the first innings, dismissed Barrington, Dexter and Parfitt for no runs.

There was another oddity that year when the MCC decided to stage a one day experimental match at Lord's under a previous lbw law and the wicket was widened with the addition of a fourth stump. In order for an lbw decision to go in the bowler's favour the ball had to pitch between two parallel lines drawn along the twenty two yards, the width of the first and fourth stumps, and then satisfy the umpire it would have hit the stumps. There is a unique photograph in the 1964 Wisden showing Shackleton bowling to Trevor Bailey. Who better than Shack to keep the ball pitching within this narrow band - he could have done this all day. The photo also shows the famous, and classic, Bailey forward defensive pose.

The West Indies won the fourth test at Headingley by a wide margin, the result never in doubt once Kanhai and Sobers had taken them from 71 for three to 214 for four in the first innings. The England bowling formula was largely as before with Trueman providing the main thrust ably backed up by Shackleton but all to no avail as the batting let them down woefully. Derek's four wickets were all batsmen in the top order.

There was then a gap of three and a half weeks between the end of the fourth test and the start of the fifth at the Oval. Hampshire welcomed back their opening bowler with open arms because they had experienced a disappointing set of results in his absence. He was now available for six county championship matches but, in fact, Hampshire's fortunes did not change dramatically. Without him, though, they would probably have been beaten by Kent and Surrey, both games being drawn, and he played a major part in the defeat of Leicestershire in a low scoring affair at Portsmouth.

On a rain affected pitch Leicestershire were all out for 66, no player reaching double figures, and, bowling unchanged, Derek took 7-31. This was a typical example of so many occasions when the wicket was green that Ingleby-Mackenzie would toss him the ball and just let him get on with the destruction. It made captaincy very easy. In the second innings Leicestershire fared little better - all out for 86 with Derek taking 3-25, again bowling without a break. There was also another highly impressive return from Cottam who took 6-10 in the second innings. Only eighteen years old he was already more than highly promising; he was giving thoroughly mature performances and probably only when Alec Kennedy made his debut way back in 1907 at the age of sixteen has a Hampshire bowler made such an impact for one so young.

Cottam vividly remembers how Derek could prise batsmen out almost on reputation alone and there was no better example of this than in the match against Leicestershire.

Dickie Bird, later to become the most famous umpire of them all, was, at the time, opening the batting for Leicestershire. In the first innings he had departed early for 3 and saw his side destroyed in very little time by the master of seam on his favourite Portsmouth wicket. When it was his turn to bat for a second time he was, according to

Cottam, a nervous wreck and, so agitated, he could hardly put his pads on. He just knew that Shack was waiting for him and that there was really nothing he could do about it no matter how hard he tried. He faced Derek and played and missed at several balls which, almost literally, shaved his stumps before being caught for 0. Bird, who achieved so much deserved fame and reputation later in life was, truthfully at best, no more than a useful batsman but probably one who could have been more prolific if he could have relaxed a little. Facing Derek that day would have done little for his confidence. Many years later, after he became an umpire, he was quoted as saying :

> "When I step across that boundary rope, I'm a different man. It's the only time I feel in total control".

This did not often apply when he was a player.

Derek was once again picked for England at the Oval but the selectors had recalled Statham and this meant he would be first change although he actually opened the bowling in the second innings with Statham due to an injury to Trueman. It was a finely poised game for the first three days but, on the fourth, the West Indies coasted to victory by eight wickets. England had greatly missed Trueman's bowling in that final innings. Whether or not he would have made such a difference as to turn the game in England's favour is conjecture but he had been their outstanding bowler that summer and figures of 34 wickets at 17.47 speak for themselves. He should, though, acknowledge the support he was given at the other end by Shackleton who, primarily, had been used as a stock, rather than as a strike, bowler. The West Indies, more than most test sides, do not like being tied down and they were frequently frustrated at scoring at a rate of only just over two runs per over against him. This hindrance to their natural attacking flair almost certainly helped Trueman.

Derek's haul of fifteen wickets in four tests against the best side in the world was highly commendable and proved that he could have been a very effective bowler for England when he was younger as he would have had that extra little nip. He had played an important part in a memorable test series and, once again, had enjoyed the big match atmosphere. Playing consistently in front of large crowds was something he had not been used to since his two tours of India. However, as it would turn out, this was to be his test swan-song and 1963 was the last year that he would play first class cricket for any side except Hampshire. The only significant change which affected him over his last few playing years was the introduction of the one day competitions which would revolutionise the game.

Chapter Thirteen

Another Onslaught from Fred

When Derek set out on his career he had to pit his skills against many fine experienced batsmen who had been playing pre war. Now, in the mid 1960s, he was bowling to a much younger generation, some of whom would continue well into the 1980s. His elegant bowling skills would tease the likes of Boycott, Amiss, Barber, Milburn, Radley and many others and the contests would often end in the bowler's favour.

Between 1964 and 1968, his last full season (he made one championship appearance in 1969) his high standards never deteriorated and, even in those late days, he was meanner than he had ever been. In his last four seasons his economy rate was permanently below 2 runs per over and, to most of the newer generation of batsmen, his feared reputation had to be treated with the utmost respect. He was, though, beginning to bowl slightly fewer overs each year but always exceeded 1,000 ! This wasn't due to a lack of stamina - he seemed inexhaustible - nor, necessarily, to the ever advancing years, but mainly because White and Cottam made it very much a three pronged seam attack. Gone were the days when Shackleton was simply THE seam attack or, at best, one of two.

The championship side of 1961 was already beginning to break up and this steady rate of disintegration would obviously continue as the decade progressed. Of the fourteen players used regularly during the 1961 triumph Baldry, Burden and Heath had already gone and so too had Harrison, although he would make one appearance in 1966. Ingleby-Mackenzie, Barnard, Gray, Horton and Wassell made their final appearances between 1965 and 1967 with Shackleton, White, Marshall and Livingstone following shortly afterwards. Only Peter Sainsbury would remain for a few more seasons and he is the only Hampshire player to have been a member of both championship teams, the second title coming in 1973.

Early retirement was not really an option for Derek as cricket was his life and basically still his sole source of income. He just continued bowling but, one day, he would have to stop and that somewhat uncertain time was fast approaching. Not surprisingly, due to the transition taking place, Hampshire's performances between 1964 and 1967 were very average and, in this four year period, they finished either eleventh or twelfth. Largely because of the brilliance of Barry Richards they advanced to fifth in 1968.

There was, by now, another bowler who was receiving plaudits as a very similar type of bowler, one, who like Derek, had entered the game as a batsman who could bowl a bit. Tom Cartwright was eleven years younger but made his debut for Warwickshire in 1952 at the age of 17. Showing a maturity well beyond his years he scored 82 and 22 not out in his first match but did not bowl on that occasion. In fact he didn't bowl regularly until 1959 when he took 80 wickets but then took a backward step the following year with 25 (expensive) wickets. He returned to form the next season and throughout the 1960s was the mainstay of the Warwickshire attack in the same way that Derek was with Hampshire. He was equally successful with Somerset for a few years when he went there in 1970.

Cartwright's playing career spanned more years than did his southern counterpart but, overall, played in fewer matches. This was because he only appeared spasmodically for Warwickshire in the early years and in only a handful of games for Somerset after 1974. He also suffered from a few injuries and these absences meant that his final wickets tally of 1536 is well below Shackleton's 2857. Their career averages, however, were very similar and, in the 1960s, there was little to choose between them.

Bryan Timms, later in his career, joined Warwickshire on a part time basis deputising as wicket keeper when A C Smith was called upon for test selection duties. For a brief period he kept wicket to Cartwright and so had the unique experience of having seen both these masters of their art from the best possible vantage point, apart from that of the unfortunate batsmen! Timms believes there was very little difference in their accuracy and they were also of very similar pace, although Cartwright had more 'oomph' in the delivery and wanted the ball to explode into the keeper's gloves. Derek was smoothness itself relying on rhythm and wrist action with the ball nipping through. If, as some have suggested, Cartwright was a little quicker it should be remembered that there was an eleven year difference in age. Shack, in his last few seasons, was on the slow side of medium.

Like Shackleton, Cartwright was also unlucky that he did not play for England more often than he did - just five matches in all. He was first picked in 1964 for the fourth test against Australia at Old Trafford and, in a tedious high scoring draw, he bowled 77 overs in the first innings and then, in the fifth test at the Oval, bowled 62 overs in the only innings. These very long spells would have taken tremendous powers of concentration and, in the two tests, he bowled 139 overs and conceded only 228 runs.

A very thoughtful and knowledgeable cricketer, Cartwright had an in built awareness of the strengths and weaknesses of batsmen which he used to his advantage. He would think them out. He had a carefully worked out planned series of deliveries often tantalising enough to lull a batsman into a false sense of security and then would come the sucker punch. He, like Derek, could dictate terms ; they would pitch the ball exactly where THEY wanted it. Hardly any delivery could be left alone and, with the uncertainty of the swing and movement off the seam, batting, especially on green wickets, would be a nightmare even for the very finest players.

Mike Smith, the former Warwickshire and England captain, suggests that, in his long experience, these two bowlers hit the seam more consistently than any others. "Neither tried any variation of length other than put it on the spot - a 'stick or twist' length, and were supreme in their styles".

Cartwright's early mentor at Warwickshire was the leg spinner, Eric Hollies, but admits that the bench mark for all aspiring seam bowlers was Derek Shackleton. When they frequently met in the 1960s Cartwright feels he was, perhaps, slightly quicker but that Derek, in his early days, would have been of a very similar pace. If there was a significant difference between the two Cartwright says that he bowled a slightly fuller length relying on swing whereas Derek would opt for movement off the seam. He confirms that due to the extreme accuracy and perfect length they could often dispense with a third man or deep fine leg. This meant there would be more fielders in the close catching positions which made life even more difficult for the batsman.

These two men are equally adamant that their style of bowling should not be described, or even dismissed, as purely defensive. Why should bowlers be penalised for bowling straight and on a perfect length ? There were certainly a lot of pale imitators but the best batsmen would generally find them out. This must not distract from the abilities of the best of their kind and they really did not come better than Cartwright and Shackleton. A medium pace seam bowler is an integral part of a well balanced attack. In any case both ended their careers with fine strike rates.

After the Oval test of 1963 there would be no more representative honours and as, a year later, he would be celebrating his 40th birthday he did have to take the prospect of retiring from the game very seriously. There was no immediate panic as he was still extremely fit and remained the king-pin of the Hampshire attack but, because his income was still only modest, the prospect of a second benefit within the next three or four years was, not only a mouth watering one, but vital as it would give him some capital to live on during what would be an uncertain period after he ended his playing days. It was because of the carrot of a second benefit that he turned down an opportunity to coach in New Zealand.

New Zealand were looking for a new national coach and word had filtered through to Colin Cowdrey. After a game against Kent at Southampton Cowdrey, over a quiet drink with Derek, asked if he would be interested coaching abroad. After some considerable deliberation and soul searching he reluctantly turned down the offer, something he has occasionally regretted. The main reason for his decision was the imminence of the second benefit. The New Zealand job was then given to Martin Horton of Worcestershire.

The significance of the second benefit cannot be over emphasised. Derek's loyalty and sheer consistency of performance could really give the county no choice and he had to ensure, as far as was possible, some sort of financial stability in later life. His income was still being supplemented by continuing to run the indoor nets at the county ground, something he enjoyed which is, perhaps, surprising in view of his reluctance to take his own net practice seriously.

As well as coaching youngsters Derek would also give tuition to older pupils and he particularly recalls a group of businessmen from the Portsmouth/Havant area, men then in their fifties. After the end of a session on a very cold winter's night Derek remembers going to his car to pack away his gear at the same time that a wealthy businessman (he believes he was a millionaire which, if true, would have been a great rarity in those pre lottery days) was putting his kit away in a Rolls Royce. Harold Butler, not to be confused with the former Nottinghamshire fast bowler, asked Derek to come and have a drink in the bar and took off an expensive sheepskin coat. Derek jokingly tried on the coat, liked the look and feel of it, and Butler said he looked really good in it. "Leave your coat, Harold!" said Derek. The reply was "I'll tell you what, Shack, if you take 100 wickets again this coming summer the coat's yours". "Well, you can wrap it up now" Derek replied.

He actually made a slow start to that particular season and, at one time, was getting a bit worried. However, the wickets soon started flowing again and he remembers that, in late July or early August, a game started at Portsmouth when he was on 96 wickets. Fielding, as he often did, at third man he saw his likely benefactor sitting near the boundary with the coat on his lap. The vision of wearing it on a winter's day was added inspiration and he was anxious to 'clinch the deal'. The required four wickets were quickly taken and, at the end of the day's play, the coat was presented to him. He still has it to this day.

Although he missed out coaching in New Zealand Derek did spend one winter abroad. He enjoyed a few months during 1966/1967 with Germiston, a Transvaal league side, coaching as well as playing and he also coached at two schools - Dawnview and Germiston High schools. As an added bonus Kathy and Caroline (Julian stayed home at boarding school) were able to go with him and, after the manager of the Germiston sports club was sacked, Kathy successfully took over the reins for a few months. A happy experience which they were quite reluctant to leave. During their visit they met up once again with Neil McCorkell who had been coaching and living there for a number of years.

His form for Hampshire during those final seasons never wavered and, in his fortieth year (1964), bowled nearly 500 more overs than any of his county colleagues and almost 300 more than anyone else in the country - Cartwright 'languishing' a mere 282 overs behind! On his actual birthday Derek took 5-35 in 28 overs against Yorkshire. John Hampshire, an attacking player by nature, scored 110 but most of his runs were obtained off White and Cottam who conceded 138 between them in 34 overs. He treated Shackleton with the utmost respect, perfectly happy to bide his time and to score from the bowling at the other end.

One of the most extraordinary matches in which Hampshire have ever been involved took place early in 1965 and it held mixed fortunes for Derek. It was a game also vividly recalled by Geoffrey Boycott. Again the opposition was Yorkshire, this time at Middlesbrough.

The wicket was described as lively but not, according to Boycott, dangerous. Yorkshire, batting first, were at one time 47 for seven with Shackleton having taken four wickets and Cottam three. Enter a bristling Trueman and, after receiving a few deliveries with which he made no contact whatsoever, he enquired of the bowler, "Shack, what the bloody 'ell's going on. Are there snakes in the wicket or what ?" He then decided, as he had successfully done in the past, to launch an assault on Shackleton to bring some respectability to the Yorkshire innings. He hit him for 26 in one over, probably the highest number of runs he ever conceded in six deliveries. Trueman then hit Cottam for a straight six and his final tally was 55 from just twenty two balls. It was the ideal innings in the circumstances finally ending when he skied a ball from Shackleton and was caught by Marshall at cover. Hampshire, in reply, were little better and led on first innings by four.

As a young man Boycott was very aware of Shackleton's reputation and he had been bowled by him for a duck in the first innings. At the start of the second innings he was genuinely concerned he would bag a pair and, at the last minute, decided to take guard a yard out of his crease. The good length ball immediately became a half volley which Boycott stroked for four. He then took an easy single only to be dismissed lbw by White. White was rampant and he, together with Shackleton, reduced Yorkshire to 12 for seven when Trueman reappeared. Ingleby-Mackenzie immediately took Shackleton off and replaced him with Cottam who trapped Trueman lbw almost straight away. Yorkshire, incredibly, were all out for 23, their lowest ever total and the lowest score made against Hampshire. These records still remain.

The match was over before lunch on the second morning - just four sessions of play. Derek remembers leaving the ground after lunch with many Yorkshire supporters arriving not believing the game had ended. Apart from the lively wicket there was another reason for the debacle. Yorkshire had chosen to use a ball with a more pronounced seam, one intended to help Trueman and Tony Nicholson. This plan backfired because, as Boycott observed, Hampshire's own seam attack "wasn't the worst in the world!".

Boycott only faced a few deliveries from Shackleton in this match but, two years later, he batted for several hours treating him with the utmost respect during a patient innings of 90 out of a total of 179. He, like so many others, confirms the great similarities between Shackleton and Cartwright and remembers the latter bowling at Trent Bridge against the 1965 South Africans. Cartwright had them in deep trouble and it took a touch of pure genius to retrieve the situation. Coming in at 16 for two, both the wickets being victims of Cartwright, and then witnessing a further deterioration to 43 for four, Graeme Pollock hit 125 out of 160 whilst he was at the crease and it took him only two hours twenty minutes. Pollock did not face Shackleton in tests but, in the same year, produced another outstanding innings against Hampshire at Southampton.

In the first innings Shackleton dismissed Pollock for 0 and the tourists were all out for 133 with Shack taking 6-29 off 17 overs. Round one to the veteran. It was a different matter second time around. Eddie Barlow hit a fine century but it was the sheer magical brilliance of the left handed Pollock that everyone remembers that day. He scored 94 effortless runs in sixty six minutes with 3 sixes and 15 fours and, going for the six which would have given him the fastest century of the season - by a considerable margin - he was caught on the boundary by Shackleton. It was a 'flat' hit rather than an attempt at a towering six and, such was the force, the 'missile' nearly drilled a hole in Derek's midriff.

Pollock was clearly one of the game's most elegant and devastating batsmen and, but for the exclusion of his country from the

International arena, would certainly have broken or set a huge number of records. The same situation would apply, later, to Barry Richards.

Although Derek had won the Brylcreem award for the best bowling performance of 1960 he had missed out narrowly on other occasions most notably with his 8-4 in 1955. He felt particularly miffed in 1965 because there were awards that year for the best performances against the tourists but excluding those in test matches. His 6-29 was the best bowling performance in matches between the counties and the South Africans but, after being invited to a London hotel with several other players, the prizes went to those involved in the tests. Whether or not there had been a misunderstanding in the first place is not clear but why invite a player to such an award ceremony if he wasn't to be rewarded ? This left a slightly sour taste and the whole affair understandably confused and annoyed Derek.

Geoffrey Boycott believes that bowlers such as Shackleton and Cartwright taught great techniques for batsmen and that concentration and great thinking were essential requisites in the battle to combat them with a reasonable hope of success. Boycott, of course, had these attributes in abundance and he believes that, even on covered wickets, a bowler like Shackleton would still be very successful because many batsmen of a later generation would not have the necessary patience to battle it out. They would probably try and attack him straight away to try and seize the initiative but "this just wasn't the way to deal with him."

Dennis Amiss, who partnered Boycott frequently for England in the 1970s, holds a similar view. He confirms that the sheer nagging accuracy of the man caused him considerable problems and that it was very difficult to 'get at him'. "He had the knack of swinging it away, with the odd ball nipping back off the seam for lbw's when you got across too much to play the outswinger" recalls Amiss. He concedes that uncovered wickets obviously helped Shackleton's style of bowling but remembers facing him on a flat wicket at Portsmouth and "he was still difficult to force away".

Amiss mentioned an occasion when his Warwickshire colleague Bob Barber set out to take Derek apart. Barber, after a not too happy time with Lancashire, developed into an attacking left handed opening batsman of the highest quality. His style did not really alter whether he was playing test, county or one day cricket. Like Dexter he could not understand the success achieved so relentlessly and consistently by Shackleton although he would surely have had an insight because of the similarities with Warwickshire's own 'mean machine', Tom Cartwright.

However, in one match, Barber decided he would hit Shack's first ball for six . He was singularly unsuccessful and was quickly bowled for eight . Henry Horton also remembers another instance, possibly in 1964. Someone from the Press suggested that Barber would not be able to hit Shackleton back over his head. After several miscued attempts he finally skied the ball and Derek took a comfortable caught and bowled. Was the pressman from Hampshire and was this a devious ploy ? This was yet another example of a class batsman coming off second best. It appeared that, unless you were prepared to slog like Trueman or were a batsman of exceptional quality like May and Pollock, you needed all the patient skills to have any chance.

Colin Milburn, another fine aggressive batsman from that decade had a miserable record against Derek being dismissed six times by him in their first eleven encounters with a top score of only 47. There was an improvement in the last three innings they were in opposition with Milburn scoring 51, 74 and 24 and he avoided being snared by the Hampshire seamer. But they were far more cautious innings; he had learned that a certain amount of restraint was required. "Ollie's" style of aggressive attacking batsmanship brightened up a somewhat negative period but England's (and, of course, Northamptonshire's) loss was huge after his serious car accident in 1969 which resulted in blindness in his left eye and, being a right handed batsman, his 'master' eye. He was never to be the same free scoring, joyous batsman again.

It is a poignant moment to reflect on Derek's similar disability which, perhaps, is the most staggering aspect of the Shackleton story. Basically from early childhood he had experienced problems with the sight in his left eye and, remarkably, during his whole cricket career he had, quite secretively from his colleagues, played largely blind in one eye - he could just pick out light and dark shades. As someone remarked in later years, when the secret was out, "How successful would he have been with two good eyes ?!"

The problem was, in fact, discovered at a very early age and, following an eye test at school, Derek was given a letter addressed to his parents advising them of the prognosis. Derek, fearing he would have to wear glasses, didn't show the letter to his mother or father and no action was taken and the condition, therefore, deteriorated. Obviously when he joined the army in 1943 something was spotted because he was assigned to the Pioneer Corps, a non combative unit. Even Kathy was not originally aware and it was only after a bit of 'mucking about' in 1954 shortly after Caroline was born that she discovered the full extent of the problem. During the horseplay Derek was hit in the eye and saw "a considerable array of stars" causing him great discomfort. Following this, just before Christmas, and after a number of further eye tests, he was admitted to the Manchester Royal Infirmary where he had an operation to withdraw fluid. This relieved the pain but did not improve the sight and he would carry this disability throughout his entire cricketing career and into retirement.

It is extremely difficult to imagine how a player could have achieved so much success with so great a disadvantage. It is impossible to believe he could have had such a long career as a batsman and without the chairman's instructions "to bowl fast" in 1948 Derek's days with Hampshire would have been short-lived, of this there can be little doubt. It is amazing that he scored as many runs as he did - nearly 10,000 at an average of just under 15 is highly commendable in the circumstances. Even so, as a bowler, it required intense concentration and this is where his calm unruffled temperament was to prove so invaluable.

Derek was a man who kept this problem to himself largely because he felt the county might have considered it to be too much of a risk to offer him a long term contract. He finally confided his secret to Henry Horton as late as 1967. Even then, a year before Derek's last full season, other players weren't told and Roy Marshall, in his autobiography, confirms he was quite unaware until after Derek retired.

After Milburn's accident he and Derek appeared together on a television programme and, whilst he gave Milburn encouragement, there was realistically little chance of Milburn carrying on as before. Derek had somehow become used to his disability over a long period and had adjusted accordingly whereas with Milburn it had been sudden. Also it was much more of a problem for a batsman and, although Milburn did return for Northamptonshire a few years later, he was but a shadow of his former ebullient self.

Largely because of his poor eyesight Derek has never particularly enjoyed driving although, in his playing days, his car was often used on away trips as a reasonably generous petrol allowance was paid. Butch White and Bryan Timms were two who would occasionally drive Derek's car which, like its owner, was absolutely immaculate. They were both given firm instructions to restrict the speed to 50 mph for economic as well as for safety reasons. Derek's simple philosophy of being prudent and sensible with his money being put into action again. Once, Timms, noticing that Derek was asleep, slowly but steadily increased the speed to 70 mph. Derek must have had an inbuilt warning system because he awoke immediately, tapped the speedometer, and said "Slow down, Timms son, you're up to 70". The journey continued on its previous sedate way, the passengers not experiencing the excitement of a ride with Colin Ingleby-Mackenzie or, in earlier days, with Alan Rayment. Timms, like all the other players, accepted this was 'just Shack'.

When Horton retired this came as quite a blow to Derek as they had been very good mates and frequently roomed together; players of similar temperament. He is another unstinting in his praise of Derek's enormous contribution to Hampshire's success. "Simply without him, Hampshire wouldn't have won the championship in 1961". He recalls his general demeanour and also a particular example of his many famous performances.

> "The late Syd Buller, the number one umpire of his time said of Derek 'he is not only immaculate with his line and length when bowling, he even folds his sweater meticulously when handing it to the umpire'."

Horton continues :

> "Immaculately turned out by his lovely wife Kathleen he would set about his business for the day of bowling out the opposition in a most unassuming way. He didn't practise very much before a match but he still wouldn't have bowled a half volley and never a long hop. As the ex Surrey and England fast bowler and coach, Alf Gover, told his protégés 'you bowl them out with the new ball and give nothing away with the old one.'"
>
> "If Derek ever did bowl a half volley the colour and sun tan would drain from his face and he would return to his mark as if he had stabbed himself through the heart."
> "I saw him bowl many famous stints but none better than when playing against the South Africans (1965) at Southampton. Before lunch he had five or six back in the pavilion before they had reached 100."

Even during those last few seasons when he was in his forties Derek just bowled and bowled, never shirking his work load and still remaining injury free.

He was awarded a thoroughly deserved second benefit in 1967 choosing the fixture against Yorkshire (now firmly established as the county of his birth) at Bournemouth at the end of July. Due to rain and an unpredictable wicket runs were hard to come by but Hampshire finally won a low scoring match by 6 wickets. Only Boycott with 90 out of 179 looked remotely comfortable and although Shackleton did not take any wickets in the Yorkshire first innings he conceded only 28 runs from 28 overs. Boycott proved his own theory that extreme patience was necessary in addition, of course, to great technique and skill. In the Yorkshire second innings, when quick runs were needed for a declaration, Shack's figures were : 4-1-5-3 with his partner Alan Castell conceding 34 runs off his four overs.

He was still almost unplayable on a wicket giving just the slightest hint of assistance. An example of this is remembered by Bob Cottam in a match against Essex at Westcliff in 1968 and there was a similar occurrence the previous year at Ilford.

In the 1967 fixture Derek had match figures of 12-94 from 49 overs, a statistic quite in line with his peak years, but when were his peak years ? He may have been slightly slower than in 1949 but the guile and cunning accumulated over all those intervening years more than compensated for the loss of speed. Twenty consecutive seasons of taking 100 wickets proved he was right at the top of his profession throughout his entire career.

At Westcliff Cottam recalls that "Shack's first delivery popped to such an extent that, with Timms standing up to the wicket, the ball took off like a leg break and was taken by me at first slip". He took 5-17 in 20 overs in Essex's first innings and, with Barry Richards scoring a brilliant 176 out of a total of 301 for four declared, Hampshire won convincingly by an innings. Although it has to be acknowledged that Essex did not have anyone remotely in Richards' class it is interesting to contrast Shackleton's match figures with those of the two Essex seamers, both of whom would later play test cricket.

	Overs	Maidens	Runs	Wickets
Shackleton	42	26	61	7
Boyce	21	1	100	1
Lever	26	2	77	1

At Bath in 1968 there was another example of Derek's uncanny perception. After opening the bowling, and to his horror straying persistently outside the leg stump, he pointed out to the umpires that the wickets were out of line. This was proved correct and the match was delayed whilst the stumps were aligned properly. The Somerset openers were really peeved as they thought that, at long last, Shack was becoming vulnerable.

His methodical mind would often result in him knowing his bowling analysis before he came off the field. On one occasion, according to Cottam, he returned to the pavilion saying that his analysis was 3-35 in 20 overs. Norman Drake, the Hampshire scorer at the time, said it was 3-36. Derek was quite adamant and, on checking the scorebook, an embarrassed and quite amazed Drake conceded he was wrong. Cottam feels this orderly mind was a way of keeping his concentration, of keeping him totally focused.

The1968 summer was to prove to be his last full season in county cricket. He finished second to Cottam in the championship averages and, for the first time since 1954, did not take the highest number of wickets. In twenty full seasons for Hampshire, such was his extraordinary consistency, he topped the averages fifteen times, excluding freak performances in 1950, 1956 and 1960 when Gray took two wickets, Rayment three and Horton two respectively. In three consecutive years - 1953, 1954 and 1955 only bowlers taking less than 40 wickets achieved a better average. In seventeen seasons he had taken more wickets than anyone else, usually by a wide margin. Therefore, Cottam's performance in taking more wickets and at a lower average was the first genuine year since 1949 that Shackleton had to play (slightly) the second fiddle.

His final first class match at Southampton and the last against a touring side saw him face to face with the visiting Australians. In this game, and on his 44th birthday, he took 5-58 in 27 overs. He still had an uncanny knack of celebrating his birthdays in some style.

He was just as capable, as he had always been, of dismissing the very best batsmen and many test players, both present and future, were among his victims that year. Greig (three times), Cowdrey, Greg Chappell, Asif Iqbal, and Sobers (all twice), Kanhai, Procter, Luckhurst, Pullar, Fletcher, Brearley, Milburn, Radley, Lewis, Barber and John Edrich and others.

He could probably have continued in the first class game - how many bowlers in their final season would take 109 wickets at 17.32 ? - but the rigours of the one day competitions would almost certainly have found him out, if only from the exertions and high demands of fielding standards. He had bowled tidily in the early years of the Gillette Cup and his 15 wickets in this competition were taken at an average of 26.73 with an economy rate of 2.35 runs per over. He had even better figures in the inaugural year of the Sunday League and his 17 wickets cost only 13.64 with an economy rate of 2.23. However, he was much less successful the following season - his 5 wickets costing almost 46 apiece and he conceded nearly 4 runs an over.

Although he played Sunday league cricket in 1969 and on a few occasions in 1970 his first class career effectively ended in 1968. Due to injuries he played one match in the championship in 1969 - at Portsmouth against Sussex just a few days before his 45th birthday. As usual he opened the bowling and his impressive figures were as follows :

Overs	Maidens	Runs	Wickets
23	10	37	2
24.5	11	58	5

Nothing had changed and this one performance ensured he topped the averages !

And so to a well deserved, if reluctant and slightly uncertain, retirement.

Chapter Fourteen

Dancing in the Dark

Derek Shackleton was, quite simply, a cricket phenomenon. Strange, perhaps, to say this about someone who represented his country on only seven occasions. As a seam bowler, though, in county cricket he reigned supreme for twenty years and, during this era, no one, but no one, could match his sheer relentless consistency. Much, quite rightly, has been written about others, such as Les Jackson and Tom Cartwright, not being selected for England more times but even their impressive final tally of wickets pale in comparison to Hampshire's adopted Yorkshireman. Only Wilfred Rhodes, from a previous distant generation, took 100 wickets in a season more often and no one in the entire history of the game beat Shackleton's record of taking 100 in twenty *consecutive* seasons. Indeed in *county championship* matches he took 100 wickets in a season on more occasions than any other player, Rhodes included and, in this competition, only Tich Freeman, Rhodes, Charlie Parker and Tom Goddard exceeded Shack's total of 2542. In all first class cricket he is the eighth highest wicket taker of all time and holds the record for the number of wickets taken since the end of the second world war. He never experienced a poor season and this almost unparalleled consistency would continue to manifest itself in his performances for Dorset in the Minor Counties League.

Derek knew no life other than cricket and, following his retirement from Hampshire, he was offered the position of coach at Canford School. This was an attractive proposition as the school was situated conveniently near to the Shackletons' new home in Ferndown which they purchased in 1969. The lingerie business and home in Totton had already been sold and, for a short period, they had been living in a flat overlooking the ground in Northlands Road. With the sale proceeds and part of the second benefit monies they were then able to buy an attractive house on the Dorset/Hampshire border where they have remained.

Probably because for over twenty years Derek had been away from home for much of the summer months Kathy had tended to handle the home finances and careful and prudent management had enabled Julian and Caroline to have a good schooling. Monies had been set aside from the benefits and from the small profits from the lingerie business.

Cricket would continue to dominate Derek's life, both as a player for Dorset and as coach at Canford. For four seasons between 1971 and 1974 he played Minor Counties cricket and just carried on bowling as he had been since 1948. Without exception during these four years he bowled more overs than anyone else and in 1974, his fiftieth year, by a huge margin.

Ken House, the Dorset captain at the time, recalls that if they fielded first he would toss the ball to Derek at 11 or 11.30 and he would bowl right through the entire pre lunch session - with few words and no complaints. His accuracy never wavered and this, together with his reputation, made it almost impossible for lesser mortals to do anything but just try and survive until he had a rest. House confirms all the qualities expounded by Derek's old colleagues at Hampshire but that he, himself, never boasted about past exploits. In his only Gillette Cup match for Dorset in 1973 he received the man of the match award for his performance against Staffordshire : 12-8-11-4.

All things have to come to an end, however, and having reached 50 he decided to finish altogether.

Derek enjoyed coaching at Canford although he found he quickly had to learn the rudiments of real or royal tennis, as this would be part of his duties. Malcolm Taylor, the previous coach, taught him the basics but arrangements were made for him to attend the famous enclosed court at Lord's. On arrival the court was heavily booked and he had to wait a day or two before he could grasp the opportunity of learning more about this somewhat complicated and little played game.

Another famous public school had a connection with the name of Shackleton. Julian had won a sports scholarship to Millfield at the age of thirteen and, when he was taken to meet the slightly eccentric cricket loving headmaster R J O Meyer, he was immediately given an opportunity in the nets. After bowling a few deliveries Julian was told "You'll do". He played in the first X1 between 1967 and 1969 heading the bowling averages in the final year with 55 wickets at 11.05. After one impressive performance (something like 4-8 off 5 overs) during his school days Julian eagerly told his Dad of his success to which the purported reply was "a bit expensive weren't you, son!".

Millfield had a reputation for producing good cricketers and, during Julian's spell there, he played with the likes of Peter Denning (future Somerset), David Graveney (Gloucestershire and Durham and later to become Chairman of the England selectors), J C Foat (Gloucestershire) and Peter Roebuck (Somerset). With the strong West Country connections Julian was persuaded to sign for Gloucestershire making his debut in 1971 when he took 4-38 against Surrey. He was in and out of the side for about eight years until he left in 1978. 'A tall slim seam bowler with a good high action' quoted one of the cricket publications. It had been assumed, at one time, that he would have signed for Hampshire and Jimmy Gray is of the very firm opinion that he would have had a more fruitful career with them. Perhaps it isn't wise to follow directly in your father's footsteps but he appears to have been given little opportunity to shine with Gloucestershire. Like Derek, Julian later joined Dorset and in the 1990s proved to be their senior and most successful bowler.

Umpiring was something which had interested Derek for some time and, in 1979, he was elected to the first class panel. With the enormous amount of bowling he had done over the years he appreciated all the pressures umpires are put under not only from inexperienced players but also from old pro's. He was a very fair appealer in his playing days but he remembers an instance as far back as 1948 and, therefore, very new to the game when he appealed optimistically for lbw against Dickie Dodds at Colchester. The vastly experienced umpire Frank Chester gave the young Shackleton a withering look as if to say 'you cheeky young whippersnapper - that was nowhere near out'.

Derek umpired for three seasons and enjoyed the continual involvement in the game. Once, when umpiring with Harold Bird in one of Yorkshire's home matches, he asked Dickie if he could stay the night in his cottage - Derek still didn't care for hotels. There was no problem with this and, after a few drinks at the end of the day's play they set off for Dickie's home. What his host omitted to mention was that there was only one bed and, quite unconcerned, said "I'm having bed, thee can sleep on the hearth-rug". Derek opted for the hotel the following night!

However, the total concentration required was difficult due, in part, to the extra strain put on his one good eye. Somehow, and this is one of the great mysteries, he overcame this disability when playing but the years were now taking their toll and an unfair burden was being placed on the right eye. During this period he did, though, have the opportunity of getting to know a new generation of players and those in the early stages of their careers included David Gower, Graham Gooch, Ian Botham and Mike Gatting.

Derek's association with the first class game came to an end after 1981 but he could look back with great satisfaction and immense pride on a very distinguished career. The art of the seam bowler is greatly undervalued, and indeed often maligned, but has been an important element in the game, particularly in England. There is a place for the very best of all types of bowlers; the problem in English county cricket, certainly since the end of the war, is that there have been too many pale imitators.

Denis Compton, writing in the 1968 Wisden, made very valid points about the general stalemate which existed between the "never ending stream of medium paced short of a length bowlers who have proved a curse on the game" and the batsmen who seem to do nothing to remove them. He had witnessed several tedious games the previous year and bemoaned the general absence of confident stroke play which he feels could have been achieved with greater use of footwork. Compton was quite right to observe that the medium pacers were a very dominant feature of the game in the mid 1960s. Only three spinners, Underwood (himself almost medium pace) and the Yorkshiremen Illingworth and Cope featured in the top fifteen of the national bowling averages for 1967 with most counties relying heavily on seam. With regard to Shackleton and Cartwright it was doubly difficult to attack them by making more use of footwork because the keeper generally stood up to the stumps.

Compton, of course, was a unique talent one to whom the word 'genius' can be safely applied. Derek has admitted that it was not easy bowling to him because he was so unorthodox and would do his utmost to put him off his length by advancing down the wicket. There is little to argue with Compton's views - the game was being strangled by so much use of seam but this shouldn't mean the medium pacer should be discarded altogether. In normal playing conditions a perfectly balanced attack would be made up of two quickies, two spinners and a quality seamer, not just an ordinary run of the mill one of which there were so many at that time.

Compton mentions an occasion in 1948 with an indirect reference to Shackleton which does warrant comment. Part of Bradman's strategy during the test series was to use Lindwall and Miller as his shock troops and then to bring on Toshack to bowl quite deliberately at leg stump making scoring extremely difficult. Norman Yardley responded by bowling "Shackleton style" and Bradman himself faced an entire over without once offering a stroke as the ball went consistently down leg side. This reference is unfair on Derek because he never deliberately bowled this line - his main aim was to get the batsman out and one of his many attributes was that a batsman was rarely given any ball he could safely leave alone. Economical yes, but never purely defensive - his main deliveries were those pitching on or just outside off stump coming back and in to the right hander off the seam and those pitching on the line of the stumps cutting away.

Compton's overall views were made with great feeling as he felt the sheer numbers of seamers were strangling the game he loved - by bowlers who would have been ineffective on covered wickets. Shackleton was, in a totally different way to Compton, unique in his own particular art. John Woodcock, writing in the 'Times' in August 1996, actually lamented the absence of quality accurate seam bowlers in England. The article was prompted by the fact that England's seamers had been bowling woefully short of a length against the talented Pakistani batting and he felt that an attack made up of say Bedser, Statham, Shackleton and Bailey would have brought the batsmen constantly on to the front foot. "Those bowlers would have known how best to exploit the conditions (at Headingley), not least because all their days were spent bowling to get sides out, rather than concentrating on containment".

How would he have fared in these days of covered wickets ? The general consensus, amongst former colleagues and opponents alike, is that he would still have taken a large number of wickets. Whether a pitch is covered or not won't affect the accuracy or length and he never bowled too short which, on a good wicket, can be so expensive against class batsmen. Another reason to suggest that Derek would have been a formidable bowler in a later era is borne out by his successes in dry summers. Pitches were not always 'green fliers' and, for example, in the dry summers of 1955 and 1959 he enjoyed huge success. The wickets were good, the outfields fast but he took 159 wickets in 1955 at an average of 13.72 and, four years later, he finished with 148 at 21.55.

What would have been interesting to see was how he would have developed in the one day game. The competitions were in their infancy when his career was coming to an end and tactics were naive at the time. It is difficult to believe that he would have remained as economical as he was in the first year of the Sunday League - he conceded just 232 runs from 104 overs. Indeed, the following year, he conceded almost as many off half the number of overs bowled. Batsmen would have been forced to attack him and, if this had come off continually, he may have had to adjust but he was an intelligent bowler and effective changes would probably have been made. Fielding, though, would have been a problem. He had a very safe pair of hands and was a competent fielder when the ball was in the near vicinity but he was never one to make extravagant efforts to stop a boundary. He was not noted for diving full length when he might have been injured and, at the same time, he may have damaged his flannels. He would go for the ball if there was a reasonable chance of stopping it but, if the odds were say 40-60, it was more than likely he would have let it go. It was contrary to his general neatness and tidiness to hurl the body around, probably quite unnecessarily.

Derek was, and is, a genuinely 'nice' man in the best sense of the word and it is probably true to say he hasn't an enemy in the world. His general nature as a man was one of the prime reasons he became such a wonderful bowler. He was totally unflappable and the equable temperament helped give him the concentration required to bowl almost all season without delivering a bad ball. This meant a complete and unyielding devotion to the job in hand. Quiet, uncomplaining, utterly professional, he was a captain's dream. He always played within the accepted rules apart from the very, very slight 'Outschoorn blemish' in 1956 and this disposition was evident in his general life. He was quite appalled to learn that he had once been associated with that dreaded delivery, the beamer. An article in a book referred to a fast bowler who, frequently and deliberately, bowled beamers but, in an effort to, perhaps, soften the criticism went on to say "Even Derek Shackleton, for example, would slip the odd one in early in his career". Derek said that, in one game against Sussex, he accidentally let one slip at George Cox who was singularly unimpressed but it was purely unintentional and the first, and only, time this had happened. One such delivery out of a career total of 159,001! Generally the beamer is extremely dangerous when delivered by someone of real pace and, as Derek remarked, "I wasn't quick enough anyway".

Those lucky enough to have seen 'Shack' during his twenty years with Hampshire will undoubtedly have a clear memory of the wonderfully smooth approach to the wicket from a slightly angled run up of twelve strides in his early days. The ball held firmly, the right arm straight, he set off on a gentle rhythmic approach, very light on his feet with the head perfectly still and with eyes set purposefully, if not menacingly, on the batsman. At the point of delivery, very close to the stumps, the wrist would be at right angles to the arm which, in a brief split second, would rise, classically high, brushing the right ear, the hand releasing the ball on its way to a spot specifically chosen by the bowler. It would hit that intended spot as though a magnet had been placed. It was the wrist action which created the sharp 'nip' which, to someone who faced him for the first time, came as a complete and somewhat unpleasant surprise. The ball will often have swung and would have pitched on a teasing length putting considerable doubt in the batsman's mind as to whether he should go forward or back. At the same time the ball was likely to have cut in to him off the seam or perhaps away from him. All this would have happened in a brief moment and the problems for the batsman were colossal. The bowler would then hitch up his flannels turn and walk unhurried, but not slowly, back to his mark.

This routine could go on for hours and, with hardly any loose deliveries, there was no respite. As one former player remarked it was probably better to chance your arm and score a quick 30 or 40 than try and hang around for an hour or so and get about 10. This certainly worked for Trueman and, a little later, for Brian Taylor of Essex.

Malcolm Heath who coaches and gives talks at Lord's to youngsters often starts by giving his brief definition of a bowler.

> "First and foremost he is a person who attacks the stumps with the ball - he is a match winner. You want a batsman out of the way and you don't want to give many runs away when you are trying to do it".

Undoubtedly this would have been Derek's philosophy.

Peter Sainsbury made a very poignant observation about an occasion very late in Derek's career when he (Sainsbury) fielded, unusually, at slip. For the majority of the fifteen years they played together he had been fielding in a short leg position from where the eyes are concentrated on the batsman rather than focused on the bowler. In 1968 he switched occasionally to the slips and, for the first time, was able to watch in fine detail Derek's beautiful run up and action. He was simply amazed at seeing what he had missed throughout all those years and could then understand the views held by previous slip fielders, in particular Jimmy Gray and Mike Barnard.

Alan Rayment, who had run a dancing school, waxed lyrical about how light Derek was on his feet, almost balletic in his approach to the stumps. "He was a Fred Astaire to Trueman's Gene Kelly. Trueman also had a most beautiful run up but somehow more intimidating".

It was also once said he could have bowled in the dark and there was an occasion well after he had finished playing, probably in the late 1970s or early 1980s, when he played in a charity match at Lord's. He had not bowled in any capacity for a few years apart from in the nets at Canford where he certainly would not have bowled off any sort of run up but, at Lord's, he was face to face with Ted Dexter again. Dexter recalls "the very first ball went like a leg break off the seam with me nowhere near it. Perhaps that was it - he was a bit too good for ordinary mortals". In the annals of cricket Dexter was not an 'ordinary' mortal. He had been a charismatic batsman, a truly handsome attacking player who averaged just under 48 for England but, as in his days with Sussex about twenty years beforehand, he found that Shack could still just turn it on at will.

Fitness also played its part and, although he was lucky in keeping free of injuries, he obviously looked after himself. It is quite ironic that, with so many players suffering from strained muscles etc in recent years notwithstanding the great emphasis on training, Derek, who hardly trained at all and for whom net practice was just a little light exercise, missed so few matches. Pre match warm up would involve combing his hair and lighting a cigarette! He ate and drank modestly and the huge number of overs bowled was the simple factor in keeping him fit.

He gave absolutely everything for Hampshire as a player and as Butch White pointed out "there were times you couldn't get the bloody ball off him!". No Hampshire player, whether batsman or bowler, had such a prolonged and uninterrupted consistency of performance in post war cricket. There were others who, over a similar length of time, gave sterling performances but for sheer high quality consistency Shackleton was supreme. In previous eras only Mead and Kennedy come into this category.

He broke and set many records although one, strangely, which eluded him was the hat trick. Considering the amount of bowling he did, the fact he was so very accurate and could whittle out tail enders with ease makes this very surprising. He, several times, took three wickets in four balls, once in a test match.

Derek was a 'cricketer's cricketer' respected equally by team mates and opponents. If he was occasionally attacked he would acknowledge the fact generously. When hit for six he would simply say "Ah that wor a good 'un" knowing "they can't go on hitting you if you are dropping it there and doing a bit".

The three skippers during his playing career fully appreciated this most valuable asset they had at their disposal. After the euphoria of the achievement of winning the first championship Desmond Eagar, his first captain and by then secretary, wrote the following in the 'Hampshire' County Magazine:

> "A great hearted cricketer who would have played many more times for England if his career had not coincided with that of Alec Bedser. To watch him run up and deliver the ball with his easy rhythmic action gives pleasure enough. To watch the subtleties of his change of pace and swing is to appreciate the accuracy of one of the great bowlers of all time. We think in Hampshire, as we always do, of Kennedy and Newman. I

> venture to believe that in twenty years time
> we shall be talking of Shackleton in the
> same breath as these other two immortal
> bowlers".

How true were Eagar's comments made all those years ago.

Derek has been described as a quiet Yorkshire gentleman with none of the abrasiveness sometimes associated with cricketers from that county. Although living in the south for half a century he still retains a gentle, but pronounced, Yorkshire accent and has also kept the traditional northern values with regard to money. He has never understood the propensity some have of squandering hard earned cash and there is a slight intolerance towards such people. He came, as is well known, from a very modest background where cash was extremely scarce and he would always be frightened of wastefulness. To those who did not know him well this could have caused a problem but, to others close to him, this was simply "Shack"; they knew that he certainly wasn't a mean spirited man and was indeed a very generous opponent. He enjoyed a beer at the end of the day's play and would pay his round although would object if he was taken advantage of - those who may have asked for an expensive 'short'.

Ray Lindwall once complained that Len Hutton had never bought him a drink and reminded him of this when they met by chance outside an hotel in Sydney. They went inside, had a most enjoyable chat for about an hour, and then went their separate ways. Lindwall suddenly realised after Hutton had gone that "he STILL hadn't bought me a drink!".

In an article about another Yorkshireman of several decades past it was suggested that a cry of "the drinks are on me" would have caused not just a stampede of willing takers but also of men in white coats! There are many similar stories of other players and, to be fair, not just those from Yorkshire, but generally there is a greater care of money earned by people in the north.

Derek had had to work hard for his money. Pounds per balls bowled would, probably, have worked out at below the national minimum wage.

A man of few words in the dressing room he would oddly, but quite frequently, explode into a song which appears to have been exclusively his own. One line is something like : "I will slap thee, Billy (belly ?) with a big flat fish". No one seems to know its origin and although his colleagues were often taken unawares when he suddenly burst forth into the ditty they would have thought there was something wrong if it was not heard once a day.

There is a very direct link between Derek's own personal human attributes and his bowling. Methodical, careful, economical, consistent, modest; words that apply to him as a man as well as to his bowling. If he had been more of an extrovert character he, almost certainly, would not have had all the patience required to produce the extraordinary bowling figures he achieved, certainly not in the manner that he did.

He was always very smart and well groomed and indeed a very good looking man. He was comfortably able to avoid the many pitfalls which can so easily attach themselves to those in the public eye and did so in a very natural way. Even the devious tabloid press of the 1990s would have been hard pressed to have found any gossip. A man with no real prejudices (apart from spendthrifts) Derek was able to mix easily with people from all backgrounds and races and they, in turn, respected him. This was never more apparent than when he went on the Commonwealth tour to India in 1950/1951.

He is essentially a private person who, in his cricketing days, 'did his talking on the cricket field'. As one former player put it "he has an inner calm grace clothed in a northern expression of life". The 'star' aspect or the 'hero' element did not sit easily with him and he did not seem to welcome media attention.

After he finished umpiring he returned to coach on a part time basis at Canford School in 1981 and remained there until he was 68 in 1992. Now he follows the game largely on television and retains an interest in his former county's fortunes which have been mixed to say the least. How, in the late 1990s, they could do with just a little of the Shackleton magic! Other than the natural misgivings of one generation towards another, which is inherent in everyone, he is not over critical of the modern game but is saddened when he sees bowlers spraying the ball all over the place. "Bowl straight, that's all they have to do. It's so simple". Not to ordinary mortals it seems.

Far too long overdue he did receive recognition for his services to cricket when he was made an Hon Member of the MCC in 1994. It would be nice to think that, when Hampshire's new stadium is completed in the year 2000, a stand will be named after him in view of his colossal contribution to the success of his adopted county. Mead and Shackleton are the two obvious candidates for such permanent recognition and would ensure that their names and deeds would be familiar to those not lucky enough to have witnessed these two greats in action.

There is still a link with Canford School as Kathy runs the tuck shop and her name and that of the school hit the national headlines in 1994. A 3000 year old stone frieze, which hung in the shop, was unexpectedly believed to be worth a lot of money. It had originally been excavated in the middle of the 19th century from the palaces of two Assyrian kings in Nineveh and Nimrud, both situated in modern day Iraq. There was some suggestion that the value may be in the region of £1m but, at the subsequent auction at Christie's, it was sold to an anonymous buyer for a staggering £7.7m! Quite amazingly the stone carving was next to the dartboard in the tuck shop and, for years, boys, practising their throwing skills, would often miss their target occasionally striking the frieze. Nobody seemed to mind for, disguised by several coats of whitewash and thought to be a plaster imitation, it never crossed anyone's mind that it once decorated the palace of a king. Kathy's and Derek's names were mentioned in many newspapers, in particular the Daily Express carrying a feature and colour photograph.

In recent years Derek's main pastime has been his garden where he can reflect, especially if the day is warm, on a long and very happy career. What would have happened if the Hampshire chairman had not delivered that instruction, all those years ago, for everyone in the nets to bowl fast? Such seemingly insignificant moments can, so often as in this case, have a huge bearing on a whole life. With the blindness in his left eye it is inconceivable Derek would have had much sustained success as a batsman and, as Desmond Eagar remarked at the time, "he bowled occasional innocuous leg breaks". He may have drifted out of the game altogether or, at best, may have held a place for a brief period with only modest success. However, what he achieved for Hampshire in post war cricket was, quite simply, monumental and, throughout the county, whether it is the large cities and towns of Southampton, Portsmouth and Bournemouth (acknowledging the latter was reluctantly "transferred" to Dorset) or in the varied beauty of the villages "Shack" is a true legend. His name is familiar in the leafy glades of the New Forest, the rolling chalk downs which sweep through central Hampshire and which look down proudly over Winchester, the historic old capital of England, the lovely areas which border Berkshire to the north and Sussex to the east and the Isle of Wight must not be overlooked for it still seems to be in a time warp; travelling there now is easy to imagine the 1950s when life seemed more gentle and "Shack" was bowling over after over in the warm summer sunshine with the gentle breeze coming from the Solent. Or was it a cold afternoon with a force eight sweeping up the Channel? No, it always seemed summer on the Island!

Derek, as in his playing days, still loves the sun and finds the long cold winters tiresome, even in the warmer south - there has never been any serious thought of returning to his northern roots. Whenever possible he and Kathy take breaks in the Canary Isles or in Malta, one of their favourite haunts. Ideally, and if they had the money, they would probably live abroad, certainly in the winter.

There are now few links with Todmorden. The Shackletons are a close-knit family with Julian (still taking wickets regularly for Dorset) being a huge help at home and able to drive his parents around. Derek still has a car but drives only on rare occasions. Caroline also lives locally and is the practice manager at a veterinary surgery.

There is no doubt that Derek is very grateful to cricket for giving him a career he loved but it should never be forgotten that, in turn, he gave a lot back to the game and for which he received only modest financial reward. It is ironic that the 1950s was arguably the decade when the standard of county championship cricket was at its highest and yet the financial rewards were sparse indeed. Of course money is not everything and there was huge enjoyment to be gained on the county circuit and most players from that era look back with great feeling and nostalgia. Nevertheless a little extra cash in the pocket would have been welcome.

Derek had the satisfaction of being one of the most respected bowlers in post war cricket and, especially when it was a 'green un', one of the most greatly feared. The Hampshire batsmen were delighted he was in their side because they, too, would have been unable to handle him. He also seemed to be worth a few points before a match even started. Very few opposition batsmen faced him with any confidence; some were as good as dismissed before they even reached the wicket! Such was his reputation.

It would not be right to say "there will never be another bowler of his ilk" but there is no doubt that he would have to be someone of quite exceptional ability and, just as importantly, someone with a quite unique temperament. In a now more aggressive age it is difficult to imagine Derek's calm nature surviving. We are in an era of high profile sport - any sport, including cricket - and the histrionics and the playing to the camera would be anathema to him. But if he had been brought up in this environment would he have been any different ? The world has changed and the game of cricket has changed and not all for the worse and the question raised is probably unanswerable.

He was a great bowler in a golden age of cricket. His closest friend in that fine Hampshire championship side, Henry Horton, simply put it :

"It was an honour and pleasure to play with such a great bowler and sportsman as Derek Shackleton, a credit to the game of cricket".

Statistics

BOWLING . All First Class Matches . Year by Year Summary .

Year	Overs	Maidens	Runs	Wickets	Ave	5wI	10wM	Best
1948	270.4	67	621	21	29.57	-	-	4-42
1949	941.2	206	2616	100	26.16	7	1	7-83
1950	976.0	234	2455	111	22.11	8	2	8.39
1950/1	570.2	145	1259	49	25.69	1	1	6-78
1951	1161.2	335	2561	130	19.70	9	1	7.89
1951/2	484.1	125	1184	51	23.21	2	-	5-36
1952	1161.1	351	2479	135	18.36	9	1	6-22
1953	1219.4	328	3070	150	20.46	10	2	9-77
1954	1069.5	391	1985	104	19.08	3	1	6-34
1955	1221.1	438	2183	159	13.72	9	2	8-4
1956	1273.0	465	2288	140	16.34	7	-	7-38
1957	1217.3	447	2429	155	15.67	14	4	7-20
1958	1320.2	505	2549	165	15.44	16	3	9-59
1959	1445.4	481	3190	148	21.55	8	2	9-81
1960	1271.5	503	2300	130	17.69	10	3	9-30
1961	1509.5	532	3017	158	19.09	12	1	6-36
1962	1717.1	678	3467	172	20.15	14	4	8-36
1963	1385.3	583	2446	146	16.75	14	4	7-30
1964	1437.0	568	2897	142	20.40	10	1	8-27
1965	1246.0	529	2316	144	16.08	10	3	7-32
1966	1306.2	575	2088	117	17.84	7	-	6-25
1967	1159.4	529	1920	114	16.84	8	1	7-37
1968	1086.5	452	1888	109	17.32	5	1	5-17
1969	47.5	21	95	7	13.57	1	-	5-58
TOTAL	26500.1	9488	53303	2857	18.65	194	38	9-30

BOWLING . Hampshire County Championship . Year by Year Summary .

Year	Overs	Maidens	Runs	Wickets	Ave	5wI	10wM	Best
1948	221.0	58	519	17	30.52	-	-	4-42
1949	863.3	191	2396	92	26.04	7	1	7-83
1950	822.3	212	1955	105	18.61	8	2	8-39
1951	1052.5	303	2350	118	19.91	9	1	7-89
1952	1051.1	312	2243	119	18.84	8	1	6-22
1953	1106.0	300	2754	133	20.70	9	2	9-77
1954	989.4	358	1834	93	19.72	3	1	6-34
1955	1112.4	410	1923	147	13.08	9	2	8-4
1956	1128.1	408	1998	126	15.85	7	-	7-38
1957	1142.4	418	2260	144	15.69	13	3	7-20
1958	1262.0	477	2469	161	15.33	16	3	9-59
1959	1291.5	442	2827	126	22.43	6	1	9-81
1960	1230.5	494	2146	128	16.76	10	3	9-30
1961	1470.3	523	2927	153	19.13	11	1	6-36
1962	1595.1	628	3214	161	19.96	14	4	8-36
1963	1025.2	457	1721	116	14.83	13	4	7-30
1964	1379.0	549	2758	138	19.98	10	1	8-27
1965	1166.0	492	2170	133	16.31	9	3	7-32
1966	1231.2	549	1917	112	17.11	7	-	6-25
1967	1115.4	512	1836	112	16.39	8	1	7-37
1968	1021.5	423	1758	101	17.40	4	1	5-17
1969	47.5	21	95	7	13.57	1	-	5-58
TOTAL	23327.3	8537	46070	2542	18.12	182	35	9-30

BOWLING . Hampshire Other First Class Matches . Year by Year Summary .

Year	Overs	Maidens	Runs	Wickets	Ave	5wI	10wM	Best
1948	49.4	9	102	4	25.50	-	-	3-47
1949	77.5	15	220	8	27.50	-	-	4-72
1950	25.0	4	87	1	87.00	-	-	1-87
1951	42.0	12	94	5	18.80	-	-	3-62
1952	44.0	19	113	9	12.55	1	-	6-41
1953	57.4	14	177	10	17.70	1	-	7-32
1954	35.0	22	41	1	41.00	-	-	1-31
1955	72.3	21	183	10	18.30	-	-	4-53
1956	94.5	40	194	8	24.25	-	-	3-56
1957	55.5	21	134	10	13.40	1	1	7-103
1958	30.0	21	27	2	13.50	-	-	2-27
1959	81.1	28	181	14	12.92	2	1	6-44
1960	41.0	9	154	2	77.00	-	-	1-12
1961	39.2	9	90	5	18.00	1	-	5-73
1962	-	-	-	-	-	-	-	-
1963	65.3	26	137	8	17.12	-	-	3-19
1964	58.0	19	139	4	34.75	-	-	2-46
1965	80.0	37	146	11	13.27	1	-	6-29
1966	75.0	26	171	5	34.20	-	-	2-49
1967	44.0	17	84	2	42.00	-	-	1-21
1968	65.0	29	130	8	16.25	1	-	5-58
1969	-	-	-	-	-	-	-	-
TOTAL	1133.2	398	2604	127	20.50	8	2	7-32

BOWLING . For Other Representative Sides . Year by Year Summary

Year	Overs	Maidens	Runs	Wickets	Ave	5wI	10wM	Best
1948	-	-	-	-	-	-	-	-
1949	-	-	-	-	-	-	-	-
1950	128.3	18	413	5	82.60	-	-	2-53
1950/1	570.2	145	1259	49	25.69	1	1	6-78
1951	66.3	20	117	7	16.71	-	-	4-31
1951/2	484.1	125	1184	51	23.21	2	-	5.36
1952	66.0	20	123	7	17.57	-	-	4-39
1953	56.0	14	139	7	19.85	-	-	3-57
1954	45.1	11	110	10	11.00	-	-	4-68
1955	36.0	7	77	2	38.50	-	-	2.58
1956	50.0	17	96	6	16.00	-	-	4-27
1957	19.0	8	35	1	35.00	-	-	1-35
1958	28.2	7	53	2	26.50	-	-	1-13
1959	72.4	11	182	8	22.75	-	-	3-51
1960	-	-	-	-	-	-	-	-
1961	-	-	-	-	-	-	-	-
1962	122.0	50	253	11	23.00	-	-	4-101
1963	294.4	100	588	22	26.72	1	-	5-42
1964	-	-	-	-	-	-	-	-
1965	-	-	-	-	-	-	-	-
1966	-	-	-	-	-	-	-	-
1967	-	-	-	-	-	-	-	-
1968	-	-	-	-	-	-	-	-
1969	-	-	-	-	-	-	-	-
TOTAL	2039.2	553	4629	188	24.62	4	1	6-78

BOWLING. Summary In First Class Cricket

	Overs	Maidens	Runs	Wickets	Ave	5wI	10wM	Best
For Hampshire in County Championship Matches								
	23327.3	8537	46070	2542	18.12	182	35	9-30
For Hampshire in Other Matches								
	1133.2	398	2604	127	20.50	8	2	7-32
For Other Representative Sides								
	2039.2	553	4629	188	24.62	4	1	6-78
Career Totals								
	26500.1	9488	53303	2857	18.65	194	38	9-30

It is believed that the 2857 wickets were taken as follows :

Bowled	828
Lbw	507
Caught at wicket	400
Stumped	25
Hit wicket	3
Other catches	1094
CAREER TOTAL	2857

BOWLING. Hampshire County Championship. Details against each county.

County	Overs	Maidens	Runs	Wickets	Ave	5wI	10wM	Best
Derbyshire	1232.2	439	2458	130	18.90	7	-	7-86
Essex	1178.1	424	2440	131	18.62	10	2	7-37
Glamorgan	1300.4	526	2395	127	18.85	9	2	9-77
Gloucestershire	1597.2	625	2905	182	15.96	12	3	9-59
Kent	1856.4	628	3821	210	18.19	14	3	7-71
Lancashire	1291.5	460	2537	136	18.65	8	1	7-51
Leicestershire	1705.0	686	3077	209	14.72	19	4	8-39
Middlesex	1735.1	608	3517	208	16.90	19	7	7-44
Northants	1276.1	509	2319	132	17.56	8	2	6-31
Notts	1688.1	603	3525	157	22.45	10	3	7-41
Somerset	1572.3	546	3146	174	18.08	13	1	8-4
Surrey	1322.4	483	2754	130	21.18	12	1	7-30
Sussex	1812.5	705	3383	229	14.77	18	2	7-48
Warwickshire	1352.1	427	2947	147	20.04	11	3	9-30
Worcestershire	1417.0	527	2629	139	18.91	6	-	6-66
Yorkshire	988.5	341	2217	101	21.95	6	1	7-78
TOTAL	23327.3	8537	46070	2542	18.12	182	35	9-30

BOWLING. For Hampshire in Other First Class Matches. Non championship.

Opponents	Overs	Maidens	Runs	Wickets	Ave	5wI	10wM	Best
Cambridge U	41.4	7	93	4	23.25	-	-	3-47
Combined Serv	62.0	15	115	6	19.16	-	-	4-72
Ireland	25.0	16	21	3	7.00	-	-	3-13
MCC	155.1	56	322	26	12.38	3	1	7-32
Oxford U	73.0	26	150	6	25.00	-	-	4-53
Rest of World	38.0	19	72	3	24.00	-	-	3-61
Yorkshire	39.2	9	90	5	18.00	1	-	5-73
Australia	154.0	54	398	14	28.42	1	-	5-58
India	128.3	48	290	14	20.71	1	-	6-41
New Zealand	53.5	23	141	4	35.25	-	-	2-27
Pakistan	35.0	22	41	1	41.00	-	-	1-31
S Africa	178.3	49	500	21	23.80	1	-	6-29
W Indies	149.2	54	371	20	18.55	1	1	7-103
TOTAL	1133.2	398	2604	127	20.50	8	2	7-32

BOWLING. Summary of performances FOR other representative sides

For	Overs	Maidens	Runs	Wickets	Ave	5wI	10wM	Best
England	346.2	96	768	18	42.66	-	-	4-72
MCC in India/ Pakistan/ Ceylon.(Excl. test match *)	455.1	118	1108	50	22.16	2	-	5-36
Commonwealth X1 in India and Ceylon	570.2	145	1259	49	25.69	1	1	6-78
MCC sides in England	127.3	40	266	14	19.00	-	-	4-27
Players v. Gentlemen	112.0	24	303	9	33.66	-	-	4-39
Other representative sides (**)	428.0	130	925	48	19.27	1	-	5-42
TOTAL	2039.2	553	4629	188	24.62	4	1	6-78

Notes.

* Bowling figures for a test match appearance in India are included under the 'England' heading, i.e. 29-7-76-1, and not under the MCC heading.

** Details under 'Other representative sides' relate to matches played in England for teams such as A E R Gilligan's X1, South of England, Rest of England etc.

BOWLING. Best Performances.

Nine wickets in an innings.

1953. 9-77 v. Glamorgan at Newport
1958 9-59 v. Gloucestershire at Bristol
1959 9-81 v. Gloucestershire at Bristol
1960 9-30 v. Warwickshire at Portsmouth

Eight wickets in an innings

1950 8-39 v. Leicestershire at Portsmouth
1955 8- 4 v. Somerset at Weston Super Mare (14-29 in match)
1962 8-36 v. Glamorgan at Cardiff
1964 8-27 v. Gloucestershire at Bristol

Seven wickets in an innings

1949 7-90 v. Derbyshire at Chesterfield
1949 7-83 v. Gloucestershire at Portsmouth
1950 7-80 v. Leicestershire at Leicester
1951 7-89 v. Leicestershire at Leicester
1953 7-32 v. MCC at Lord's
1956 7-62 v. Surrey at Guildford
1956 7-38 v. Warwickshire at Edgbaston
1956 7-48 v. Sussex at Eastbourne
1957 7-20 v. Leicestershire at Leicester
1957 7-81 v. Nottinghamshire at Cowes, IOW
1957 7-51 v. Lancashire at Old Trafford, Manchester
1957 7-60 v. Lancashire at Old Trafford, Manchester (14-111 in match)
1957 7-103 v.West Indies at Southampton
1958 7-34 v. Surrey at Guildford
1958 7-39 v. Glamorgan at Southampton
1958 7-71 v. Kent at Canterbury
1959 7-86 v. Derbyshire at Derby
1962 7-95 v. Surrey at Guildford
1962 7-78 v. Yorkshire at Bradford
1963 7-71 v. Kent at Southampton
1963 7-30 v. Surrey at Southampton
1963 7-31 v. Leicestershire at Portsmouth
1964 7-44 v. Middlesex at Lord's
1964 7-97 v. Gloucestershire at Bournemouth
1965 7-67 v. Warwickshire at Bournemouth
1965 7-32 v. Warwickshire at Bournemouth (14-99 in match)
1965 7-89 v. Leicestershire at Leicester
1965 7-41 v. Nottinghamshire at Nottingham
1967 7-37 v. Essex at Ilford

BOWLING. Record at Specific Venues in UK. First Class Matches.

Venues	Overs	Maidens	Runs	Wickets	Ave	5wI	10wM	Best
Aldershot	49.4	9	102	4	25.50	-	-	3-47
Basingstoke	125.1	53	261	13	20.07	1	-	5-64
Bath	215.1	90	402	25	16.08	1	-	6-42
Birmingham	604.5	183	1316	60	21.93	3	-	7-38
Blackpool	29.3	15	42	6	7.00	1	-	6-42
Bournemouth	3642.1	1372	7211	337	21.39	20	1	7-32
Bradford	204.1	71	510	27	18.88	3	1	7-78
Brentwood	36.0	9	98	4	24.50	-	-	4-98
Bristol	639.5	277	1029	78	13.19	4	2	9-59
Bristol (Imp)	62.0	27	68	8	8.50	-	-	4-25
Burton	79.0	22	194	10	19.40	-	-	4-36
Canterbury	708.5	217	1557	83	18.75	2	-	7-71
Cardiff Arms Park	167.3	75	300	21	14.28	1	-	8-36
Cardiff Sophia Gdns	32.0	16	53	2	26.50	-	-	2-53
Cheltenham	45.4	15	101	6	16.83	1	-	5-61
Chesterfield	241.1	73	529	25	21.16	1	-	7.90
Clacton	46.4	18	93	7	13.28	1	-	5-57
Coalville	120.5	57	181	10	18.10	1	-	5-62
Colchester Garrison A	28.0	12	36	2	18.00	-	-	2-24
Colchester	8.0	2	10	-	-	-	-	0-10
Coventry Courtaulds	99.3	35	194	6	32.33	-	-	3-61
Cowes IOW	389.0	155	645	47	13.72	5	1	7-81
Derby	254.3	78	578	29	19.93	2	-	7-86
Dublin	25.0	16	21	3	7.00	-	-	3-13
Dudley	137.5	63	219	15	14.60	1	-	5-70
Eastbourne	174.0	57	326	35	9.31	5	1	7.48
Ebbw Vale	32.5	19	40	6	6.66	1	-	5.32
Frome	8.0	1	17	0	-	-	-	0-6
Gillingham	123.0	49	207	14	14.78	1	-	6-59
Glastonbury	49.0	21	75	4	18.75	-	-	2-25
Gloucester	68.0	23	115	4	28.75	-	-	3-53
Guildford	322.4	115	627	37	16.94	4	-	7-34
Harrogate	14.0	7	15	0	-	-	-	0-15
Hastings	340.0	104	741	39	19.00	1	-	5-44
Hinckley	50.0	26	63	5	12.60	-	-	3-32
Hornsey	50.0	15	118	5	23.60	-	-	4-77
Horsham	59.4	18	118	8	14.75	1	-	5-70
Hove	517.1	223	934	59	15.83	3	-	6-66
Hull	127.1	39	287	15	19.13	-	-	4.58
Ilford	49.0	25	94	12	7.83	2	1	7-37
Kettering	59.0	21	127	6	21.16	1	-	6-85
Kingston	34.0	9	78	4	19.50	-	-	3-57
Leeds	175.5	48	360	15	24.00	-	-	4-57
Leicester Aylestone Rd	18.0	9	17	1	17.00	-	-	1-17
Leicester Grace Rd	633.0	219	1348	79	17.06	8	1	7-20
Leyton	51.0	17	91	2	45.50	-	-	1-14
Liverpool	123.1	41	211	11	19.18	1	-	5-109
Lord's	1286.2	444	2640	160	16.50	13	6	7-32
Loughborough	67.0	24	146	12	12.16	1	-	6-49
Maidstone	31.0	9	77	4	19.25	-	-	4-77

Manchester	520.4	184	1016	57	17.82	4	1	7-51
Middlesbrough	31.5	15	71	8	8.87	1	-	6-64
Neath	47.0	28	46	9	5.11	1	-	6-20
Newport	81.0	33	169	14	12.07	1	1	9-77
Northampton	473.1	149	1046	40	26.15	2	-	6-75
Nottingham	763.4	232	1668	75	22.24	6	2	7-41
Oval	466.5	171	898	39	23.02	3	1	6-34
Oxford	41.0	12	94	2	47.00	-	-	1-34
Peterborough	84.0	32	152	14	10.85	1	-	5-21
Portsmouth	4454.4	1638	8713	475	18.34	36	7	9-30
Romford	194.2	68	382	24	15.91	1	-	5-47
Rushden	54.0	18	89	6	14.83	-	-	4-33
Scarborough	39.2	9	90	5	18.00	1	-	5-73
Southampton	3992.1	1463	8320	411	20.24	29	7	7-30
Stourbridge	25.0	8	44	3	14.66	-	-	3-33
Swansea	228.2	67	539	20	26.95	1	-	6-90
Taunton	389.5	113	906	49	18.48	3	-	5-43
Torquay	15.4	5	32	4	8.00	-	-	3-28
Wellingborough	67.1	27	104	11	9.45	2	1	6.44
Westcliff	153.3	67	296	20	14.80	3	1	6-96
Weston-Super-Mare	27.1	14	29	14	2.07	2	1	8-04
Worcester	595.5	217	1090	65	16.76	2	-	6-66
Worksop	89.0	40	183	8	22.87	-	-	3-37
Worthing	116.4	46	202	14	14.42	1	1	6-34
Yeovil	39.0	19	59	5	11.80	1	-	5-17
TOTAL	25445.4	9218	50860	2757	18.44	191	37	9-30

BOWLING . Record at Specific Venues in India , Pakistan and Ceylon

Venues	Overs	Maidens	Runs	Wickets	Ave	5wI	10wM	Best
Ahmedabad	40.1	9	87	7	12.42	-	-	4-23
Amritsar	22.0	6	36	5	7.20	1	-	5-36
Bahawalpur	31.0	9	61	1	61.00	-	-	1-61
Bangalore	35.5	16	95	6	15.83	-	-	4-44
Baroda	11.0	3	24	0	-	-	-	0-11
Bombay	134.2	26	314	7	44.85	-	-	3-41
Calcutta	55.0	19	91	5	18.20	-	-	3-20
Colombo	103.0	24	260	8	32.50	-	-	4-62
Dehra Dun	52.0	19	71	5	14.20	-	-	3-38
Hyderabad	70.0	24	151	6	25.16	-	-	3-35
Indore	37.0	5	84	2	42.00	-	-	2-43
Jamsedpur	68.5	22	155	8	19.37	1	-	5-64
Kanpur	17.0	3	46	0	-	-	-	0-17
Karachi	51.0	9	137	7	19.57	-	-	4-50
Lahore	24.0	4	82	2	41.00	-	-	2-82
Lucknow	20.0	6	50	4	12.50	-	-	3-42
Madras	140.5	37	343	17	20.17	1	1	6-78
Nagpur	34.3	8	63	6	10.50	-	-	3-30
New Delhi	51.0	11	135	2	67.50	-	-	1-41
Poona	29.0	5	70	0	-	-	-	0-8
Sialkot	27.0	5	88	2	44.00	-	-	2-71
TOTAL	1054.3	270	2443	100	24.43	3	1	6-78

BATTING . All First Class Matches . Year by Year Summary

Year	M	Inn	NO	Runs	Hst	Ave	50s	Ct
1948	16	23	3	228	63	11.40	1	8
1949	26	48	9	914	87*	23.43	3	11
1950	29	44	3	686	73	16.73	2	9
1950/1	20	20	5	297	55*	19.80	1	7
1951	31	45	8	705	58	19.05	3	5
1951/2	16	20	3	306	66	18.00	1	4
1952	29	46	6	558	29	13.95	-	9
1953	31	47	8	512	65	13.12	1	10
1954	30	43	4	420	45*	10.77	-	15
1955	31	47	7	525	50	13.12	1	18
1956	31	34	9	386	64	15.44	1	19
1957	29	41	7	492	64	14.47	2	8
1958	29	36	9	347	47	12.85	-	11
1959	32	42	8	599	66*	17.61	1	16
1960	30	32	9	391	56*	17.00	2	11
1961	33	42	15	341	42	12.62	-	12
1962	34	45	19	406	44*	15.61	-	13
1963	27	36	17	263	34	13.84	-	4
1964	29	37	19	308	50*	17.11	1	10
1965	30	32	3	235	46	8.10	-	7
1966	27	25	8	223	42*	13.11	-	4
1967	28	35	13	282	29*	12.81	-	6
1968	28	31	5	142	39	5.46	-	3
1969	1	1	-	8	8	8.00	-	1
TOTAL	647	852	197	9574	87*	14.61	20	221

BATTING . Hampshire County Championship . Year by Year Summary

Year	M	Inn	NO	Runs	Hst	Ave	50s	Ct
1948	14	21	3	150	27	8.33	-	6
1949	24	44	8	844	87*	23.44	3	10
1950	24	38	2	612	73	17.00	2	8
1951	27	39	6	665	58	20.15	3	4
1952	24	39	4	496	29	14.17	-	9
1953	27	41	8	461	65	13.96	1	8
1954	27	39	3	385	45*	10.69	-	14
1955	28	43	7	466	47	12.94	-	16
1956	28	31	9	299	35	13.59	-	15
1957	27	39	7	478	64	14.93	2	8
1958	27	33	9	329	47	13.70	-	11
1959	28	39	7	574	66*	17.93	1	15
1960	29	30	9	379	56*	18.04	2	11
1961	32	42	15	341	42	12.62	-	12
1962	32	43	18	404	44*	16.16	-	13
1963	20	24	9	188	30	12.53	-	3
1964	28	35	18	296	50*	17.41	1	9
1965	28	32	3	235	46	8.10	-	6
1966	25	24	7	223	42*	13.11	-	3
1967	27	33	12	243	29*	11.57	-	6
1968	26	28	4	126	39	5.25	-	3
1969	1	1	-	8	8	8.00	-	1
TOTAL	553	738	168	8202	87*	14.38	15	191

BATTING. Hampshire Other First Class Matches . Year by Year Summary

Year	M	Inn	NO	Runs	Hst	Ave	50s	Ct
1948	2	2	-	78	63	39.00	1	2
1949	2	4	1	70	21	23.33	-	1
1950	1	1	1	0	0*	-	-	-
1951	1	1	-	9	9	9.00	-	1
1952	1	2	1	29	23*	29.00	-	-
1953	2	3	-	11	6	3.66	-	2
1954	1	1	-	4	4	4.00	-	1
1955	2	3	-	59	50	19.66	1	1
1956	2	1	-	3	3	3.00	-	4
1957	1	1	-	0	0	0.00	-	-
1958	1	1	-	0	0	0.00	-	-
1959	2	1	-	4	4	4.00	-	1
1960	1	2	-	12	11	6.00	-	-
1961	1	-	-	-	-	-	-	-
1962	-	-	-	-	-	-	-	-
1963	2	4	2	54	34	27.00	-	-
1964	1	2	1	12	12	12.00	-	1
1965	2	-	-	-	-	-	-	1
1966	2	1	1	0	0*	-	-	1
1967	1	2	1	39	20*	39.00	-	-
1968	2	3	1	16	8	8.00	-	-
1969	-	-	-	-	-	-	-	-
TOTAL	30	35	9	400	63	15.38	2	16

BATTING. For Other Representative Sides . Year by Year Summary

Year	M	Inn	NO	Runs	Hst	Ave	50s	Ct
1948	-	-	-	-	-	-	-	-
1949	-	-	-	-	-	-	-	-
1950	4	5	-	74	42	14.80	-	1
1950/1	20	20	5	297	55*	19.80	1	7
1951	3	5	2	31	14	10.33	-	-
1951/2	16	20	3	306	66	18.00	1	4
1952	4	5	1	33	12	8.25	-	-
1953	2	3	-	40	26	13.33	-	-
1954	2	3	1	31	18*	15.50	-	-
1955	1	1	-	0	0	0.00	-	1
1956	1	2	-	84	64	42.00	1	-
1957	1	1	-	14	14	14.00	-	-
1958	1	2	-	18	11	9.00	-	-
1959	2	2	1	21	15	21.00	-	-
1960	-	-	-	-	-	-	-	-
1961	-	-	-	-	-	-	-	-
1962	2	2	1	2	1*	2.00	-	-
1963	5	8	6	21	8	10.50	-	1
1964	-	-	-	-	-	-	-	-
1965	-	-	-	-	-	-	-	-
1966	-	-	-	-	-	-	-	-
1967	-	-	-	-	-	-	-	-
1968	-	-	-	-	-	-	-	-
1969	-	-	-	-	-	-	-	-
TOTAL	64	79	20	972	66	16.47	3	14

BATTING. Summary In First Class Cricket

	M	Inn	N O	R	Hst	Ave	50s	Ct
For Hampshire in County Championship Matches								
	553	738	168	8202	87*	14.38	15	191
For Hampshire in Other Matches								
	30	35	9	400	63	15.38	2	16
For Other Representative Sides								
	64	79	20	972	66	16.47	3	14
CAREER TOTALS								
	647	852	197	9574	87*	14.61	20	221

Derek Shackleton's batting dismissals were as follows :

Bowled	122
Caught	402
LBW	79
Hit wkt	1
Run out	14
Stumped	37
Other	0
(Not out)	197
Total Innings	852

BATTING. Hampshire County Championship. Details against each county.

County	M	Inn	NO	Runs	Hst	Ave	50s	Ct
Derbyshire	29	43	10	516	58	15.63	1	11
Essex	30	38	9	425	87*	14.65	1	14
Glamorgan	35	39	12	465	84	17.22	3	14
Gloucestershire	38	48	12	500	47	13.88	-	12
Kent	41	55	11	562	56*	12.77	2	9
Lancashire	31	46	15	473	45	15.25	-	11
Leicestershire	41	52	9	578	50*	13.44	1	11
Middlesex	37	55	9	559	41	12.15	-	13
Northants	27	38	16	483	64	21.95	1	4
Notts	40	50	14	654	57*	18.16	1	13
Somerset	39	47	9	392	45	10.31	-	23
Surrey	32	46	9	463	67	12.51	2	11
Sussex	42	52	6	592	73	12.86	1	14
Warwickshire	32	43	9	603	53	17.73	1	13
Worcestershire	30	42	10	506	45*	15.81	-	10
Yorkshire	29	44	8	431	66*	11.97	1	8
TOTAL	553	738	168	8202	87*	14.38	15	191

BATTING. For Hampshire in Other First Class Matches. Non championship.

Opponents	M	Inn	NO	Runs	Hst	Ave	50s	Ct
Cambridge U	1	1	-	15	15	15.00	-	-
Combined Serv	2	3	1	96	63	48.00	1	3
Ireland	1	-	-	-	-	-	-	-
MCC	4	3	1	21	16*	10.50	-	4
Oxford U	2	2	1	6	6	6.00	-	1
Rest of World	1	1	-	8	8	8.00	-	-
Yorkshire	1	-	-	-	-	-	-	-
Australia	4	7	2	33	12	6.60	-	4
India	3	5	2	72	23*	24.00	-	-
New Zealand	2	3	-	37	21	12.33	-	-
Pakistan	1	1	-	4	4	4.00	-	1
S Africa	4	5	-	74	50	14.80	1	3
W Indies	4	4	2	34	34	17.00	-	-
TOTAL	30	35	9	400	63	15.38	2	16

BATTING. Summary of performances FOR other representative sides

For	M	Inn	N O	R	Hst	Ave	50s	Ct
England	7	13	7	113	42	18.83	-	1
MCC in India/ Pakistan/ Ceylon (Excl. test match*)	15	18	2	275	66	17.18	1	4
Commonwealth X1 in India and Ceylon	20	20	5	297	55*	19.80	1	7
MCC sides in England	5	6	1	113	64	22.60	1	1
Players v. Gentlemen	3	4	1	40	25	13.33	-	-
Other representative sides (**)	14	18	4	134	26	9.57	-	1
TOTAL	64	79	20	972	66	16.47	3	14

Notes.

* Batting figures for a test match appearance in India are included under the ‘England’ heading, i.e. 10 and 21 not out, and not under the MCC heading.

** Details under ‘Other representative sides’ relate to matches played in England for teams such as A E R Gilligan’s X1, South of England, Rest of England etc.

BATTING Scores of 50 and above.

1948	63	Hampshire v. Combined Services at Aldershot
1949	87*	Hampshire v. Essex at Bournemouth
1949	84	Hampshire v. Glamorgan at Bournemouth
1949	58	Hampshire v. Surrey at Portsmouth
1950	73	Hampshire v. Sussex at Portsmouth
1950	67	Hampshire v. Surrey at Guildford
1950/51	55*	Commonwealth X1 v.Bombay Governor’s X1 at Bombay
1951	58	Hampshire v. Derbyshire at Portsmouth
1951	57*	Hampshire v. Nottinghamshire at Bournemouth
1951	52	Hampshire v. Kent at Southampton
1951/52	66	MCC v. Maharashra at Poona
1953	65	Hampshire v. Glamorgan at Portsmouth
1955	50	Hampshire v. South Africa at Southampton
1956	64	MCC v. Surrey at Lord’s
1957	64	Hampshire v. Northamptonshire at Bournemouth
1957	53	Hampshire v. Warwickshire at Southampton
1959	66*	Hampshire v. Yorkshire at Bournemouth
1960	56*	Hampshire v. Kent at Canterbury
1960	54*	Hampshire v. Glamorgan at Cowes IOW
1964	50*	Hampshire v. Leicestershire at Leicester

BATTING. Record at Specific Venues in UK. First Class Matches.

Venues	M	Inn	NO	Runs	Hst	Ave	50s	Ct
Aldershot	2	2	-	78	63	39.00	1	2
Basingstoke	3	3	-	36	21	12.00	-	1
Bath	6	8	-	32	11	4.00	-	1
Birmingham	16	21	6	258	45	17.20	-	5
Blackpool	1	2	1	30	29*	30.00	-	-
Bournemouth	93	125	34	1402	87*	15.40	5	37
Bradford	7	10	2	87	38	10.87	-	2
Brentwood	1	1	-	0	0	0.00	-	-
Bristol	15	18	3	150	38	10.00	-	6
Bristol (Imp)	1	1	-	37	37	37.00	-	-
Burton	2	3	-	6	5	2.00	-	1
Canterbury	18	23	5	268	56*	14.88	1	4
Cardiff Arms Park	6	6	1	40	14*	8.00	-	-
Cardiff Sophia Gdns	1	2	-	5	5	2.50	-	-
Cheltenham	2	3	2	19	9	19.00	-	-
Chesterfield	6	9	2	93	26	13.28	-	3
Clacton	2	2	1	23	20*	23.00	-	1
Coalville	2	1	-	1	1	1.00	-	-
Colchester Garrison A	1	-	-	-	-	-	-	-
Colchester	1	1	-	9	9	9.00	-	1
Coventry Courtaulds	2	3	1	44	26	22.00	-	-
Cowes IOW	7	8	2	102	54*	17.00	1	3
Derby	6	8	-	125	14	15.62	-	3
Dublin	1	-	-	-	-	-	-	-
Dudley	3	4	1	72	38*	24.00	-	-
Eastbourne	4	7	-	64	14	9.14	-	2
Ebbw Vale	1	1	-	8	8	8.00	-	-
Frome	1	2	-	5	4	2.50	-	-
Gillingham	2	2	-	0	0	0.00	-	-
Glastonbury	1	2	-	4	4	2.00	-	-
Gloucester	2	1	-	3	3	3.00	-	-
Guildford	8	15	1	156	67	11.14	1	1
Harrogate	1	1	-	3	3	3.00	-	-
Hastings	11	13	2	101	26	9.18	-	-
Hinckley	1	1	-	42	42	42.00	-	-
Hornsey	1	1	-	15	15	15.00	-	2
Horsham	1	1	-	5	5	5.00	-	-
Hove	11	16	3	205	26	15.76	-	1
Hull	3	6	3	103	36*	34.33	-	1
Ilford	1	1	1	1	1*	-	-	1
Kettering	1	1	1	42	42*	-	-	-
Kingston	1	2	-	14	11	7.00	-	-
Leeds	3	4	2	2	1*	1.00	-	2
Leicester Aylestone Rd	1	1	-	0	0	0.00	-	-
Leicester Grace Rd	15	24	2	330	50*	15.00	1	5
Leyton	1	2	1	31	18*	31.00	-	2
Liverpool	3	5	2	61	23	20.33	-	1
Lord's	29	38	6	391	64	12.21	1	7
Loughborough	2	2	-	29	28	14.50	-	1
Maidstone	1	2	-	5	5	2.50	-	-

Manchester	12	18	6	150	34*	12.50	-	5
Middlesbrough	1	1	-	0	0	0.00	-	-
Neath	1	-	-	-	-	-	-	-
Newport	2	3	1	42	27	21.00	-	-
Northampton	10	15	9	151	37	25.16	-	3
Nottingham	19	24	5	370	46*	19.47	-	1
Oval	10	12	7	47	14	9.40	-	3
Oxford	1	1	1	0	0*	-	-	1
Peterborough	2	2	-	47	47	23.50	-	1
Portsmouth	99	121	21	1405	73	14.05	4	40
Romford	5	7	2	79	25	15.80	-	1
Rushden	1	1	1	7	7*	-	-	-
Scarborough	1	-	-	-	-	-	-	-
Southampton	94	137	33	1565	53	15.04	3	41
Stourbridge	1	2	1	19	13*	19.00	-	-
Swansea	6	5	2	51	22	17.00	-	1
Taunton	10	13	4	150	45	16.66	-	8
Torquay	1	1	1	18	18*	-	-	-
Wellingborough	1	2	2	23	12*	-	-	-
Westcliff	3	3	1	36	17	18.00	-	1
Weston-Super-Mare	1	1	-	0	0	0.00	-	-
Worcester	12	15	4	176	45*	16.00	-	4
Worksop	2	4	2	20	14*	10.00	-	1
Worthing	4	8	-	75	27	9.37	-	1
Yeovil	1	1	1	3	3*	-	-	2
TOTAL	611	812	189	8971	87*	14.40	18	210

BATTING. Record at Specific Venues in India, Pakistan and Ceylon

Venues	M	Inn	NO	Runs	Hst	Ave	50s	Ct
Ahmedabad	2	3	-	40	23	13.33	-	1
Amritsar	1	2	1	28	22	28.00	-	-
Bahawalpur	1	1	-	0	0	0.00	-	-
Bangalore	1	1	-	3	3	3.00	-	-
Baroda	1	1	-	16	16	16.00	-	-
Bombay	6	5	2	128	55*	42.66	1	2
Calcutta	3	3	-	63	32	21.00	-	1
Colombo	3	5	2	37	19*	12.33	-	1
Dehra Dun	2	3	1	57	39*	28.50	-	1
Hyderabad	2	1	-	8	8	8.00	-	-
Indore	1	1	-	43	43	43.00	-	1
Jamsedpur	2	1	1	4	4*	-	-	-
Kanpur	1	1	-	2	2	2.00	-	2
Karachi	1	2	-	22	17	11.00	-	-
Lahore	1	1	-	17	17	17.00	-	-
Lucknow	1	1	-	5	5	5.00	-	-
Madras	2	2	-	1	1	0.50	-	-
Nagpur	1	1	-	0	0	0.00	-	-
New Delhi	2	3	1	47	21*	23.50	-	1
Poona	1	1	-	66	66	66.00	1	-
Sialkot	1	1	-	16	16	16.00	-	1
TOTAL	36	40	8	603	66	18.84	2	11

One Day Cricket Competitions

Gillette Cup

BOWLING

Year	Overs	Maidens	Runs	Wickets	Ave	Best
1964	20.0	5	64	3	21.33	2-58
1965	32.1	11	78	3	26.00	2-26
1966	46.0	11	102	5	20.40	3-12
1967	36.0	11	77	3	25.66	3-31
1968	24.0	5	44	1	44.00	1-26
1969	11.5	3	36	0	—	0-36
TOTAL	170.0	46	401	15	26.73	3-12

BATTING

	M	Inn	NO	R	Hst	Ave	Ct
1964	2	2	1	9	5*	9.00	1
1965	3	2	-	15	13	7.50	-
1966	4	3	-	41	22	13.66	1
1967	3	1	1	2	2*	—	1
1968	2	1	-	0	0	0.00	1
1969	1	-	-	-	-	—	-
TOTAL	15	9	2	67	22	9.57	4

For additional statistics for the Gillette Cup Competition see details under 'Dorset'.

John Player Sunday League

BOWLING

	Overs	Maidens	Runs	Wickets	Ave	Best
1969	104.0	24	232	17	13.64	3-24
1970	59.0	7	228	5	45.60	2-18
TOTAL	163.0	31	460	22	20.90	3-24

BATTING

	M	Inn	NO	R	Hst	Ave	Ct
1969	13	5	5	17	10*	—	2
1970	8	2	1	2	2	2.00	2
TOTAL	21	7	6	19	10*	19.00	4

Minor Counties Cricket With Dorset CCC

BOWLING

Year	Overs	Maidens	Runs	Wickets	Ave
1971	372.2	180	591	43	13.74
1972	264.4	128	348	33	10.55
1973	274.2	126	425	26	16.35
1974	309.0	143	417	36	11.58
TOTAL	1220.2	577	1781	138	12.91

BATTING

Year	Inn	NO	R	Hst	Ave
1971	9	4	80	24	16.00
1972	3	2	27	17*	27.00
1973	12	6	72	22	12.00
1974	8	4	24	17	6.00
TOTAL	32	16	203	24	12.69

Gillette Cup Competition with Dorset

BOWLING

Year	Overs	Maidens	Runs	Wickets	Ave
1973	12.0	8	11	4	2.75

BATTING

Year	M	Inn	NO	R	Hst	Ave	Ct
1973	1	1	1	18	18*	—	1

In this game Derek won the Man of the Match award.

INDEX